Origins and Development of Congress

SECOND EDITION

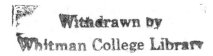

Congressional Quarterly Inc.

Congressional Quarterly Inc., an editorial research service and publishing company, serves clients in the fields of news, education, business and government. It combines specific coverage of Congress, government and politics by Congressional Quarterly, founded in 1946, with the more general subject range of an affiliated service, Editorial Research Reports, founded in 1923 and merged with Congressional Quarterly in 1956.

Congressional Quarterly publishes the CQ *Weekly Report* and a variety of books, including college political science textbooks under the CQ Press imprint. CQ also publishes information directories and reference books on the federal government and elections, including *The Guide to Congress* from which *Origins and Development of Congress* is taken. In addition, CQ publishes paperback books that are designed as timely reports to keep journalists, scholars and the public abreast of developing issues, events and trends.

CQ publishes *The Congressional Monitor,* a daily report on present and future activities of congressional committees. CQ Direct Research is a consulting service that performs contract research and maintains a reference library and query desk for clients.

Editor: Barbara R. de Boinville
Contributors: William Korns, Mary Cohn, Irwin B. Arieff, Michael D. Wormser, Lynda McNeil
Designer: Mary McNeil
Cover: Richard A. Pottern
Photo Credits: Library of Congress, pp. 8, 94, 190.

Library of Congress Cataloging in Publication Data

Main entry under title:

Origins and development of Congress.

   Bibliography p.
   Includes index.
   1. United States.   Congress — History. I. Congressional Quarterly, inc.
JK1021.074 1982   328.73'09   82-7372
ISBN 0-87187-235-8   AACR2

Table of Contents

PREFACE

Since the first edition of *Origins and Development of Congress* was published in 1976, significant changes have occurred in Congress in terms of party leadership, legislative initiatives and institutional reforms. Jimmy Carter's election secured Democratic control of the White House and both chambers of Congress for the first time since Lyndon Johnson's presidency. But the Republicans bounced back in the 1980 elections. They put their candidate, Ronald Reagan, in the White House with 50.7 percent of the vote and picked up 12 new seats in the Senate and 33 in the House. The GOP had won control of the Senate for the first time in 28 years and weakened the Democrats' hold on the House.

The new edition traces these shifts in the balance of power and the effects of changing executive-legislative relations on the course of important legislation. Amid highly charged debate, the Senate ratified two treaties with Panama relinquishing American control over the Panama Canal. Congressional debate on a new U.S.-Soviet arms limitation treaty was equally contentious, but the Soviets' invasion of Afghanistan in December 1979 put SALT II on a back burner.

Infrequently, legislation passed by Congress is declared unconstitutional by the Supreme Court. This happened January 30, 1976, when the court unanimously voided key portions of the 1971 and 1974 campaign finance reform bills, although it left intact the 1974 provisions for public financing of presidential campaigns. The new edition explains the restructuring of the Federal Election Commission as well as changes in financial disclosure requirements and limits on campaign spending under the Federal Election Campaign Act Amendments of 1976 and 1979.

The second edition of *Origins and Development of Congress* describes the leaders and legislation that have shaped Congress since 1789. But perhaps most importantly it shows how Congress as an institution has changed through the years. Since the publication of the first edition, major organizational and procedural changes have taken place. In 1977 the Senate streamlined its operations by reducing the number of committees from 31 to 25. Fifteen standing committees with revised jurisdictions remained after the reorganization, the most sweeping overhaul since the Legislative Reorganization Act of 1946. The committee roster rose to 16 with the elevation of the Select Small Business Committee to permanent status in 1981.

One of the most important changes in Senate procedures concerned the filibuster, a popular tool since the 1890s to thwart majority rule. In 1917 the Senate adopted its first cloture rule limiting debate, and since then Rule 22 has been revised significantly four times (1949, 1959, 1975 and 1979). The 1979 rules change permitted no more than 100 hours of debate once cloture had been invoked.

Institutional reforms in the late 1970s affected Congress' public image as well as its internal operations. In March 1979 the House approved gavel-to-gavel broadcast coverage of its proceedings. The signal produced by the House-operated system could be distributed to radio and television stations nationwide. But the Senate was more reticent to go on the air; in 1981 it delayed action on a proposal to open the chamber to TV cameras and radio microphones.

Although both chambers adopted new ethics codes in 1977, a few members' conduct marred the effort to upgrade the images of the House and Senate. In March 1978 former Representative Richard Hanna pleaded guilty to one count of conspiracy to defraud the government; his was the only conviction in a two-and-one-half year government investigation into South Korean influence-peddling in Congress. In October 1979 Senator Herman Talmadge was "denounced" for financial misconduct, and in 1980 an undercover FBI political corruption investigation, dubbed "Abscam" for "Arab scam," led to the conviction of six representatives and one senator. All later resigned, were defeated, or, in the case of Representative Michael "Ozzie" Myers, were expelled.

These are some of the recent developments in Congress that have been included in the second edition. New material also has been introduced on the constitutional origins of the House and Senate and their historical evolution since the first Congress. To highlight important points in the text, 24 boxes have been added on such subjects as the *Federalist Papers* (p. 90), the 20th Amendment to the Constitution (pp. 141-142) and. famous filibusters (p. 261). The footnotes have been moved from the back of the book to the end of each chapter for easier reference, and the bibliography and index have been expanded. The updated content and improved internal design make the second edition a more comprehensive and readable history of the 193-year-old Congress.

Barbara R. de Boinville
May 1982

INTRODUCTION

The 55 delegates who gathered in Philadelphia in the summer of 1787 faced a challenge of no mean proportions: How were they to devise a system of government that would bind 13 sovereign and rival states into one firm union without threatening the traditional freedoms for which the American colonists so recently had fought?

Americans, with their predominantly English heritage, were wedded to the principles of representative government and personal freedom, which had developed gradually in England from the signing of the Magna Carta in 1215. They had gone to war against the mother country to preserve their freedoms from the encroachments of centralized power.

But independence from Britain had brought new problems. Americans' allegiance still was directed toward their own states. The former colonists were reluctant to yield state sovereignty to any superior governmental power. The Articles of Confederation, the first basic law of the new nation, reflected this widespread distrust of centralized power. Under the Articles, the United States was little more than a league of sovereign states, bickering and feuding among themselves. The states retained control over most essential governmental functions, and Congress — in which each state had one vote — was the sole organ of central government. So limited were its powers that it could not levy taxes or regulate trade, and it had no sanction to enforce any of its decisions.

The inadequacies of the Articles of Confederation, brought into sharp focus by Shays' Rebellion in 1786, provided new impetus to an already growing movement for change that culminated in the Philadelphia Convention the following year. The delegates there voted to create a new national governing system consisting of supreme legislative, judicial and executive branches. [1]

In the Constitution that emerged from these deliberations, the concept of government by consent of the governed formed the basic principle; accountability was the watchword. The rights of the people were to be protected by diffusing power among rival interests.

1

The Constitution strengthened central authority, but national powers were carefully enumerated; all other powers were reserved to the states and the people. The Constitution provided for a president, to be chosen by electors in each state, a national judiciary and a legislature of two chambers. The House of Representatives was to be popularly elected, while the Senate — which shared certain executive powers with the president — was to be chosen by the individual state legislatures. Under the terms of the so-called "Great Compromise" between the large and small states, representation in the House was to be proportional to a state's population, while in the Senate each state was to have two votes. The national plan finally agreed to by the convention delegates in Philadelphia, along with the Constitution's separation of powers between the three branches of government, created a system of checks and balances.

Writing in *The Federalist*, James Madison explained the delicate relationship between the federal and state governments and the division of power within the system. He stated:

> In the compound republic of America, the power surrendered by the people is first divided between two distinct governments, and then the portion allotted to each subdivided among distinct and separate departments. Hence a double security arises to the rights of people. The different governments will control each other at the same time that each will be controlled by itself. [2]

Madison on the Constitution

"If men were angels, no government would be necessary. If angels were to govern men, neither external nor internal controls on government would be necessary. In framing a government which is to be administered by men over men, the great difficulty lies in this: you must first enable the government to control the governed; and in the next place oblige it to control itself. A dependence on the people is, no doubt, the primary control on the government; but experience has taught mankind the necessity of auxiliary precautions."

— James Madison, *The Federalist*, No. 51

The final draft of the Constitution provided a broad framework for the new government. Thus for nearly 200 years the document has proved flexible enough to meet the nation's changing needs without extensive formal revision. Although many modern governmental practices would seem alien to the authors of the Constitution, the basic structure continues to operate in much the way they planned it. Madison realized the importance of "maintaining in practice the necessary partition of power among the several departments." This could best be done, he wrote, "by so contriving the interior structure of the government as that its several constituent parts may, by their mutual relations, be the means of keeping each other in their proper places." [3]

Separate Roles of House and Senate

The House, because of its popularity with the people, was expected by Alexander Hamilton to be "a full match if not an overmatch for every other member of the government." [4] The Senate was originally designed to serve as a restraining influence on the House. But each chamber was given special power not shared by the other. The Senate's special authority over appointments and treaties was counterbalanced by the right of the House to originate all revenue bills.

At first the House, under the leadership of Madison and later under Henry Clay, was the pre-eminent chamber of Congress, but the Senate soon emerged as a powerful legislative force. In the years preceding the Civil War, it was the chief forum for the discussion of national issues, and in the post-Reconstruction era it became the dominant arm of the government. The House, as its membership increased, was compelled to adopt a variety of procedures that diminished the power of individual representatives but assured its ability to act when action was desired. The Senate remained a comparatively small body, which found elaborate institutional structures unnecessary for the legislative deliberation that it saw as its paramount function.

In his book, *Congressional Government*, written in 1885, Woodrow Wilson stated:

> It is indispensable that besides the House of Representatives which runs on all fours with popular sentiment, we should have a body like the Senate which may refuse to run with it at all when it seems to be wrong — a body which has time and security enough to keep its head, if only now and then and but for a little while, till other people have had time to think. The Senate is fitted to do

3

deliberately and well the revising which is its properest function, because its position as a representative of state sovereignty is one of eminent dignity, securing for it ready and sincere respect, and because popular demands, ere they reach it with definite and authoritative suggestion, are diluted by passage through the feelings and conclusions of the state legislatures, which are the Senate's only immediate constituents. [5]

Wilson's initial concept of the Senate, written long before he became president, might have been satisfactory to the framers of the Constitution, but in the 20th century it would no longer serve. As the Progressive era advanced, an increasingly restive public demanded more genuinely popular government, and in 1912 the Senate reluctantly agreed to a constitutional amendment providing for the direct election of senators. The House, too, felt the pressures of the times: the power of the Speaker that "Czar" Thomas B. Reed had established in 1890 was dismantled in 1910 under the banner of popular rule.

The Seventeenth Amendment, by taking senatorial elections out of the hands of the state governments, blurred the constitutional distinction between the Senate and House. From the time of the amendment's adoption in 1913, the Senate came more and more to resemble the lower chamber. At times it appeared to be the more representative legislative body. Both chambers, however, repeatedly have been subject to charges that they fail to represent the will of the electorate.

Although most members of Congress run for office today as Republicans or Democrats, the absence of unity within the national parties precludes party responsibility for legislative decisions. Moreover, the institutional characteristics of Congress itself often prevent a legislative majority from working its will. Campaigns in the 1960s and 1970s against the rigid seniority system, the Senate filibuster rule and secrecy in congressional committee sessions and in other activities all represented attempts to make Congress more accountable to the people. The same goal prompted demands for reapportionment of the House of Representatives to make congressional districts more nearly equal in population.

Congress and Presidential Power

The growth of presidential power in the 20th century, spurred by a major economic depression, two world wars and the Korean and

Indochina conflicts, posed a threat to the viability of Congress as a coequal branch of government. As the volume and complexity of government business increased, legislative initiative shifted from Capitol Hill to the White House, and Congress with its antiquated procedures often found that it was no match for the tremendous resources of the executive branch.

By passing reorganization acts in 1946 and 1970 and a comprehensive budget law in 1974, Congress sought to restore its equality in the three-branch federal system provided by the Constitution. And repeated clashes between Congress and the executive branch over spending and the federal budget and the war and treaty powers reflected congressional resistance to what lawmakers saw as executive encroachment upon the powers delegated to Congress by the Constitution. One turning point was Congress' overriding of President Nixon's veto of the War Powers Act of 1973, the first legislation ever enacted that defined the president's constitutional role in making war.

Another power struggle, and ultimately a constitutional confrontation, between the two branches occurred over the Watergate scandal that drove Nixon from office. In June 1972 five men (two of whom were employees of the Committee for the Re-election of the President) broke in and attempted to burglarize the Democratic National Committee headquarters at the Watergate office-hotel complex in Washington, D.C. Although Nixon denied any knowledge of the break-in, he became implicated in the cover-up of the affair. Before its resolution after two years of sensational disclosures and mounting national agony, the scandal had tested the powers of the presidency, Congress and the Supreme Court. The Court played a crucial role by ruling unanimously that the president had no power to withhold evidence in a criminal trial. Nixon obeyed the court and surrendered the evidence — certain White House tape recordings — which led to House Judiciary Committee approval of three articles of impeachment against him and, 16 days after the court decision, to his resignation on Aug. 9, 1974.

The scandal weakened the presidency. In both the Ford and Carter administrations that followed, members of Congress appeared to delight in displaying their independence from the White House. The administration of Jimmy Carter was the first in eight years in which both the presidency and Congress were in the hands of the same party. Though there were no divisive wars or major scandals under Carter, the president's inability to work with his own party to solve the increasingly complex domestic problems of the economy and energy scarcity further encouraged Congress to go its own way. And the hostage crisis with Iran and the unchecked aggressive actions and military buildup of the Soviet Union led Congress to act more assertively on foreign policy issues as well.

With a more cohesive and unified Republican Party in control of the White House and the Senate in 1981, Congress appeared to be somewhat less anxious to assert its independence, at least in foreign affairs. It remained to be seen whether this was momentary or evidence that the pendulum had begun to swing back under President Reagan toward greater executive branch control of Congress.

Notes

1. Carl Van Doren, *The Great Rehearsal: The Story of the Making and Ratifying of the Constitution of the United States* (New York: Viking Press, 1948), p. 35.
2. Alexander Hamilton, James Madison, and John Jay, *The Federalist Papers*, with an introduction by Clinton Rossiter (New York: Mentor, 1961), p. 323.
3. Ibid., p. 320.
4. Ibid., p. 403.
5. Woodrow Wilson, *Congressional Government* (1885; reprint ed., Cleveland: Meridian, 1956), pp. 154-155.

Part I

Constitutional Beginnings

Benjamin Franklin, Thomas Jefferson, John Adams
and Robert Livingston (from left) draft the
Declaration of Independence.

Chapter 1

COLONIAL BACKGROUND

When the Federal Convention met in Philadelphia in 1787 to consider revising the Articles of Confederation, the reasons for seeking a more effective form of national government for the newly independent United States of America seemed manifest and pressing. The exact form that government should take was by no means clear, however, and substantial compromise was required before agreement could be reached.

What finally emerged as the Constitution of the United States nevertheless reflected in good measure the shared experience of men who had grown up in a colonial America that was predominantly English in origin and who had finally rebelled against English sovereignty when that seemed the only way to preserve the basic rights and freedoms they had come to expect as a part of their English heritage.

Almost a century passed between Columbus' voyage of discovery in 1492 and Sir Walter Raleigh's attempt in 1587 to plant the first English settlement in the New World — the ill-fated "Lost Colony" on Roanoke Island in what is now North Carolina. [1] By then, Spain had seized the Caribbean and much of South and Central America (with its gold and silver) and had placed outposts in Florida. But at the beginning of the 17th century most of North America was still unexplored, Spain's power was on the wane and England was primed for colonial venture.

English Dominance

Private initiative was the prime mover behind the settlement of America by the English during the 17th century, when all of the original 13 colonies except one (Georgia) were founded. Several were started by promoters with an eye to profits or the creation of new feudal domains. Religious strife underlay the "Great Migration" of Puritans to New England (and the West Indies) during the repressive reign of Charles I (1625-49). [2] Poverty drove many others to take a chance on America.

Whatever the motive for settlement, it was entirely a private undertaking, receiving little help from the state other than a charter to the land to be settled.

The English achieved their dominant position along the Atlantic seaboard in two waves of colonization. Virginia, Maryland and the New England colonies were founded before 1642, when the outbreak of civil war in England absorbed Britain's energies. After restoration of the monarchy in 1660, the English added New York, New Jersey, Pennsylvania, Delaware and the Carolinas. Georgia, the 13th colony, was founded in 1733. By 1700 the colonies had a population of 200,000 — largely of English origin — stretched along a thousand miles of coast from Maine to the Carolinas.

Roots of Self-Government

By the time Jamestown was founded in 1607, the English had already attained significant rights and privileges. English justice was grounded on a solid body of common law that included the right to trial by jury. No English subject could be deprived of life, liberty or property without due process in the courts. The first colonists brought with them the models of English courts and other organs of local government.

The long struggle in England for the right of self-government also was well-advanced by the beginning of the 17th century. The Crown still was supreme, and it would take the beheading of Charles I in 1649 and the dethroning of James II in 1688 to assure Parliament ascendancy over the King. Already, though, the two houses of Parliament — the Lords and the Commons — symbolized the principle of government by law and representative assembly, and this principle, too, was soon transplanted to America. In 1619 the Virginians (then numbering about 1,000) elected 22 "burgesses" — the first English elected representatives in the New World — to a General Assembly. [3] After Virginia became a royal colony in 1624, the governor and his council were appointed by the King, but popular representation in the lower house of the Virginia Assembly — the House of Burgesses — was retained.

The organizers of the Massachusetts Bay Company carried governing matters considerably further when they voted to transfer the entire enterprise and its charter as "one body politique and corporate" to New England. [4] On their arrival in 1630, the officers promptly established themselves as the government of the Bay Colony, subject only to annual election thereafter by the stockholder-colonists. The founders of Massachusetts thereby asserted a right to full self-government that neither the King nor Parliament had contemplated or would be prepared to challenge for another 50 years.

The great distance that separated England from America was itself a major factor in promoting a spirit of independence and self-reliance among the early colonists. Many of those drawn to America were predisposed to resist authority, and this attitude was reinforced by the free availability of land and the harshness of frontier living. In New England, where entire congregations of Puritans had often emigrated and settled together in a town of their own, the town meeting became a unique instrument of self-government that was exceptionally democratic for the times.

Origins of Conflict with England

England left the colonies pretty much to themselves initially, but it was not for lack of self-interest. Under the prevailing economic doctrine of the times — mercantilism — the central goal of any nation-state was self-sufficiency, and it was taken for granted that all profits of empire should accrue to the benefit of the mother country. Thus the English were quick to try to monopolize the trade in Virginia tobacco, the first American product to find a wide market. And in 1660 they initiated systematic efforts to exploit colonial trade with the first of a series of Acts of Trade and Navigation.

These laws were designed to maximize English profits on the transport of imports to and exports from the colonies and on the marketing of major colonial products. They required all trade between England and the colonies to be carried by English or colonial-built ships manned by English subjects; stipulated that imports of goods to the colonies from other countries in Europe first had to be landed and reloaded at English ports; and prohibited the export of certain colonial products to countries other than England. Tobacco was the first of these enumerated items, and eventually every important American export except salt fish was added to the list.

The trade acts were not without some benefit to the colonies. But in exchanging their raw products for English manufactures, the colonists rarely found the terms of trade to their advantage. When tobacco prices collapsed in the 1660s, for example, Virginians had no recourse against the English merchants who raised the prices of goods sent in exchange. This situation was aggravated by England's continuing refusal to permit

The Colonial Settlements In . . .

Virginia. The Virginia Company of London, a joint stock company with a charter from James I, founded the first permanent English settlement in America at Jamestown in 1607. After severe initial setbacks, the company discovered tobacco to be a thriving crop and profitable export and began to attract new settlers with "head rights" to 50 acres of land. The company was dissolved in 1624 when Virginia became a royal colony.

Maryland. In 1632 Charles I gave a proprietary charter to Maryland (originally a part of Virginia) to Sir George Calvert, who wanted a feudal domain for his family that would serve also as a refuge for English Catholics. Maryland became a royal colony in 1692 but was restored to the Calvert family in 1715.

Massachusetts. A small band of Pilgrims founded Plymouth in 1620. Ten years later John Winthrop and other organizers of the Massachusetts Bay Company settled Boston and nearby towns. The Bay Colony remained a self-governing Puritan commonwealth until its charter was annulled in 1684. In 1691 Massachusetts became a royal colony, incorporating Plymouth and Maine as well.

Connecticut. Thomas Hooker led a group of Puritans from the Massachusetts Bay Colony to found Hartford in 1636. Saybrook, New Haven and other Puritan settlements were joined in 1662 when Charles II granted Connecticut its own charter as a self-governing colony. The colony retained that status until 1776.

Rhode Island. Providence was founded in 1636 by Roger Williams, a strong believer in religious freedom who had been banished from the Bay Colony for opposing the conformist rule of Governor Winthrop. In 1644 the settlements federated as Rhode Island and Providence Plantations. They obtained a royal charter in 1663 and remained a self-governing colony until the Revolution.

New Hampshire. Between 1623 and 1640 Antinomians, Puritans and Anglicans settled on land granted to John Mason by Charles I. These settlements were annexed by Massachusetts until 1679, when Massachusetts became a royal colony. The governor of Massachusetts served also as governor of New Hampshire from 1699 to 1741.

New York. The Dutch West Indies Company founded New Netherland with posts at Albany (1624) and Manhattan (1626). The

... 17th and 18th Century America

colony was seized by the English in 1664 and renamed New York as part of a grant by Charles II to his brother, the Duke of York, of all land between the Connecticut and Delaware rivers. The Duke ran the colony without an assembly until 1683; as James II, he made it a royal colony in 1685.

New Jersey. In 1665 the Duke of York gave the land between the Hudson and Delaware rivers to Lord John Berkeley and Sir George Carteret, former governor of the Isle of Jersey. It became a royal colony in 1702 and had the same governor as New York until 1738.

Pennsylvania. William Penn, a Quaker convert, received proprietary title to Pennsylvania from the Duke of York in 1681. Penn attracted settlers from the Continent as well as England with promises of political and religious liberty and the offer of land on generous terms. German Mennonites were among the first to come, settling Germantown in 1683. Pennsylvania prospered under Penn's tolerant rule, and it remained a proprietary colony until the Revolution.

Delaware. The town of Lewes on the Delaware Bay was settled first by the Dutch in 1631 and then by the Swedes, until the Dutch regained control in 1655. The area was conquered by the English in 1664 and was included in the grant to the Duke of York, who sold it to William Penn in 1682. Known as the "Lower Counties," Delaware had its own assembly after 1704 but had the same proprietary governor as Pennsylvania until 1776.

Carolinas. In 1663 Charles II gave proprietary title to all land between Virginia and Florida to the Carolina proprietors, a group of promoters led by Sir John Colleton and the Earl of Shaftesbury. Charleston was founded in 1670 by settlers from England and Barbados. Later, French Huguenots and Scots came to settle. South Carolina, a plantation colony like Virginia, and North Carolina, an area of small farms, became royal colonies in 1729.

Georgia. General James Oglethorpe and other English philanthropists envisioned the territory known as Georgia as a refuge for debtors. They founded Savannah in 1733, and in the next eight years brought over approximately 1,800 charity colonists. Many of these settlers, however, moved on to South Carolina. When Georgia became a royal colony in 1752, it had a total population of little more than 2,000 residents.

its coins to circulate in the colonies. To get specie (gold or silver), the colonists had to sell their products in the West Indies or other markets.

The trade acts were met with widespread evasion in the colonies. Smuggling, bribery and the use of false documents were commonplace. New Englanders, who ran a chronic deficit in their balance of trade with England, were especially resourceful in evading the trade acts. Massachusetts went so far as to refuse to obey them, asserting that the laws of England "do not reach America" because the colonies were unrepresented in Parliament. For this and similar acts of defiance against English authority, the Bay Colony's charter was annulled in 1684. [5]

When James II came to the throne in 1685, England moved to strengthen its colonial administration by consolidating the New England colonies, New York and New Jersey into one Dominion of New England. For three years these colonies were ruled by Sir Edmund Andros as governor-general with the aid of an appointed council but no representative assembly. The colonists bridled at being taxed without their consent and were quick to oust Andros and other dominion officials as soon as they received word of the Glorious Revolution of 1688 and the expulsion of James from England. The concept of the Dominion was promptly abandoned.

The accession of William and Mary in 1689 marked the beginning of a transfer of power from the British Crown to Parliament and a series of colonial wars that ended in 1763 with the English in control of all of North America east of the Mississippi River. Mercantilist aims continued to dominate English colonial policy throughout this period, and new restrictions were placed on colonial trade. But the American colonies continued to grow in population, economic strength and political assertiveness.

Growth of the Colonies

Between 1700 and 1760 large families and new immigrants boosted the colonial population from 200,000 to about 1,700,000. Persons of English stock were in the majority overall and among the colonial leaders. The first Adams arrived in 1636, the first Washington in 1656, the first Franklin in 1685. Other major ethnic groups in 1760 were the Scots-Irish (estimated at 280,000) and Germans (170,000), whose forebears had started coming to America toward the end of the 17th century. Finding the best land along the seaboard already taken, most of them had moved on to settle the back country.

Even more numerous in the American population of 1760 were an estimated 310,000 black slaves. The Spaniards brought the first African slaves to the New World in the 16th century; a Dutch ship brought the first 20 to Virginia in 1619. The English saw nothing wrong in slavery, and the Puritans regularly took Indians as slaves and sold them in the West Indies.

Slaves helped to meet a chronic shortage of labor in colonial America at a time when most colonists wanted and usually could obtain their own land. Slavery eventually declined in the North, where it became unprofitable, but it flourished in the plantation economy of the South. The number of slaves in Virginia, the Carolinas and Georgia grew rapidly during the 18th century. Americans vied with the English slave traders in meeting the demand. Yankee slavers were especially successful in trading New England rum for Africans, who then were sold in the West Indies for sugar and molasses with which to make more rum.

Profits from slave labor and the slave trade thus added to a prosperity that was sustained by a rise in prices for colonial produce in England and the rest of Europe. In 1731 exports leaving Charleston included 42,000 barrels of rice, 14,000 barrels of pitch, tar and turpentine, and 250,000 deerskins. Virginia and Maryland shipped more tobacco, while Pennsylvania found a growing market for its wheat and flour. The fur trade was centered in New York. The New England colonies exported large quantities of ship timber and lumber of all types along with fish and meat.

Most of the colonial products were not competitive with those of England, but when competition did appear, restrictions followed. The Woolens Act of 1699 barred sale of colonial cloth outside the place where it was woven. Parliament in 1732 banned the export of hats from one colony to another. To protect English exports of iron and steel products, the colonies in 1750 were ordered to stop building various kinds of mills. After the British West Indies complained that the Americans were buying cheaper sugar and molasses from the French, Parliament passed the Molasses Act of 1733, placing a stiff duty on imports from the French islands. For the most part, however, these restrictions were poorly enforced and easily evaded by the Americans.

Governors vs. Assemblies

As the American population and economy grew, so did the problems of English colonial administration. All of the colonies were

17

permitted to elect their own assemblies after the Dominion of New England collapsed in 1689, but only Connecticut and Rhode Island (self-governing colonies) retained the right to elect their governors as well. The governors of the eight royal colonies (Virginia, Massachusetts, New York, New Hampshire, New Jersey, North Carolina, South Carolina, Georgia) were appointed by the King and those of the three proprietary colonies (Maryland, Pennsylvania, Delaware) with the King's approval.[6] It was the colonial governors who had primary responsibility for enforcing English laws and regulations in America.

The governors were armed with great legal authority. Long after the Crown had been stripped of such prerogatives in England, the colonial governors had the right of absolute veto over colonial legislation, the authority to terminate and dissolve assemblies and the power to dismiss judges and create courts. But the real power of the governors was effectively limited by their dependence on the colonial assemblies in almost all cases for their salaries and operating revenues. In *Great Britain and the American Colonies,* Jack Greene described the governors' plight:

> [M]any governors chose simply not to "consider anything further than how to sit easy," and to be careful "to do nothing, which upon a fair hearing ... can be blamed." Because the surest way to "sit easy" was to reach a political accommodation with local interests, they very frequently aligned themselves with dominant political factions in the colonies. Such governors sought to avoid disputes with the lower houses by taking especial care not to challenge their customary privileges and, if necessary, even quietly giving way before their demands.[7]

The powers of the assemblies, though nowhere carefully defined by charter or statute, grew steadily. In time the assemblies claimed and exercised the right to lay taxes, raise troops, incur debts, issue currency, and otherwise initiate all legislation. They commonly passed only short-term revenue bills, stipulated in detail how appropriations were to be spent, tacked riders on essential money bills and vied with the governors for control of patronage.

Claiming prerogatives similar to those of the British House of Commons, the assemblies made the most of their power of the purse to extract concessions from the governors. When one governor asked for a fixed revenue for five years, the assembly demanded the right to appoint every official to be paid from the grant.

Some governors came to feel "impotent to carry out either imperial directions or their own projects against the exorbitant power" of the assemblies. "The too great and unwarrantable encroachments of the assemblies," declared Gouverneur Lewis Morris of New Jersey, "make it necessary that a stop some way or other should be put to them, and they reduced to such proper and legal bounds as is consistent with his majesty's prerogative and their dependence." [8]

If the governors found it impolitic to veto certain colonial measures, such legislation still could be killed by royal decree. Acts so vetoed included those that discriminated against the various religious minorities, assessed duties on the products of neighboring colonies, authorized unbacked issues of paper currency and restricted the burgeoning slave trade. But preventing the assemblies from taking unwanted action was not the same as winning their support for imperial projects, as the English found out during the wars they waged against the French.

During these wars, English requisitions on the colonies for men, money and supplies were honored by the assemblies slowly, if at all, especially in those colonies that did not feel threatened. The larger states, such as New York and Pennsylvania, were notorious for continuing to trade with the French while France was warring with England. All of the colonies resisted imperial direction to some degree, however, and cherished their independence one from another. Not one of the state assemblies ratified the Albany Plan of Union of 1754, although it had been drafted primarily by Benjamin Franklin with the approval of representatives from seven of the 13 colonies. The Albany Plan of Union was designed to create "one general government" in America.

Colonial Frustrations

The French and Indian War (1754-63) doubled the national debt of England (to £130 million) and quadrupled the prospective cost (to £300,000 a year) of administering the greatly enlarged empire in America, thereby helping to put the government of King George III, crowned in 1760, on a collision course with the colonies. To the mercantilists in Parliament, it now seemed logical to plug the loopholes in England's trade controls on the colonies and to make the colonists pay a share of the costs of imperial overhead. The shift in English colonial policy began in 1763 when George Grenville became prime minister.

Grenville's first step was to set aside the claims of Virginia and other colonies to portions of the vast lands taken from the French. By

Four Wars in the Colonies ...

Between 1689 and 1763 the Colonies became embroiled in four wars born of the imperial rivalries of England, France and Spain.

At the outset, French Canada was only sparsely settled and Spanish Florida not at all, but the French had built a lucrative fur trade with the Indians in the Great Lakes region while La Salle had sailed down the Mississippi in 1682 and claimed Louisiana. Most of the fighting that ensued, however, involved New England and New York.

King William's War — 1689-1697. (War of the League of Augsburg, in Europe). When William of Orange became King of England, the English joined a continental alliance against Louis XIV of France. In America, French and Indian soldiers raided English settlements in New York, New Hampshire, and Maine. New Englanders captured the French base at Port Royal, Nova Scotia, but an English attempt to take Quebec failed. The Treaty of Ryswick restored Port Royal to the French.

Queen Anne's War — 1702-1713. (War of Spanish Succession). In America, the French and their Indian allies raided frontier settlements in Massachusetts and New Hampshire. The French captured the English post of St. John's, Newfoundland, while the English retook Port Royal; expeditions against Quebec and Montreal failed. In the Treaty of Utrecht the French accepted British sovereignty over Nova Scotia and Hudson's Bay, and the English inherited Spain's monopoly over the slave trade with its colonies.

the Proclamation of 1763, the entire region between the Appalachians and the Mississippi, south of Quebec and north of Florida, was reserved for the Indians. And the English adhered to this policy despite strong pressures from highly placed speculators (including Benjamin Franklin), who promoted the settlement of such proposed inland colonies as Vandalia, Charlotiana and Transylvania.

At the same time, Parliament began to strengthen enforcement of trade controls. Admiralty courts, which tried smuggling cases without juries, could now move such trials to Halifax in Nova Scotia at considerable cost to those whose goods and ships were detained. Colonial issues of paper money, which had been permitted during the war, were banned by the Currency Act of 1764. And to lighten the British tax load, Grenville pushed three other laws through Parliament.

... Fomented by European Rivalries

King George's War — 1745-1748. (War of the Austrian Succession). The major military event in America was the capture of Louisbourg, a French fortress on Cape Breton Island, by an army of 4,000 militiamen led by William Pepperell, a Maine merchant. Under the Treaty of Aachen, England restored Louisbourg to France in exchange for Madras in India but paid the cost of the colonial campaign.

French and Indian War — 1754-1763. (Seven Years War). In America this worldwide conflict focused on upper New York state and western Pennsylvania where the French built several forts. The English fared badly until William Pitt came to power in 1758 and reorganized the war effort under new and younger generals. The French were dislodged from Fort Duquesne (renamed Pittsburgh), Fort Niagara and Fort Ticonderoga. In 1759 the English took Quebec, then Montreal the next year. The English also defeated the French in India and the West Indies and, after Spain entered the war in 1762, took Havana and Manila.

The Treaty of Paris was signed by Great Britain, France and Spain on February 10, 1763. (Twenty years later another treaty was signed in Paris; the Treaty of Paris of 1783 ended the Revolutionary War.) The 1763 agreement left England the dominant power in North America. France ceded Canada and all claims east of the Mississippi to England and gave Louisiana to Spain. England also got Spanish Florida in exchange for Havana, and Manila reverted to Spanish control.

— The Revenue Act of 1764, designed to defray the expenses of defending, protecting and securing the colonies, cut in half the widely evaded duty laid on foreign molasses in 1733 but placed new duties on such colonial imports as wine, silk and linen.

— The Quarterly Act of 1765, which required the colonies to contribute to the upkeep of the 10,000 troops England planned to station in America.

— The Stamp Act of 1765, which required that revenue stamps costing up to 20 shillings be affixed to all licenses, legal documents, leases, notes and bonds, newspapers, pamphlets, almanacs, advertisements and other documents issued in the colonies.

None of these measures sat well with the Americans, but opposition focused on the Stamp Act as the first direct tax ever laid on the colonies by Parliament. Americans felt they could be taxed only by their own assemblies and that the Stamp Act, which was taxation without representation, was unconstitutional. The Virginia House of Burgesses so resolved at the urging of Patrick Henry, while the Massachusetts House of Representatives called for the convening of an intercolonial conference.

The Stamp Act Congress, held in New York in October 1765, was attended by 28 delegates from nine colonies. They affirmed their allegiance to the Crown, asserted their right as English subjects not to be taxed without their consent, noted that the colonists were not represented in the House of Commons, and concluded that "no taxes ever have been or can be constitutionally imposed on them, but by their respective legislatures." The delegates urged Parliament to repeal the Stamp Act and other recent laws that had "a manifest tendency to subvert the rights and liberties of the colonists."

Grenville insisted that Parliament represented and acted in behalf of all English subjects. But he could not ignore the sharp drop in exports that followed a colonial boycott of English goods or the attacks on royal officials by colonial mobs calling themselves "Sons of Liberty." When it became clear in 1766 that the Stamp Act could not be enforced, it was repealed. But Parliament, through a Declaratory Act, asserted its authority to legislate for the colonies "in all cases whatsoever" and declared colonial resolves to the contrary "utterly null and void." [9]

The Intolerable Acts

After repeal of the Stamp Act, Chancellor of the Exchequer Charles Townshend proposed an increase in customs receipts as a way of raising the needed revenue. Parliament passed laws in 1767 laying new duties on imports by the colonies of paper, lead, glass, paint and tea; reorganizing the customs service in America; and authorizing broad use of general search warrants, known as Writs of Assistance, to ferret out violations. The Townshend Acts were greeted by a new outbreak of protests. Colonial merchants revived their nonimportation agreements, and the adverse effect on English business again persuaded Parliament to retreat. When Lord North came to power in 1770, all of the Townshend duties except the one on tea were repealed. Most of the colonists were appeased, trade revived and for three years England and the colonies lived in relative harmony.

To American radicals like Samuel Adams of Massachusetts, this period of relative calm only foreshadowed future attacks on colonial liberties by Parliament. The English had begun to pay the salaries of the royal governors and other officials from their increased customs receipts, thus freeing them from the hold of the assemblies. Adams, Patrick Henry, Thomas Jefferson and many others, who now questioned the right of Parliament to legislate for the colonies in any respect, formed committees of correspondence that became the underground of the colonial resistance movement.

The quiet years ended abruptly in 1773 when the faltering East India Company was authorized to dump a surplus of tea on the American colonies by undercutting the price of tea smuggled in from Holland. Colonial merchants, foreseeing ruinous competition, joined the radicals in protesting the Tea Act, and there was virtual unanimity in the colonies in favor of boycotting the first shipments. In Boston, however, Adams and John Hancock urged direct action, and on Dec. 16, 1773, a mob disguised as Indians boarded three tea ships and dumped their cargoes into the harbor.

The "Boston Tea Party" alarmed many Americans who opposed British policy, and it also provoked the English government into a series of coercive acts that drove the colonists together. On March 26, 1774, the House of Commons ordered the port of Boston closed until the city paid for the tea that was thrown into the harbor. That order was followed by laws revising the Massachusetts charter to strengthen England's authority and transferring to England the trials of colonists charged with murder.

To these so-called Intolerable Acts Parliament added one that alienated most of Protestant America by giving to the French-Canadian — and Catholic — royal province of Quebec all of the land west of the Appalachians lying north of the Ohio River and east of the Mississippi. The Quebec Act of June 22, 1774, was regarded as another punitive measure by most colonists and helped to muster broad support for a "general congress of all the colonies" proposed by the Virginia and Massachusetts assemblies. [10]

First Continental Congress

Every colony except Georgia, whose governor blocked the selection of delegates, was represented at the First Continental Congress, which met in Philadelphia on Sept. 5, 1774. Describing the Congress in a letter to his wife, John Adams wrote: "The business of the Congress is tedious beyond expression. This assembly is like no other that ever existed. . . . Every man upon every question must show his oratory, his criticism and his political ability."[11] Conservative Joseph Galloway of Pennsylvania hoped to conciliate the English, while radical Samuel Adams wanted to defy all British controls. As the session continued, more and more delegates joined in the movement to protest and repudiate British policies toward the colonies.

The turning point came when Paul Revere arrived with the Suffolk Resolves, adopted by a convention of towns around Boston, which called on Massachusetts to arm itself against efforts to "enslave America" and urged Congress to adopt economic sanctions against England. To Galloway, these "inflammatory resolves . . . contained a complete declaration of war against Great Britain." Others agreed with Galloway, but most delegates felt compelled to register their support of Massachusetts. By a vote of six colonies to five they set aside Galloway's plan (based on the Albany Plan of Union of 1754) to give Parliament and a colonial legislature joint control over American affairs, and endorsed the Suffolk Resolves.[12]

The Congress then adopted a Declaration of Rights and Grievances against all British acts to which "Americans cannot submit" and approved a wide-ranging nonimportation, nonconsumption and nonexportation agreement as "the most speedy, effectual and peaceable" means of swaying England. Locally elected committees were directed to enforce this commercial boycott by publicizing violations so that "all such foes to the rights of British-America may be publicly known and universally condemned as the enemies of American liberty." On Oct. 22, 1774, the Continental Congress adjourned, after agreeing to meet again the following May if necessary.

King George III declared that the colonies were "now in a state of rebellion; blows must decide whether they are to be subject to this country or independent." While the Earl of Chatham and Edmund Burke hoped conciliation was possible, they firmly believed "that the British Parliament was supreme over the colonies, that the authority of the empire could not be surrendered."[13] In the colonies patriot forces began to gather arms and supplies and to train militia. In Massachusetts, rebels soon controlled all of the colony except Boston, where the governor, Gen. Thomas Gage, was installed with 5,000 English troops.

The Albany Plan of Union

The Albany Congress of 1754 was initiated by the British in an effort to nail down the wavering friendship of their longtime allies, the six Indian nations of the Iroquois Confederacy. The Iroquois had come under increasing pressure from the French on the western frontier. The Americans who represented the seven colonies that took part — Massachusetts, New Hampshire, Connecticut, Rhode Island, New York, Pennsylvania and Maryland — were more ambitious and adopted a Plan of Union drafted largely by Benjamin Franklin of Pennsylvania.

The plan called on Parliament to create "one general government" in America, to be administered by a "president-general" appointed by the Crown as executive officer. There also was to be a "grand council" of delegates elected by the various assemblies. The number of delegates from any one colony was to be dependent upon the size of the financial contribution which that colony made. This was Franklin's clever scheme. Under the Albany Plan, the government was to have the sole authority to make war and peace with the Indians, regulate trade with the tribes, control the purchase of Indian lands, raise troops for the common defense and levy "such general duties, imposts or taxes ... as may be collected with the least inconvenience to the people."

Both the British government and the colonial assemblies opposed the Albany Plan as involving too large a grant of power. Britain was not prepared to give the colonies that much autonomy, while the assemblies were not ready to share their power to tax. Not a single assembly accepted the plan."The different and contrary reasons of dislike to my plan made me suspect that it was really the true medium," Franklin later wrote, "and I am still of the opinion it would have been happy for both sides of the water if it had been adopted." *

As it was, the Albany Plan reflected a growing awareness of the need for a common approach to administration of the expanding American colonies. Rejection of the plan was a major landmark that led to the Constitutional Convention of 1787.

* Carl Van Doren, *Benjamin Franklin* (Greenwood Press, 1973), p. 223.

On April 19, 1775, Gage sent 1,000 of his soldiers to destroy the patriots' stores in Lexington and Concord. They were met by Minutemen, and shooting broke out. British casualties numbered 247 dead and wounded before Gage's forces could get back to Boston. This encounter turned out to be the opening shots of the Revolutionary War, although more than a year would pass before the Americans were sufficiently united to declare their independence.

Notes

1. Charles M. Andrews, *The Colonial Period of American History*, 4 vols., *The Settlements*, vol 1. (New Haven: Yale University Press, 1934), I: 23.
2. Ibid., p. 375.
3. Ibid., p. 185.
4. Ibid., p. 368.
5. Andrews, *The Colonial Period of American History*, vol. 4, *England's Commercial and Colonial Policy*, (New Haven: Yale University Press, 1938), IV: 150.
6. For a discussion of royal, proprietary and self-governing colonies and differences in colonial government, see Alfred H. Kelly and Winfred A. Harbison, *The American Constitution: Its Origins and Development*, 5th ed. (New York: W. W. Norton & Co., 1976), pp. 7-25.
7. Jack P. Greene, ed., *Great Britain and the American Colonies, 1606-1763* (New York: Harper Paperbacks, 1970), p. xxxix.
8. Ibid., p. xii.
9. Edmund S. Morgan, *The Birth of the Republic, 1763-89* (Chicago: University of Chicago Press, 1956), p. 31.
10. Ibid., pp. 60-61.
11. L. H. Butterfield, ed., *Adams Family Correspondence*, 4 vols., *December 1761-May 1776*, vol. 1 (Cambridge, Mass.: Belknap Press, 1963), I: 166.
12. Edmund Cody Burnett, *The Continental Congress* (New York: W. W. Norton & Co., 1964), pp. 42-50.
13. Ibid., p. 61.

Chapter 2

REVOLUTION AND CONFEDERATION

When the Second Continental Congress met on May 10, 1775, in Philadelphia, most of the delegates still hoped to avoid war with England and were reluctant to opt for independence. But faced with pleas for help from Massachusetts, the delegates agreed in mid-June to raise a Continental Army of 20,000 men, to ask the colonies for $2 million (in proportion to their population) for the army's support, and to make George Washington, a delegate from Virginia, the army's commander in chief.

The Congress, however, also approved a petition to George III drafted by John Dickinson of Delaware asking for "a happy and permanent reconciliation" between the colonies and England. The delegates also adopted a Declaration of the Causes of Necessity of Taking up Arms, drafted by Dickinson and Jefferson, in which they disavowed any desire for independence, but resolved "to die free men rather than live slaves." [1]

King George's response of Aug. 23 was to proclaim a state of rebellion in America. The British then began to hire mercenaries in Germany and to incite the Iroquois against the colonials, while Congress authorized an expedition against Canada and efforts to contact other nations for aid. Yet the legislatures of five of the colonies took positions against independence that autumn. Pennsylvania's delegation to the Continental Congress was told to "utterly reject any proposition . . . that may cause or lead to a separation from our mother country or a change in the form of this government." [2]

The British gave no signs of retreating, however, and the appearance in January 1776 of Thomas Paine's pamphlet "Common Sense" fueled colonial sentiment for independence. Paine argued that it was time for Americans to stand on their own feet, for there was "something absurd in supporting a continent to be perpetually governed by an island," and "it is evident that they belong to different systems: England to Europe, America to itself." Paine also put the onus for the colonies' troubles on King George rather than on Parliament. [3]

Declaration of Independence

Pressure on the Congress to act reached a climax on June 7, 1776, when Richard Henry Lee of Virginia introduced a resolution stating that "these United Colonies are, and of right ought to be, free and independent States." [4] Jefferson, Adams, Franklin, Roger Sherman and Robert Livingston were named to draw up a declaration, but it was largely Jefferson's draft that was presented on June 28. Lee's resolution was adopted on July 2; Jefferson's Declaration then was debated and slightly amended (to strike out an indictment of the British slave trade, for example) before it was approved July 4 by all of the delegations to the Congress except New York's, which later voted for it after receiving new instructions.

The greater part of the Declaration — and the most important to Americans at that time — consisted of a recitation of every grievance against English colonial policy that had emerged since 1763. The grievances were presented as facts to prove that George III was seeking "the establishment of an absolute Tyranny over these States" and to justify the colonists' decision to dissolve "all political connection" with Britain. But it was the preamble that was to exert the greatest influence on others as a statement of political philosophy with universal appeal. Rooted in the concept of natural rights as developed by such English philosophers as Thomas Hooker and John Locke, the preamble made these assertions:

> We hold these truths to be self-evident, that all men are created equal, that they are endowed by their Creator with certain unalienable Rights, that among these are Life, Liberty and the pursuit of Happiness. That to secure these rights, Governments are instituted among Men, deriving their just powers from the consent of the governed. That whenever any Form of Government becomes destructive of these ends it is the Right of the People to alter or to abolish it, and to institute new Government, laying its foundation on such principles and organizing its powers in such form, as to them shall seem most likely to effect their Safety and Happiness.

In conclusion, the signers, who styled themselves "the Representatives of the United States of America, in General Congress, Assembled," declared that "these United Colonies are, and of Right ought to be, Free and Independent States," that as such "they have full Power to levy War, conclude Peace, contract Alliances, establish Commerce, and to do all other Acts and Things which Independent States may of right do," and that in support of this stand "we mutually pledge to each other our Lives, our Fortunes and our Sacred Honor."

Formation of State Governments

The Declaration of Independence committed the colonies to wage a war that was already under way and that would drag on for more than five years before England gave up the struggle. The Declaration also put an end to tolerance of the many Americans who remained loyal to the King. Tories who refused to sign an oath of allegiance to the United States suffered imprisonment and confiscation of property; as many as 80,000 fled to Canada and England. At home, the Declaration put to immediate test the ability of the patriots to govern.

As early as the fall of 1774, Massachusetts had set up a provisional government in response to the Coercive Acts. As revolutionary sentiment grew, patriots took control of provincial assemblies and conventions, and the royal governors and judges began to leave. New Hampshire adopted a constitution in January 1776, South Carolina followed suit in March, and on May 10 the Continental Congress advised all of the colonies to form new governments. All except Massachusetts and the self-governing charter colonies of Connecticut and Rhode Island had done so by July 4, 1777, the first anniversary of the signing of the Declaration of Independence. Four days later, Vermont, not previously a separate colony, declared its independence and adopted a constitution. Connecticut and Rhode Island did not get around to replacing their colonial charters with state constitutions until 1818 and 1842, respectively. *(See box, p. 33)*

The new state constitutions of the Revolutionary period emerged in various ways. Those of South Carolina, Virginia and New Jersey were drafted by legislative bodies without explicit authorization and put into effect without popular consent. Those of New Hampshire, Georgia, Delaware, New York and Vermont were authorized but were not submitted to the voters for approval. In Maryland, Pennsylvania and North Carolina the constitutions were authorized and ratified by the voters. Only Massachusetts and New Hampshire (which wrote a new constitution in 1784 to replace the one adopted in 1776) employed what

Major Military Developments . . .

The Revolutionary War was waged and won under severe handicaps. One-third of the colonists were opposed to the cause of independence to the end, according to John Adams, and more than a few collaborated openly with the British. Apathy was widespread and parochialism common; those not in the direct line of fire were often unwilling either to fight the war or to help pay for it.

As commander in chief, George Washington was plagued by problems of maintaining an effective military force, and the Continental Congress had little power to requisition money and supplies for the colonial armies. The war was financed largely by depreciated paper money. Without subsidies and loans from France, and that country's military intervention in 1778, the war might have been lost.

However, England also was sharply divided by the war, and the opposition increased in Parliament as time went on. The British were forced to hire German mercenaries to supplement the 15,000 regulars sent to America. Transporting and directing such a force over a distance of 3,000 miles became more and more difficult.

Major developments in the war were:

1775. Washington took command after the Battle of Bunker Hill on June 17; the British occupied Boston until they evacuated the city March 17, 1776. Meanwhile, Americans under Ethan Allen and Benedict Arnold took Montreal on Nov. 13. They were badly beaten at Quebec on Dec. 31.

1776. The British launched three campaigns. Gen. Clinton sailed for the Carolinas, but was fended off at Charleston June 28 and withdrew. Gens. Carleton and Burgoyne marched for Albany, but were stopped at Fort Ticonderoga in October. Gen. Howe sailed for New York, inflicting heavy losses there on Washington's forces; New York stayed in British hands from Sept. 15 to the end of the war. Washington retreated across the Delaware, recrossing it the night of Dec. 25 to surprise and capture 1,000 Hessians at Trenton.

1777. In August Howe sailed up the Chesapeake Bay with 15,000 men, defeated Washington at Brandywine Creek and occupied Philadelphia

...In the Revolutionary War

Sept. 25. Washington set up winter quarters at Valley Forge. Meanwhile, Burgoyne attacked Albany, suffered a series of reverses, and surrendered Oct. 17 at Saratoga. Burgoyne's defeat led to a French-American treaty of alliance, signed Feb. 6, 1778.

1778. The British offered wide concessions to end the war short of independence, but Congress rejected the offer June 17. No decisive battles were fought.

1779. The British captured Savannah Dec. 29, 1778, but Americans under Benjamin Lincoln successfully defended Charleston. Spain joined the war against England June 21 but did not enter into alliance with the Americans.

1780. On May 12 the British captured Charleston and 5,000 troops — the worst American defeat of the war. Benedict Arnold defected to the British in September.

1781. Americans under Nathaniel Greene beat Lord Cornwallis at Cowpens, S.C., on Jan. 17. Cornwallis moved north to fortify Yorktown, Va., where American and French troops surrounded the town on land and sea; Cornwallis surrendered on Oct. 17.

1782. The House of Commons resolved on March 4 to end the struggle. Congress named John Adams, envoy to the Netherlands; John Jay, envoy to Spain; Benjamin Franklin, envoy to Paris and Henry Laurens, a peace commissioner, to negotiate jointly with the French. Jay, suspicious of the French, persuaded the others to enter separate negotiations with the British. On Nov. 30, a preliminary treaty was signed pending an Anglo-French accord.

1783. The Treaty of Paris was signed Sept. 3 and approved by Congress on Jan. 14, 1784. It validated the former colonies' independence and claims to the West and fixed the boundary with Canada along the St. Lawrence and the Great Lakes. It also validated private debts to England and stated that Congress would "earnestly recommend" to the states that they restore property confiscated from Tories. England then gave West and East Florida back to Spain. The last British troops left New York Nov. 25. Washington resigned Dec. 23 to take "leave of all the employments of public life."

was to become the standard method of electing a constitutional convention and putting the product to a vote of the people.

Although they varied in detail, the new constitutions reflected a number of concepts held in common by Americans of the period. All were written, because the unwritten British constitution had become a source of such great contention between the colonists and England. All included or were accompanied by some kind of "Bill of Rights" to secure those English liberties that George III had violated, such as freedom of speech, press and petition, and the rights of habeas corpus and trial by jury. All paid tribute to the doctrine of separation of powers among the legislative, executive and judiciary, as it had been developed in England after the revolution of 1688 and expounded by Montesquieu's *Spirit of Laws*, published in 1748.

Separation did not mean balance, however, and most of the constitutions betrayed the colonists' great fear of executive authority, born of their many conflicts with the Crown and the royal governors. Executive power was weakened in every state except New York, Massachusetts and New Hampshire, and the governors of only two states were given the power of veto. In most cases the state legislature appointed the judiciary, although efforts were made to protect the independence of judges by preventing their arbitrary removal.

Power under most of the colonial constitutions was lodged in the state legislatures. Ten of these were bicameral (Pennsylvania, Georgia and Vermont had one house), with the lower house predominant. Virginia's constitution provided, for example, that: "All laws shall originate in the House of Delegates, to be approved of or rejected by the Senate, or to be amended, with consent of the House of Delegates; except money bills, which in no instance shall be altered by the Senate, but wholly approved or rejected." [5]

All of the constitutions recognized the people as sovereign, but few entrusted them with much power. The Pennsylvania constitution, written by radicals who came to power early in 1776 after a major reapportionment of the colonial assembly, was the most democratic and was later copied by Vermont. It replaced the governor and the upper chamber with an executive council, from whose ranks a president was chosen. Its members could serve no more than three years in seven while assemblymen were limited to four years in seven, to guard against establishing an aristocracy. There were no property qualifications for voting or for holding office.

First State Constitutions

	Date Adopted
New Hampshire (1st)	Jan. 6, 1776
South Carolina (1st)	March 26, 1776
Virginia	June 29, 1776
New Jersey	July 2, 1776
Delaware	Aug. 22, 1776
Pennsylvania	Sept. 28, 1776
Maryland	Nov. 11, 1776
North Carolina	Dec. 18, 1776
Georgia	Feb. 5, 1777
New York	April 20, 1777
Vermont*	July 8, 1777
South Carolina (2nd)	March 19, 1778
Massachusetts	June 15, 1780
New Hampshire (2nd)	June 13, 1784

* Vermont became a state in 1791.

Most other states adhered to prerevolutionary limits on suffrage. Ownership of some amount of property was generally required as a qualification to vote and more usually was required to hold office. The property qualification to become a state senator in New Jersey and Maryland was 1,000 pounds, in South Carolina, 2,000 pounds. Most states also imposed religious qualifications for public office.

Articles of Confederation

When Richard Henry Lee called for a declaration of independence on June 7, 1776, he proposed also that "a plan of confederation be prepared and transmitted to the respective Colonies for their consideration and approbation." [6] On June 11 Congress agreed and named a committee of 13 (one from each colony) to undertake the task. The plan that was recommended, based on a draft by John Dickinson, was presented on July 12, but it was not until Nov. 15, 1777, that Congress, after much debate and some revision, adopted the Articles of Confederation and Perpetual Union.

The Articles reflected the dominant motive of Americans who were rebelling against British rule: to preserve their freedoms from the encroachments of centralized power. Even as the Congress set up under the Articles was struggling with tenuous authority to prosecute the war (and it gave Washington dictatorial powers over the army in December 1776), few of the delegates or other American leaders were prepared to entrust a national government with any power that would diminish the sovereignty and independence of the states. Thus the scope of federal authority was not a central consideration in the design of the confederation.

What was at issue was the relative standing of 13 rival and jealous states. Would they be represented equally in the national legislature, as they were in the Continental Congress and as the smaller states desired, or in proportion to their population, as the larger states wished? The cost of a national government would have to be shared, but on what basis — wealth, the total population of each state or, as the southerners insisted, on the population of the white population only? States without claims to lands west of the Appalachians thought Congress should control the area; those with claims were reluctant to give them up.

As finally adopted, the Articles conferred less authority on the national government than had the proposal envisioned by the Albany Plan of Union of 1754. The Articles did little more than legalize what Congress already was doing by sufferance of the states. The Congress remained the sole organ of government; the states retained their equality, each having one vote; and of the specific powers delegated to Congress, the most important could not be exercised without the assent of nine of the 13 states.

The delegated authority included the power to declare war, enter treaties and alliances, raise an army and a navy, regulate coinage and borrow money. Congress was empowered also to regulate Indian affairs, establish a postal service and adjudicate disputes between the states. But it had no power to tax (other than to charge postage); the costs of government would be allocated to the states in proportion to the value of their land and improvements as determined by Congress. The states also were to be assigned quotas for troops in proportion to the number of white inhabitants. But Congress was not empowered to compel compliance.

The Articles provided that Congress was to be composed of from two to seven delegates from each of the states (and from Canada if it chose to join). The delegates were to be selected annually and paid by the states, but they could serve for no more than three years in any six. Members of Congress were barred from holding any federal post for pay and were immune from arrest while in attendance and from legal action for anything said in debate — provisions that later were incorporated in the Constitution. A Committee of the States (with one delegate from each) was authorized to act for Congress during a recess on matters that did not require the assent of nine states.

Congress was authorized to appoint committees and civil officers necessary for managing the affairs of the United States. After ratification of the Articles of Confederation, Robert Livingston was named secretary of foreign affairs, Robert Morris became superintendent of finance, and Gen. Benjamin Lincoln was appointed secretary of war. But the Articles made no provision for a federal executive or judiciary, and they gave Congress no sanction by which to enforce any of its decisions. Control of taxation and tariffs was left to the states, and unanimous consent of the states was required for the adoption of amendments.

Final ratification was delayed by the reluctance of Maryland, New Jersey and Delaware to act until the states with western claims agreed to cede them to the national government. Cession of state claims did not actually begin until 1784, but it was clear by the beginning of 1781 that the states would cede, and Maryland, the last holdout, ratified the Articles on March 1, 1781. Congress proclaimed them to be in effect the same day.

Defects of the Confederation

Adoption of the Articles of Confederation did nothing to relieve the chaotic state of federal finances. Of $10 million requisitioned by Congress in the first two years, the states paid in less than $1.5 million. From 1781 to 1786 federal collections averaged half a million dollars a year, barely enough to meet current expenses. After two years as superintendent of finance, Robert Morris resigned in 1783, saying "our public credit is gone." [7] The foreign debt of the United States increased from less than $8 million in 1783 to more than $10 million in 1789, plus almost $1.8 million in unpaid interest.

35

Congress recognized the need for some independent financial authority even before the Articles took effect. Early in 1781 it had asked the states for authority to levy a duty of 5 percent on all imports. But it took unanimous agreement to amend the Articles, and the proposal died in 1782 when Rhode Island rejected it. In 1783 Congress again asked for the power to levy import duties, and this time New York refused to give its approval.

Peace put an end to the destruction and drain of war, but it also underscored the weakness and disunity of the now sovereign and independent American states. As agreed in the peace treaty with England, Congress in 1783 recommended that the states restore the property confiscated from the Loyalists, but few of them complied. And instead of helping British merchants to recover their prewar debts (as the treaty obligated them to do), many of the states enacted laws making recovery more difficult. The British, in turn, refused to evacuate several posts on the American side of the border with Canada.

The inability of Congress to force the states to comply with terms of the peace treaty contributed to the refusal of England, France and Spain to enter commercial treaties with the Confederation. Lacking any authority over trade, Congress was unable to retaliate when the British in 1783 closed Canada and the British West Indies to American shipping; the attempts of the states to retaliate individually failed completely. The weakness of the Confederation also encouraged Spain to close the Mississippi River to American ships in 1784 and to intrigue for the secession of frontier areas north of the Floridas.

Congress was equally powerless to help resolve a postwar conflict between debtors and creditors that was aggravated by an economic depression and a shortage of currency. Most of the states stopped issuing paper money and attempted to pay their war debts by raising taxes. At the same time, merchants and other creditors began to press for the collection of private debts. Squeezed on all sides, debtors (who were mostly farmers) clamored for relief through state laws to put off the collection of debts and to provide cheap money.

In response to this pressure, seven of the states resorted to paper money issues in 1786, during the worst of the depression. In Rhode Island debtors fared relatively well; many creditors, compelled by law to accept repayment in highly depreciated paper money, fled the state. But in Massachusetts, where the commercial class was in power, the state government refused to issue paper money and pressed forward with a deflationary program of high taxes; cattle and land were seized for debts, debtors crowded the jails and all petitions for relief were ignored.

Out of this turmoil came Shays' Rebellion of 1786, an uprising of distressed farmers in central Massachusetts led by Daniel Shays. Although the rebellion was put down by state militia in fairly short order, sympathy for the rebels was widespread. Their leaders were treated leniently, and a newly elected legislature acted to meet some of their demands. But the rebellion aroused the fears of many Americans for the future, and it pointed up another weakness of the Confederation — Congress had been unable to give Massachusetts any help. The rebellion also gave a strong push to the growing movement for governmental reform.

Notes

1. Edmund Cody Burnett, *The Continental Congress* (New York: W. W. Norton & Co., 1964), pp. 85-87.
2. Ibid., p. 127.
3. Ibid., pp. 131-137.
4. Ibid., p. 171.
5. Charles Ramsdell Lingley, *The Transition in Virginia from Colony to Commonwealth* (New York: Columbia University Press, 1910), p. 172.
6. Burnett, *The Continental Congress*, p. 171.
7. Andrew C. McLaughlin, *The Confederation and the Constitution, 1783-1789*, with a foreword by Henry Steele Commager (New York: Collier Books, 1962), p. 51.

Chapter 3

THE CONSTITUTION

The state of the union under the Articles of Confederation had become a source of growing concern to leading Americans well before Shays' Rebellion shook the confidence of a wider public. In voluminous correspondence beginning as early as 1780, George Washington, John Jay, Thomas Jefferson, James Madison, James Monroe and many others expressed their fears that the union could not survive the strains of internal dissension and external weakness without some strengthening of central authority.

It was clear to Washington, writing in 1783, "that the honor, power and true interest of this country must be measured by a Continental scale, and that every departure therefrom weakens the Union, and may ultimately break the band which holds us together." He urged all patriots "to avert these evils, to form a Constitution that will give consistency, stability, and dignity to the Union and sufficient powers to the great Council of the Nation for general purposes." [1]

How to form such a constitution was not yet clear. Opinions varied widely as to what would be "sufficient powers . . . for general purposes." Alexander Hamilton, in 1780, thought Congress should be given "complete sovereignty" over all but a few matters.[2] But Congress had ignored proposals of its committees in 1781 that it seek authority to use troops "to compel any delinquent State to fulfill its Federal engagement" and to seize "the property of a State delinquent in its assigned proportion of men and money." [3] While there was general agreement on congressional authority to levy a federal import duty, the effort to amend the Articles foundered on the rule of unanimity.

At Hamilton's urging, the New York Assembly asked Congress in 1782 to call a general convention of the states to revise the Articles. The Massachusetts Legislature seconded the request in 1785. Congress studied the proposal but was unable to reach any agreement. Then,

Virginia and Maryland in 1785 worked out a plan to resolve conflicts between the two states over navigation and commercial regulations. This gave Madison the idea of calling a general meeting on commercial problems. In January 1786 the Virginia Assembly issued the call for a meeting in Annapolis in September.

Nine states named delegates to the Annapolis convention, but the dozen persons who assembled represented only five states — New York, New Jersey, Pennsylvania, Delaware and Virginia. Rather than seek a commercial agreement from so small a group, Madison and Hamilton persuaded the delegates on Sept. 14 to adopt a report that described the state of the Union as "delicate and critical." The report recommended that the states appoint commissioners to meet the next May in Philadelphia "to devise such further provisions as shall appear to them necessary to render the constitution of the Federal Government adequate to the exigencies of the Union." [4]

The proposal was deliberately vague. Madison and Hamilton knew there was strong opposition to giving the central government much more power. Some officials even preferred the alternative of dividing the union into two or more confederations of states with closer economic and political ties. Southerners were convinced that this was the ultimate objective of John Jay's offer to Spain to give up free navigation of the Mississippi in return for trading concessions of interest to New England. James Monroe, a Virginia delegate to Congress, saw it as part of a scheme "for dismembering the Confederacy and throwing the states eastward of the Hudson into one government." [5]

The Virginia Assembly, prodded by Madison and Washington, agreed on Oct. 16, 1786, to send delegates to Philadelphia, and six other states took similar action before Congress, on Feb. 21, 1787, moved to retain control of the situation. It passed a resolution endorsing the proposed convention for the purpose of reporting to Congress and the several legislatures on its recommendations. Officially, therefore, the convention was to be no more than advisory to Congress.

Soon after the Philadelphia convention opened on May 25, 1787, the delegates were asked to decide whether to try to patch up the Articles of Confederation or to ignore them and draw up a new plan of government.

Congress, the state legislatures and many of the delegates expected the session in Philadelphia to do no more than draft proposals to revise the Articles in a way that would somehow strengthen the Confederation

Twelve of the 13 Original Colonies...

All of the states except Rhode Island (whose upper house balked) were represented at the Constitutional Convention of 1787, which met at the State House in Philadelphia from May 25 to Sept. 15. The states appointed a total of 74 delegates, but only 55 attended, and their comings and goings held the average attendance to little more than 30.

Delegates

The 55 delegates who took part included many of the most distinguished men in America. Eight had signed the Declaration of Independence, seven had been governors of their respective states and 39 had served in the Congress of the Confederation. More than half were college graduates, and at least 33 were attorneys at law. Most of them had held prominent positions in the Revolutionary War, and all were well-respected men of substance in their states. A majority were under the age of 50 (five were under 30) and only four were 60 or over.

George Washington, then 55, and Benjamin Franklin, the oldest delegate at 81, were the most influential Americans of the time. General Washington, who had not wanted to participate at the convention as a delegate but had yielded for fear that his absence might be construed as indifference to the outcome, was the unanimous choice to preside at the convention. He took a limited but effective part in the deliberations. Those credited with the greatest influence were Gouverneur Morris and James Wilson of Pennsylvania, James Madison of Virginia and Roger Sherman of Connecticut, each of whom spoke well over 100 times.

Rules

The convention adopted its rules of procedure on May 28 and 29. There was some talk of the larger states getting more votes than the smaller, but the convention followed the custom under the Articles of Confederation in giving each state one vote. The rule provided that seven states would constitute a quorum. This rule was amended to permit reconsideration of any vote — a step taken many times during the convention. Reconsideration was made easier by a rule of secrecy providing that "nothing spoken in the House [was to] be printed or otherwise published or communicated without leave." Secrecy was essential, Madison wrote Jefferson, "to secure unbiased discussion within doors and to prevent

... Attended the Constitutional Convention

misconceptions and misconstructions without." * The official journal, limited to a report of formal motions and votes, was closed until 1819. Madison's shorthand notes, withheld until 1840, provided the fullest account.

Procedure

The convention began by moving into Committee of the Whole to debate the Virginia resolutions, which called for a national government with a bicameral legislature, an executive and a judiciary. The smaller states then rallied behind the New Jersey Plan, which proposed only modest revisions in the Articles of Confederation. After that plan was defeated June 19, the members reverted to convention, and a threatened deadlock was broken by the "Great Compromise" of July 16 giving each state an equal vote in the Senate. On July 24 a Committee of Detail (Nathaniel Gorham, Oliver Ellsworth, Edmund Randolph, John Rutledge and Wilson) was appointed to draft a constitution based on agreements already reached. The convention then took a ten-day recess during which Washington went fishing near Valley Forge. On Sept. 8 a Committee of Style was named to polish the wording and arrange the articles. The final document was put before the convention on Sept. 17.

The Signing

At this point, Franklin said he hoped "every member of the Convention who may still have objections to it [the Constitution], would, with me, on this occasion doubt a little of his own infallibility, and ... put his name to this instrument." ** He moved that the Constitution be signed by the unanimous consent of the states present. The motion was approved as was one change increasing representation in the House from one member for every 40,000 inhabitants to one for every 30,000 — a change supported by Washington in his only speech at the convention. The Constitution was signed by all but three of the 42 delegates still in attendance: George Mason, Edmund Randolph and Elbridge Gerry. After agreeing that the Constitution should be submitted to special conventions of the states for ratification, the convention adjourned.

*Charles Warren, *The Making of the Constitution* (Boston: Little, Brown & Co., 1928), p. 135.
** Ibid., p. 709.

without altering the system of state sovereignty. But Madison and others who had worked to bring about the convention were convinced of the need for fundamental reform.

The Virginia Plan

These nationalists had come prepared, and on May 29 they seized the initiative. Edmund Randolph, acting for the Virginians, introduced 15 resolutions that added up to a plan for a new "National Government" of broad powers. The Virginia Plan called for a "National Legislature" of two houses, one to be elected by the people and the other by members of the first; a "National Executive" to be chosen by the Legislature; and a "National Judiciary." The Legislature would have power to legislate in all cases where the states were "incompetent" or would interrupt "the harmony of the United States," and to "negate" state laws contrary to the articles of union. And the states would be represented in both chambers in proportion to their wealth or their white population.[6]

The convention moved at once into Committee of the Whole to consider the Randolph resolutions. The proposals clearly envisaged a central government that, unlike that of the Confederation, would operate directly upon the people and independently of the states. It was to be a "national government" in contrast to the "merely federal" system that had been tried and found wanting. What the Virginians had in mind, though, was a system in which national and state governments would exercise dual sovereignty over the people within separate and prescribed fields. Randolph said that his plan "only means to give the national government power to defend and protect itself — to take, therefore, from the respective legislatures of states no more sovereignty than is competent to this end."[7]

Such a dual system was unknown in 1787. To many delegates the term "national government" implied a unitary or consolidated regime of potentially unlimited powers that would extinguish the independence of the states. However, on May 30, with only Connecticut opposed and New York divided, they adopted Randolph's proposition "that a National Government ought to be established consisting of a supreme Legislative, Executive and Judiciary." This opening commitment by most of the delegates then present reflected the air of crisis in which they met.[8]

The next step of the Committee of the Whole was to take up and approve several of the specific proposals of the Virginia Plan. As the debate proceeded, some members from smaller states became alarmed by

Legislative Nomenclature

The Constitutional Convention continued to speak of the "Legislature of the United States" and its "first branch" and "second branch" until those terms were changed in the Aug. 6 report of the Committee of Detail to the "Congress of the United States," the "House of Representatives" and the "Senate." The term "Congress" was taken from the Articles of Confederation. "House of Representatives" was the name of the first branch in five states (the others being called the Assembly, House of Delegates and House of Commons). The second branch was called the "Senate" in all but two states.*

Provisions of the Constitution relating to both the House and Senate referred to "each House" in keeping with English usage. But the terms "upper house" and "lower house" to denote the Senate and the House, which also were taken from English usage, were not included in the Constitution.

* Charles Warren, *The Making of the Constitution* (Boston: Little, Brown & Co., 1928), p. 388.

the insistence of the larger states on proportional representation in both houses of the proposed national Legislature. Under one formula, Virginia, Pennsylvania and Massachusetts — the three most populous states — would have held 13 of 28 seats in the Senate as well as a similar share of seats in the House. This spelled domination to those accustomed to the equality of states that prevailed in the Congress of the Confederation and in the convention as well.

To Luther Martin of Maryland, such a plan meant "a system of slavery which bound hand and foot 10 states of the Union and placed them at the mercy of the other three." John Dickinson declared that "we would rather submit to a foreign power than submit to be deprived of an equality of suffrage in both branches of the Legislature, and thereby be thrown under the domination of the large states." New Jersey would "never confederate" on such a basis, said William Paterson, for "she would be swallowed up." He would "rather submit to a monarch, to a despot, than to such a fate." [9]

The New Jersey Plan

On June 11 the convention voted six states to five to constitute the Senate on the same proportional basis as the House. That decision led Paterson and others to draft a purely federal alternative to the Virginia Plan. The New Jersey Plan, presented June 15, proposed amending the Articles of Confederation to give Congress authority to levy import duties and to regulate trade. It would have provided also for a plural executive, to be chosen by Congress, and a federal judiciary. It proposed that treaties and acts of Congress "shall be the supreme law," and that the executive be authorized to "call forth the power of the Confederated States" to enforce the laws if necessary. But the plan would have left each state with an equal voice in Congress and most of the attributes of sovereignty.

Paterson argued that his plan "accorded first with the powers of the convention, and second with the sentiments of the people.... Our object is not such a Government as may be best in itself, but such a one as our constituents have authorized us to prepare and as they will approve."

The nationalists rejected this concept of their responsibility. Randolph said he was not "scrupulous on the point of power. When the Republic was at stake, it would be treason to our trust not to propose what we found necessary." As Hamilton put it, the Union was in peril, and "to rely on and propose any plan not adequate to these exigencies, merely because it was not clearly within our powers, would be to sacrifice the means to the end.... The great question is what provisions shall we make for the happiness of our country?" [10]

Madison was the last to speak against the New Jersey Plan, pointing up serious problems of the Confederation for which it offered no solution. On June 19 the delegates were asked to decide whether the Randolph resolutions "should be adhered to as preferable to those of Mr. Paterson." [11] Seven states voted yes and only three states no. That settled the issue of partial vs. total reform; a clear majority of the delegates were now committed to abandoning the Articles and to drafting a new constitution.

The Great Compromise

The task was to take three months. There were few points of unanimity among the 55 men participating. Delegates from the same state frequently were divided; as a result, states occasionally were unable to cast votes on constitutional proposals. The records of the convention also reveal that, although the nationalists won over a majority to their cause at an early stage, the original Virginia Plan was unacceptable in many of its details. The Constitution could not have been written without some degree of willingness on all sides to compromise in the interests of designing a workable and acceptable plan.

This became evident soon after defeat of the New Jersey Plan when the small states continued to demand and the large states to oppose equal representation in the Senate. On July 1 the convention split five to five on this issue. Faced with a deadlock, the convention named a committee to seek a compromise. It proposed on July 5 that, in return for equality of state representation in the Senate, the House be given sole power to originate money bills, which the Senate could accept or reject but not modify. This formula was finally approved July 16, five states to four, with Massachusetts divided and New York not voting because two of its three delegates had departed, never to return. On July 24 a five-member Committee of Detail was appointed to draft the Constitution according to the resolutions adopted by the convention. The draft presented Aug. 6 included changes and additions that were refined through the following month. On Sept. 8 another committee was named to revise the style and arrange the articles.

Without the Great Compromise the convention would have collapsed. As Madison pointed out, however, "the great division of interests" in America was not between the large and small but between the northern and southern states, partly because of climate but "principally from the effects of having or not having slaves." [12] Although the southerners were mostly supporters of a strong central government, they were determined to limit its power to discriminate against the South's special interests in slavery, agricultural exports and western expansion. This stand necessitated other compromises that accounted for some of the key provisions of the new plan of government.

What finally emerged Sept. 17 as the Constitution of the United States was a unique blend of national and federal systems based on republican principles of representative and limited government. It met the basic objective of the nationalists by providing for a central government of ample powers that could function independently of the states. It also met the concerns of states' rights supporters by surrounding that government with checks and balances to prevent the tyranny of any one branch.

The text of the Constitution does not follow the order in which the separate provisions were developed. The convention moved generally from decisions on broad principles to questions of detail and precision. But the interdependent nature of the various parts of the plan made for frequent reconsideration of decisions in one area to take account of subsequent decisions in another but related area. As a result, many of the provisions were altered or added in the final weeks of the convention. How the major provisions were developed is described in the following chapters in Part I.

Notes

1. Charles Warren, *The Making of the Constitution* (Boston: Little, Brown & Co., 1928), p. 12.
2. Ibid., pp. 6-7.
3. Ibid., p. 8.
4. Ibid., p. 23.
5. Ibid., p. 25.
6. James Madison, *Notes of Debates in the Federal Convention of 1787*, with an introduction by Adrienne Koch (Athens, Ohio: Ohio University Press, 1966), p. 30.
7. Warren, *The Making of the Constitution*, p. 150.
8. Madison, *Notes of Debates in the Federal Convention*, p. 36.
9. Warren, *The Making of the Constitution*, pp. 216-18; Andrew C. McLaughlin, *The Confederation and the Constitution, 1783-1789*, with a foreword by Henry Steele Commager (New York: Collier Books, 1962), p. 144.
10. Warren, *The Making of the Constitution*, p. 223.
11. Ibid., p. 232.
12. Ibid., p. 257.

Chapter 4

THE STRUCTURE OF CONGRESS

The convention's early decision that a national government, if formed, should consist of three branches — legislative, executive and judicial — was undisputed. This division of governmental functions had been recognized from early colonial times and was reflected in most of the state constitutions. The failure of the Articles of Confederation to separate the functions was generally recognized as a serious mistake. The decision by the convention in favor of three branches of government also implied broad acceptance of the principle of separation of powers, although most of the provisions of the Constitution that gave effect to this principle were adopted on practical rather than theoretical grounds.

The Virginia Plan had called for a national legislature of two houses, according to the practice initiated by the English Parliament and followed by most of the colonial governments and retained by 10 of the 13 states. The Continental Congress and the Congress of the Articles of Confederation were unicameral, but once the convention had decided to abandon the Articles there was little question that the new Congress should be bicameral. As George Mason saw it, the minds of Americans were settled on two points — "an attachment to republican government [and] an attachment to more than one branch in the Legislature." [1] Only Pennsylvania dissented when the Committee of the Whole voted for two houses, and the convention confirmed the committee's decision June 21 by a vote of seven states to three.

Election to the House

The nationalists insisted that the new government rest on the consent of the people rather than on the state legislatures. They felt it was essential that at least "the first branch," the House, be elected "by the people immediately," as James Madison put it. The government "ought to possess ... the mind or sense of the people at large," said James Wilson, and for that reason "the Legislature ought to be the most exact transcript of the whole society." The House "was to be the grand depository of the democratic principles of the Government," George Mason declared.[2]

Those who were suspicious of a national government preferred election of the House by the state legislatures. "The people immediately should have as little to do" with electing the government as possible, according to Roger Sherman, because "they want information and are constantly liable to be misled." Elbridge Gerry was convinced that "the evils we experience flow from the excess of democracy," while Charles Pinckney thought "the people were less fit judges" than the legislatures to choose members of the House.[3] The proposal for election by state legislatures twice was defeated, however, and popular election of the House was confirmed June 21 by a vote of nine states to one.

Election to the Senate

The Virginia Plan proposed that the House elect the "second branch" from persons nominated by the state legislatures. Few delegates supported this plan because it would have made the Senate subservient to the House. Most agreed with Gouverneur Morris that the Senate should "check the precipitation, changeableness and excesses of the first branch." [4] (The concept of the Senate's role as that of representing the states emerged later, after the decision in favor of equal representation.) Neither was there any support for Madison's and Wilson's view that the people should elect the Senate as well as the House. Election of senators by the state legislatures was carried unanimously in the Committee of the Whole on June 7 and confirmed June 25 by a convention vote of nine states to two.

Basis of Representation

The Virginia Plan called for representation of the states in both the House and Senate in proportion to their wealth or free population. This proposal led to the revolt of the small states, which was resolved by a vote on July 16 for equal representation of the states in the Senate. While the principle of proportional representation in the House was never seriously challenged, the idea of basing Senate representation on wealth or the free population raised numerous questions and led to adoption of important qualifications.

To retain southern support for proportional representation in the Senate, Wilson had proposed on June 11 that the House be apportioned according to a count of the whole number of free citizens and three-fifths of all others (meaning slaves), excluding Indians not paying taxes. This formula (first proposed in Congress in 1783) was adopted with only New Jersey and Delaware opposed. Then on July 9 the convention decided that the new Congress should have the power "to regulate the number of representatives upon the principles of wealth and number of inhabitants." [5] Since southerners regarded slaves as property, this led northerners who wanted representation in the House to be based on population alone to ask why slaves should be counted at all.

As a result, on July 11 the convention voted six states to four to exclude blacks from the formula worked out June 11. At this point Gouverneur Morris proposed that the power of Congress to apportion the House according to wealth and numbers be subject to a proviso "that direct taxation shall be in proportion to representation." [6] This proviso, which was adopted without debate, cast the slave issue in a different light: the South would have to pay additional taxes for any increases in representation it gained by counting slaves. The northerners then dropped their opposition to the three-fifths count demanded by the southerners, and on July 13 the convention restored that provision.

Because it was agreed finally that representation was to be based solely on population (counting all whites and three-fifths of the blacks), the word "wealth" was deleted from the provision adopted July 9. This solution to the issue gave five free voters in a slave state a voice in the House equivalent to that of seven free voters in a non-slave state, according to Massachusetts delegate Rufus King, but it was "a necessary sacrifice to the establishment of the Constitution." [7]

Size of Congress

The convention committee that recommended equal representation in the Senate on July 5 also proposed that each state have one vote in the House for every 40,000 inhabitants. This proposal precipitated the debate on representation, during which it was decided to let Congress regulate the future size of the House to allow for population changes and the admission of new states. Upon reflection by the delegates, however, it was feared that under such an arrangement a majority in Congress would be able to block a reapportionment plan or change the basis of representation for slaves. Thus northerners and southerners now agreed that the periods between reapportionments and the rules for revising representation in the House ought to be fixed by the Constitution.

Edmund Randolph was the first to propose a regular census, and on July 13 the convention adopted the plan, finally incorporated in Article I, Section 2, linking the apportionment of representatives to an "enumeration" every 10 years of the "whole number of free persons . . . and three fifths of all others." On Aug. 8 it was decided that the number of representatives "shall not exceed one for every 40,000," a figure that was lowered to 30,000 on the last day of the convention. Until the first census was taken, the size of the House was fixed at 65 representatives, allotted as set forth in Article I.[8]

The size of the Senate was fixed on July 23 when the convention adopted a proposal (which Maryland alone voted against) that the body should "consist of two members from each state, who shall vote per capita." A proposal to allow each state three senators had been turned down on the ground that it would penalize poorer and more distant states and that "a small number was most convenient for deciding on peace and war," as Nathaniel Gorham put it.

The idea that senators should vote individually rather than as a delegation came from Elbridge Gerry, who wanted to "prevent the delays and inconveniences" that had occurred in Congress in voting under the unit rule.[9] Although this provision was at odds with the decision that the states should be equally represented in the Senate, it was accepted with little objection and included in Article I, Section 3.

Terms of Office

There was strong attachment in the convention to the tradition of annual elections — "the only defense of the people against tyranny," according to Gerry. But Madison argued that representatives would need more than one year to become informed about the office and the national interests, and his proposal of a three-year term for the House was adopted June 12. Many delegates continued to press for more frequent elections, however. "The Representatives ought to return home and mix with the people," said Sherman, adding that "by remaining at the seat of Government they would acquire the habits of the place, which might differ from those of their constituents." The convention reconsidered the question June 21 and compromised on biennial elections and a two-year term for representatives.[10]

The delegates also changed their minds about the Senate, agreeing first to a term of seven years, although the terms of state senators varied from two years to a maximum of five. When this decision was reviewed, alternatives of four, six and nine years were considered. Charles Pinckney opposed six years. Senators would be "too long separated from their constituents, and will imbibe attachments different from that of the state," he argued. But having decided on biennial elections for the House, the convention voted June 26 to make it a six-year term in the Senate, with one-third of the membership to be elected every two years.[11]

Qualifications of Voters

The Aug. 6 report of the convention's Committee of Detail stated that the qualifications of electors for the House should be the same as those required by the states for "the most numerous branch" of their own legislatures. Because property and other voting qualifications varied widely from state to state, no uniform standard seemed feasible. When Gouverneur Morris proposed giving Congress power to alter the qualifications, Oliver Ellsworth objected: "The clause is safe as it is — the states have staked their liberties on the qualifications which we have proposed to confirm." [12] A proposal by Morris and others to limit the franchise to those who owned land was rejected, and on Aug. 8 the convention adopted the committee's proposal without dissent.

Regulation of Elections

The Committee of Detail also proposed that the states regulate the times and places of electing senators and representatives, but that Congress retain the power to change these regulations. The states should not have the last word in this regard, said Madison, since "it was impossible to foresee all the abuses that might be made of the discretionary power." The convention adopted this provision on Aug. 9 but amended it Sept. 14 by adding the qualification: "except as to the places of choosing Senators," who were to be elected by the state legislatures. The purpose of the change was to "exempt the seats of government in the states from the power of Congress." [13]

Qualifications of Members

The convention decided in June on a minimum age of 30 for senators and 25 for representatives. The Committee of Detail added two more qualifications: United States citizenship (three years for the House, four for the Senate) and residence within the state to be represented. Fearful of making it too easy for foreigners to be elected, the convention lengthened the citizenship requirement to seven years for representatives and nine years for senators, after voting down 14 years as likely, in Ellsworth's view, to discourage "meritorious aliens from emigrating to this country." [14]

Some delegates wanted to require residence in a state for a minimum time — from one to seven years. Mason feared that "rich men of neighboring states may employ with success the means of corruption in some particular district and thereby get into the public councils after having failed in their own state." But these proposals were voted down, and it was left that "no person shall be a representative [or senator] who shall not, when elected, be an inhabitant of that state in which he shall be chosen." [15]

The convention debated the desirability of a property qualification for office. Most of the state constitutions required members of their legislatures to own certain amounts of property. John Dickinson doubted the wisdom of a "policy of interweaving into a Republican Constitution a veneration of wealth." But on July 26, by a vote of eight states to three, the convention instructed the Committee of Detail to draft a property qualification. As written, this would have given Congress authority to establish "uniform qualifications . . . with regard to property." When the provision was debated on Aug. 10 it was rejected, and further efforts to include a property qualification ended.[16]

There was even less disposition to include a religious qualification, although all of the states except New York and Virginia imposed such a qualification on state representatives. The convention's outlook on this point was made clear when, in debating an oath of office on Aug. 30, the delegates adopted without dissent Charles Pinckney's proviso (which became a part of Article VI) that "no religious test shall ever be required as a qualification to any office or public trust under the United States." [17] Thus the only qualifications established by the Constitution for election to Congress were those of age, citizenship and residence.

Pay of Members

The Virginia Plan wanted members of the National Legislature to be paid "liberal stipends" without saying who should pay them. To the nationalists, however, one of the weaknesses of the Confederation was that members of Congress were paid by their states. So on June 12, after submitting "fixt" for "liberal," the Committee of the Whole agreed that in the case of representatives "the wages should be paid out of the National Treasury." Ellsworth dissented and on June 22 moved that the states pay their salaries. This change was opposed by Randolph who said it would create a dependence that "would vitiate the whole system." Hamilton agreed: "[T]hose who pay are the masters of those who are paid." Ellsworth's motion was rejected, four states to five.

When the pay of senators was discussed on June 26, Ellsworth again moved that the states pay. Madison argued that this would make senators "the mere agents and advocates of state interests and views, instead of being the impartial umpires and guardians of justice and general good." Ellsworth's motion was again defeated, five states to six. Despite the vote, the Aug. 6 report of the Committee of Detail provided that the pay of senators and representatives should be "ascertained and paid" by the states. But Ellsworth and others by now had changed their minds, and on Aug. 14 the convention voted nine states to two to pay members out of the national Treasury.

Whether the amount of pay should be fixed in the Constitution was another matter. To let Congress set its own wages, said Madison, "was an indecent thing and might, in time, prove a dangerous one." Ellsworth proposed five dollars a day. Others thought the decision should be left to Congress, although Sherman was afraid the members would pay themselves too little rather than too much, "so that men ever so fit could not serve unless they were at the same time rich." On Aug. 14 the convention voted to give Congress full authority to fix its own pay by law.[18]

Length of Service

Because of the attachment of several states to the theory of rotation in office, the Articles of Confederation had provided that "no person shall be capable of being a delegate for more than three years in any term of six years."[19] This rule had forced out of Congress some of its better members and was widely criticized. The Virginia Plan proposed, nevertheless, that members ought not to be eligible for re-election indefinitely after the expiration of their initial term of service, and that they should be subject to recall. But this provision was eliminated in the Committee of the Whole, without debate or dissent, and no further effort was made to restrict the eligibility of representatives or senators for re-election.

Whether members of Congress should be eligible to hold other offices was more controversial. Under the Articles, a delegate was not "capable of holding any office under the United States for which he, or another for his benefit, receives any salary, fees or emolument of any kind." [20] The Congress had appointed many delegates to diplomatic and other jobs, however, and the practice had created much resentment.

The office-seeking propensities of state legislators also raised general concern. The Virginia Plan proposed making any member of Congress ineligible for any office established by a particular state, or under the authority of the United States, during this term of service and for an unspecified period after its expiration.

Although this provision, with a period of one year inserted in the blank, was adopted in the Committee of the Whole on June 12, the convention reconsidered and modified it several times before the final form was approved on Sept. 3. Delegates who wanted to shut the door on appointments saw them as a source of corruption. "What led to the appointment of this Convention?" asked John Mercer, who answered: "The corruption and mutability of the legislative councils of the states." Those opposed to too many strictures feared they would discourage good men from running for Congress. "The legislature would cease to be a magnet to the first talents and abilities," said Charles Pinckney.[21]

The compromise that emerged was a twofold disqualification. First, a member could not be appointed during his term to a federal office created during his term or to a federal office for which the pay was increased during the member's term. Second, no one holding federal office could be a member of Congress at the same time. The provision, incorporated in Section 6 of Article I, made no reference to state office or to ineligibility following expiration of a member's term.

Rules and Regulation of Congress

Article I included four provisions for the regulation of the House and Senate that originated with the Committee of Detail and were modified only slightly by the full convention:

— "Each House shall be the Judge of the Elections, Returns and Qualifications of its own Members. . . ." The constitutions of eight of the states contained this language, and it was agreed to without debate.

— "Each House may determine the Rules of its Proceedings, punish its Members for disorderly Behaviour, and, with the Concurrence of two-thirds, expel a Member." This provision was amended by the two-thirds vote requirement for expulsion. The change, proposed by Madison because "the right of expulsion was too important to be exercised by a bare majority of a quorum," was approved unanimously.

— "Each House shall keep a Journal, and from time to time publish the same. . . ." This language stemmed from a similar provision in the Articles of Confederation. When Madison proposed giving the Senate some discretion in the matter, Wilson objected: "[T]he people have a right to know what their agents are doing or have done, and it should not be in the option of the legislature to conceal their proceedings." [22] The convention voted to require publication of the Journals of each House, "excepting such parts as may in their judgment require secrecy." The clause also provided for recording the "yea" and "nay" votes of members, although some delegates objected that "the reasons governing the votes never appear along with them."

— "Neither House, during the Session of Congress, shall, without the Consent of the other, adjourn for more than three days, nor to any other Place than that in which the two Houses shall be sitting." This was agreed to after brief debate. Most of the state constitutions had similar provisions, reflecting a common reaction against the practice of royal governors to suspend and dissolve the state assemblies.

Notes

1. Charles Warren, *The Making of the Constitution* (Boston: Little, Brown & Co., 1928), p. 159.
2. Ibid., pp. 160, 162.
3. Ibid., p. 161.
4. Ibid., p. 195.
5. James Madison, *Notes of Debates in the Federal Convention of 1787*, with an introduction by Adrienne Koch (Athens, Ohio: Ohio University Press, 1966), p. 257.
6. Warren, *The Making of the Constitution*, p. 290.
7. Ibid., p. 292.
8. Ibid., pp. 294-298.
9. Ibid., p. 345.
10. Ibid., p. 242.
11. Ibid., p. 243.

12. Ibid., p. 401.
13. Ibid., p. 409.
14. Ibid., pp. 415-416.
15. Ibid., pp. 414-415.
16. Ibid., pp. 417-419.
17. Ibid., p. 426.
18. Ibid., pp. 445-451.
19. Merrill Jensen, *The Articles of Confederation* (Madison: University of Wisconsin Press, 1940), p. 264.
20. Ibid.
21. Warren, *The Making of the Constitution,* pp. 615-616.
22. Ibid., p. 431.

Chapter 5

POWERS OF CONGRESS

The resolutions introduced May 29 by Edmund Randolph of Virginia reflected the great concern of the nationalists with the powerlessness of Congress under the Articles of Confederation to protect the interests of the United States at large. James Dickinson warned against the "prejudices, passions and improper views of the state legislatures," and James Madison deplored "a constant tendency in the states to encroach on the federal authority, to violate national treaties, to infringe the rights and interests of each other, to oppress the weaker party within their respective jurisdiction." [1] Delegates at the Constitutional Convention of 1787 felt it was essential that, in addition to adequate authority to legislate for the general interests of the Union, the new national government should possess the power to restrain the states and to compel their obedience.

The Virginia resolutions proposed that the National Legislature be empowered:

"to enjoy the Legislative Rights vested in Congress by the Confederation and moreover to legislate in all cases to which the separate States are incompetent, or in which the harmony of the United States may be interrupted by the exercise of individual Legislation;

"to negate all laws passed by the several States, contravening in the opinion of the National Legislature the articles of Union; and

"to call forth the force of the Union against any member of the Union failing in its duty under the articles thereof."

When these proposals were first discussed May 31, some delegates wanted an exact enumeration of such powers before voting, but the first of the Virginia resolutions was approved after brief debate without dissent. The second, granting a power to negate state laws — which was akin to the royal disallowance of colonial laws — also was approved easily. When the third resolution was called up, however, Madison moved to set it aside because he feared that "the use of force against a state would look more like a declaration of war than an infliction of punishment." [2] Although the New Jersey Plan contained a similar provision, there was no further consideration of this power by the convention.

On June 8 Charles Pinckney proposed that the power to nullify state laws be extended to all such laws Congress should judge to be improper. Such an expansion would enslave the states, Elbridge Gerry argued, and the motion was rejected, seven states to three. Strong opposition then developed to any power to negate state laws, although Madison continued to defend it as the most certain means of preserving the system. On July 17 the convention reversed its earlier action by voting seven states to three against the power to veto. The problem of securing conformity of the states to national law finally was resolved by adoption of a "supremacy" clause and a specific prohibition on certain types of state laws.

The convention on July 17 also reconsidered the first of the Virginia resolutions. Roger Sherman proposed as a substitute that Congress be empowered "to make laws binding on the people of the United States in all cases which may concern the common interests of the Union; but not to interfere with the Government of the individual States in any matters of internal police which respect the Government of such States only, and wherein the general welfare of the United States is not concerned." This formulation, in which the term "general welfare" made its first appearance in the convention, seemed too restrictive to most delegates; it was rejected, eight states to two. Then, by a vote of six states to four, the convention inserted in the resolution approved May 31 the additional power to legislate "in all cases for the general interests of the Union." [3]

The Committee of Detail found this broad grant of legislative authority too vague and unlimited and decided to replace it with an enumeration of specified powers. Eighteen of these powers were listed in the committee's Aug. 6 report, which also spelled out certain powers to be denied to Congress and to the states. These powers and prohibitions were finally incorporated in Sections 8, 9 and 10 of Article I of the Constitution.

Power to Tax

The committee's first proposal — that Congress "shall have the power to lay and collect taxes, duties, imposts and excises" — was adopted Aug. 16 without dissent. The convention then became embroiled in the issue of paying off the public debt and decided to amend the tax clause to provide that Congress "shall fulfill the engagements and discharge the debts of the United States and shall have the power to lay and collect taxes. . . ." Pierce Butler objected that this language would require Congress to redeem at face value all government paper, including that held by "bloodsuckers who had speculated on the distresses of others and bought up securities at heavy discounts." [4] He thought Congress should be free to buy up such holdings at less than full value.

As a result, the convention dropped the language added to the tax clause and adopted in its place the declaration found in Article VI: "All debts contracted and engagements entered into before the adoption of this Constitution shall be as valid against the United States under this Constitution as under the Confederation." (The question of full or partial redemption, which was to become a major issue in the First Congress, was left unresolved.) Some delegates then argued that the power to tax should be linked explicitly to the purpose of paying the debt. Their position led to further amendment of the tax clause on Sept. 4 to provide that Congress "shall have power to lay and collect taxes, duties, imposts and excises, to pay the debts and provide for the common defense and general welfare of the United States."

It was to be argued later that inclusion of the words "general welfare" was intended to confer an additional and unlimited power on Congress. The records of the convention indicate, however, that when it was decided to qualify the power to tax by adding the words "to pay the debts," it became necessary to make it clear that this was not the only purpose for which taxes could be levied. "To provide for the common defense and general welfare" was taken from the Articles of Confederation and used to encompass all of the other specific and limited powers vested by the Constitution in Congress.[5]

In settling the basis for representation in the House, the convention had linked the apportionment of "direct taxes" as well as representatives to a count of all whites and three-fifths of the blacks. When this provision was reconsidered Aug. 20, Rufus King asked, "What was the precise meaning of direct taxation?" According to Madison "no one answered." [6] The only direct taxes in use at that time were land and capitation or poll taxes. Because southerners feared that Congress might seek to levy a special tax on slaves, the Committee of Detail recommended and the convention later adopted a further provision: "No Capitation, or other direct, Tax shall be laid, unless in Proportion" to the count required by Section 2. Another concession to the South incorporated in Section 9 of Article I was a prohibition of levies on exports.

Power to Regulate Commerce

A lack of uniformity in duties and commercial regulations under the Articles of Confederation severely handicapped trade among the states and with other countries. To Madison and many others, it was as essential to the new plan of government that Congress have the power to regulate commerce as it was that it have the power to tax. It soon became clear, however, that the southern states would not accept a Constitution that failed to protect their vested interest in slave labor and agricultural exports from the burdensome restrictions that a Congress controlled by northerners might seek to impose.

As a result, the Committee of Detail proposed that Congress be given the power to regulate commerce with foreign nations and among the several states, subject to two limitations: a ban on taxing exports and a prohibition on efforts to tax or outlaw the slave trade. The general power to regulate commerce was approved on Aug. 16 without dissent. (The words "and with the Indian Tribes" were added Sept. 4.) The proposed limitations met with considerable opposition, however.

In keeping with mercantilist doctrines, it was common practice at that time for governments to tax exports. The idea of prohibiting such action was novel. "To deny this power is to take from the common government half the regulation of trade," argued James Wilson of Philadelphia. It also would deny Congress the power to menace the livelihood of the South by taxing exports of rice, tobacco and indigo on which its economy was largely dependent. Some northerners, however, considered this concession to the South as wise as it was necessary. Massachusetts delegate Gerry said the convention already had given Congress "more power than we know how will be exercised." On Aug. 21, by a vote of seven states to four, the convention agreed that "No Tax or Duty shall be laid on Articles exported from any State." This provision was placed in Section 9 of Article I in the final draft.[7]

The second limitation on the power to regulate commerce provided that no tax or duty was to be laid on the migration or importation of such persons as the several States shall think proper to admit; nor shall such migration or importation be prohibited. The limitation was designed to meet the South's objection to any interference with the slave trade, although those words were carefully avoided. Luther Martin thought it was "inconsistent with the principles of the Revolution and dishonorable to the American character to have such a feature in the Constitution." [8] But most other delegates, including those opposed to slavery, argued that it was a political rather than a moral issue.

Some northerners as well as southerners agreed with Oliver Ellsworth of Connecticut that "the morality or wisdom of slavery" should be left to the states to determine. "Let us not intermeddle," he said, predicting that "slavery, in time will not be a speck in our country." Many others agreed with George Mason that the "infernal traffic" in slaves was holding back the economic development of the country and that for this reason the national government "should have power to prevent the increase of slavery." Since the provision reported by the Committee of Detail was clearly unacceptable to many delegates, a committee was named to seek a compromise.[9]

The panel now proposed that Congress be barred from prohibiting the slave trade until the year 1800, but that it have power to levy a duty on slaves as on other imports. Both provisions were approved Aug. 25, the first by a vote of seven states to four (after the year 1800 had been changed to 1808), and the second after limiting the duty to $10 per person. These provisions concerning slaves, incorporated in the first clause of Section 9 of Article I, further limited Congress's power to regulate commerce.

Still another limit on the commerce power sought by the South and recommended by the Committee of Detail would have required a two-thirds vote of both houses of Congress to pass a navigation act. England had used such laws to channel colonial imports and exports into British ships and ports, and southerners now feared that the North, where shipping was a major interest, might try to monopolize the transport of their exports by a law requiring them to be carried aboard American ships.

Northern delegates were strongly opposed to the two-thirds proposal, and in working out the compromise on the slave trade they succeeded in having it dropped. As a result, Pinckney moved to require a two-thirds vote of both houses to enact any commercial regulation. This motion was rejected Aug. 29 by seven states to four, and the convention confirmed the decision to drop the proposed two-thirds rule for navigation acts. Mason, one of three delegates who refused to sign the Constitution, later argued that a bare majority of Congress should not have the power to "enable a few rich merchants in Philadelphia, New York and Boston to monopolize the staples of the Southern States." [10]

A relatively minor limitation on the power to regulate commerce was adopted to allay the fear of Maryland that Congress might require ships traversing the Chesapeake Bay to enter or clear at Norfolk or another Virginia port in order to simplify the collection of duties. As approved Aug. 31 and added to Section 9, Article I, the added language provided that "No Preference shall be given by any Regulation of Commerce or Revenue to the Ports of one State over those of another; nor shall Vessels bound to or from one State be obliged to enter, clear or pay Duties in another."

War and Treaty Power

The Articles of Confederation had given Congress the exclusive right and power of deciding issues of peace and war. The Committee of Detail proposed giving to the new Congress as a whole the power to make war and giving to the Senate alone the power to approve treaties. Subsequently, the treaty power was divided between the president and the Senate, but in discussing the war-making power on Aug. 17, Pinckney favored giving that authority exclusively to the Senate. "It would be singular for one authority to make war, and another peace," he reasoned. Butler, on the other hand, felt the war power should rest with the president, "who will have all the requisite qualities and will not make war but when the Nation will support it." Neither view drew any support, and the convention voted to give Congress the power "to declare war." The word "declare" had been substituted for "make" in order to leave the president free to repel a sudden attack. Sherman said, "The Executive should be able to repel, and not commence, war." [11]

On Aug. 18 the convention agreed to give Congress the power "to raise and support Armies," "to provide and maintain a Navy," and "to make Rules for the Government and Regulation of the land and naval Forces." All of these provisions were taken from the Articles of Confederation. Gerry, voicing the old colonial fears of a standing army, wanted a proviso that "in time of peace" the army should consist of no more than two or three thousand men, but his motion was unanimously rejected. On Sept. 5, however, the convention added to the power to "raise and support Armies" the proviso that "no Appropriation of Money to that Use shall be for a longer Term than two Years." This was intended to quiet fears similar to those that had led the British to require annual appropriations for the army.[12]

The convention approved without dissent the power, proposed by the Committee of Detail and included in Section 8, Article I, "to provide for calling forth the Militia to execute the Laws of the Union, suppress Insurrections and repel Invasions." But a further proposal by Mason that Congress have the power to regulate the militia alarmed the defenders of state sovereignty. To Gerry this was the last point remaining to be surrendered. Others argued that the states would never allow control of the militia to get out of their hands.

The shortcomings of the militia during the Revolutionary War were a bitter memory to most of the delegates, however, and they shared the practical view of Madison that "as the greatest danger to liberty is from large standing armies, it is best to prevent them by an effectual provision for a good militia." [13] So on Aug. 23 the convention adopted the provision, as later incorporated in Section 8, giving Congress power "to provide for organizing, arming, and disciplining the Militia, and for governing such Part of them as may be employed in the Service of the United States. . . ."

Special Status of Money Bills

The committee named to resolve the issue of equal or proportional representation in the Senate had proposed as a compromise that each state have one vote in the Senate, but that the House originate all bills to raise and appropriate money or pay government salaries and that the Senate be denied the right to amend such bills. Included in the proposal was the phrase, "No money shall be drawn from the public Treasury, but in pursuance of appropriations to be originated in the first branch." Seven states at this time required that money bills originate in the lower house, but only four of those states forbade amendment by the upper house. Although some delegates objected that such a provision would be degrading to the Senate, it was approved July 6 by a vote of five states to three.

The Committee of Detail phrased the provision as follows: "All bills for raising or appropriating money, and for fixing the salaries of the officers of Government, shall originate in the House of Representatives, and shall not be altered or amended by the Senate." Madison feared the provision would promote "injurious altercations" between House and Senate; others insisted that it was necessary because the people "will not agree that any but their immediate representatives shall meddle with their purse." [14] The convention's division on the question reflected contrasting concepts of the Senate as likely to be the most responsible branch or the most aristocratic one, to be strengthened or checked accordingly.

But on Aug. 8 the convention reversed itself and dropped the provision. A compromise adopted Sept. 8 by a vote of nine states to two provided that "All bills for raising revenue shall originate in the House of Representatives, and shall be subject to alterations and amendments by the Senate; no money shall be drawn from the Treasury but in consequence of appropriations made by law." The first clause, slightly revised, was incorporated in Section 7, while the second clause was made one of the limitations on the powers of Congress listed in Section 9, Article I.

The Constitution thus gave the House exclusive power to originate any bill involving taxes or tariffs, but it did not extend that power to include appropriations bills. However, the House assumed that additional power on the basis of the consideration it had received in the convention; it became the recognized prerogative of the House to originate spending as well as revenue bills.

Admission of New States

As early as 1780 the Continental Congress had resolved that lands ceded to the United States "shall be disposed of for the common benefit of the United States, and be settled and formed into distinct republican States, which shall become members of the Federal Union, and have the same rights of sovereignty, freedom and independence as the other States." By 1786 the Congress of the Confederation was in possession of all land south of Canada, north of the Ohio, west of the Allegheny Mountains and east of the Mississippi. Guidelines for governing this great territory were laid down by Congress in the Northwest Ordinance of July 13, 1787.

The Ordinance provided that, upon attaining a population of 5,000 free male inhabitants of voting age, the territory would be entitled to elect a legislature and send a nonvoting delegate to Congress. No less than three or more than five states were to be formed out of the territory. Each state was to have at least 60,000 free inhabitants to qualify for admission to the Union "on an equal footing with the original States in all respects whatever." And the Ordinance declared that "there shall be neither slavery nor involuntary servitude in the said territory...." [15]

At the same time as this farsighted plan was being approved in New York by the Congress of the Confederation, Gouverneur Morris and other eastern delegates to the Constitutional Convention in Philadelphia were arguing strongly against equality for the new states. "The busy haunts of men, not the remote wilderness, are the proper school of political talents," said Morris. "If the western people get the power into their hands, they will ruin the Atlantic interests. The back members are always most adverse to the best measures." [16]

Among those opposing this view were the delegates of Virginia and North Carolina, whose western lands were to become Kentucky and Tennessee. Mason argued that the western territories "will either not unite with or will speedily revolt from the Union, if they are not in all respects placed on an equal footing." In time, he thought they might well be "both more numerous and more wealthy" than the seaboard states. Madison was certain that "no unfavorable distinctions were admissible, either in point of justice or policy." [17]

In the light of that debate, the Committee of Detail proposed on Aug. 6 that Congress have the power to admit new states upon the consent of two-thirds of the members present of each house and, in the case of a state formed from an existing state, upon the consent of the legislature of that state. New states were to be admitted on the same terms as the original states. But when this proposal was considered Aug. 29, the convention adopted a motion by Morris to drop the provision for equality of admission.

Morris and Dickinson then offered a new draft, eliminating the condition of a two-thirds vote in favor of a simple majority, which was adopted and became the first clause of Section 3, Article IV. It provided simply that new states could be admitted by Congress. Although this provision of the Constitution was silent as to the status of the new states, Congress was to adhere to the principle of equality in admitting them.

The convention then adopted the provision governing territories set out in the second clause of Section 3, Article IV. Madison had first proposed adding such a provision to the Constitution to give a legal foundation to the Northwest Ordinance, since the Articles of Confederation had given Congress no explicit power to legislate for territories. A proviso ruling out prejudice to any claims of the United States or of a particular state was added because some delegates feared that, without it, the terms on which new states were admitted might favor the claims of a state to vacant lands ceded by Britain.

Power of Impeachment

It was decided early in the convention that the chief executive should be "removable on impeachment and conviction of malpractice or neglect of duty." [18] Who should impeach and try him, however, depended on how he was to be chosen. So long as Congress was to elect the president — and that decision stood until Sept. 4 — few delegates were willing to give Congress the additional power to remove him. The final decision to have the president chosen by presidential electors helped to resolve the problem.

The Virginia Plan called for the national judiciary to try "impeachments of any National officers," without specifying which branch of government would impeach. Because all the state constitutions vested that power in the lower house of the assembly, the Committee of Detail proposed removal of the president on impeachment by the House and conviction by the Supreme Court "of treason, bribery or corruption." No action was taken on this proposal until the special committee, in advancing the plan for presidential electors, suggested that the Senate try all impeachments and that conviction require the concurrence of two-thirds of the members present.

When this plan was debated Sept. 8, Pinckney opposed trial by the Senate on the ground that if the president "opposes a favorite law, the two Houses will combine against him, and under the influence of heat and faction throw him out of office." [19] Nevertheless, the convention adopted the formula for impeachment by the House, trial by the Senate, and conviction by a two-thirds vote. It also extended the grounds for impeachment from treason and bribery to "other high crimes and other misdemeanors" and made the vice president and other civil officers similarly impeachable and removable. These provisions were incorporated in Sections 2 and 3 of Article I and in Section 4 of Article II.

Miscellaneous Powers

The Committee of Detail proposed that Congress retain the power granted in the Articles "to borrow money and emit bills on the credit of the United States." But state emissions of paper money in 1786 had contributed greatly to the alarms that had led to the calling of the convention, and most delegates agreed with Ellsworth that this was a "favorable moment to shut and bar the door against paper money." [20] So the words "and emit bills" were struck when this provision was approved Aug. 16.

Most of the other powers of Congress specified in Section 8 of Article I — concerning naturalization and bankruptcy, coinage, counterfeiting, post offices, copyrights, inferior tribunals, piracies and the seat of government — were approved with little debate. The final provision of Section 8, one of the most sweeping grants of power in the entire Constitution, also attracted little attention at the time. That clause authorized Congress "to make all Laws which shall be necessary and proper for carrying into Execution the foregoing Powers, and all other Powers vested by this Constitution in the Government of the United States, or in any Department or Officer thereof." The intent of this grant was simply to enable Congress to enact legislation giving effect to the specified powers. No member of the convention suggested that it conferred powers in addition to those previously specified in the article. But the meaning of the clause and of the words "necessary and proper" was to become the focus of the controversy between broad and strict constructionists of the Constitution that began with the passage by the First Congress of a law creating a national bank.

Limits on Congressional Power

Section 9 of Article I imposed eight specific limitations on the powers of Congress. Those relating to the slave trade, capitation taxes, sport taxes, preference among ports and appropriations have been discussed in connection with the powers to tax, regulate commerce and originate money bills. The other three were adopted as follows:

— On Aug. 28 Pinckney moved to adopt a provision in the Massachusetts Constitution that barred suspension of the writ of habeas corpus except on the most urgent occasions and then for a period not to exceed one year. This was amended and adopted to provide that "the Privilege of the Writ of Habeas Corpus shall not be suspended, unless when in Cases of Rebellion or Invasion the public Safety may require it."

— On Aug. 22 Gerry proposed a prohibition on the passage of bills of attainder and ex post facto laws. Some delegates objected that such a provision would imply an improper suspicion of Congress and that it was unnecessary. The convention agreed, however, that "No Bill of Attainder or ex post facto Law shall be passed." A subsequent motion by Mason, to delete ex post facto laws on the ground that the ban might prevent Congress from redeeming the war debt at less than face value, was rejected unanimously.

— On Aug. 23 the convention adopted the two provisions that make up the final clause of Section 9, Article I, both of which were taken from the Articles of Confederation. The bar to titles of nobility was proposed by the Committee of Detail. The bar to acceptance of emolument, office or title from foreign governments without the consent of Congress was urged by Pinckney to help keep American officials independent of external influence.

Pinckney and others proposed adding to the Constitution a number of provisions similar to those contained in the Bills of Rights of the various states. On Sept. 12 Gerry moved to appoint a committee to draft a Bill of Rights, but 10 states voted no. Anxious to complete their work and return home, the delegates were in no mood to spend more time on something most of them believed to be unnecessary since none of the powers to be vested in Congress seemed to countenance legislation that might violate individual rights.

The omission of a Bill of Rights later became a major issue in seeking the states' approval of the Constitution and led to assurances by those favoring ratification that guarantees would be added to the Constitution promptly once the new system of government was established.

Notes

1. Charles Warren, *The Making of the Constitution* (Boston: Little, Brown & Co., 1928), pp. 166, 316.
2. James Madison, *Notes of Debates in the Federal Convention of 1787*, with an introduction by Adrienne Koch (Athens, Ohio: Ohio University Press, 1966), p. 45.
3. Warren, *The Making of the Constitution*, pp. 314-315.
4. Ibid., p. 469.
5. Ibid., pp. 473-475.
6. Ibid., p. 497.
7. Ibid., pp. 573-574.
8. Ibid., p. 575.
9. Ibid., p. 575-576.
10. Ibid., p. 583.
11. Madison, *Notes of Debates in the Federal Convention*, pp. 475-477.
12. Ibid., pp. 482, 580.
13. Ibid., p. 516.
14. Warren, *The Making of the Constitution*, pp. 665-666.
15. Henry Steele Commager, ed., *Documents of American History*, 2 vols, *To 1898*, vol 1. (Englewood Cliffs, N.J.: Prentice-Hall, 1973), I: 128.
16. Warren, *The Making of the Constitution*, p. 594.

17. Ibid., pp. 594-595.
18. Ibid., p. 661.
19. Ibid., p. 662.
20. Madison, *Notes of Debates in the Federal Convention*, p. 471.

Chapter 6

THE EXECUTIVE BRANCH

No question troubled the convention more than the powers and structure to be given the executive in the new government. The office did not exist under the Articles of Confederation, which placed the executive function in Congress. A longstanding fear of executive authority had led Americans "to throw all power into the Legislative vortex," as James Madison explained it. Under most of the state constitutions, the executives were indeed "little more than cyphers, the Legislatures omnipotent." [1] How much more authority and independence to give the national executive remained in dispute until the very end of the convention.

The Virginia Plan had recommended a national executive chosen by the legislative branch for a fixed term. He would be ineligible for reappointment and empowered with "a general authority to execute the National laws" as well as "the Executive rights vested in Congress by the Confederation." Debate on these proposals disclosed a spectrum of views. Many delegates were wary of a return of executive authority like that exercised by the royal governors or by the King. Roger Sherman thought the executive should be "nothing more than an institution for carrying the will of the Legislature into effect." Gouverneur Morris, on the other hand, believed the executive should be "the firm guardian of the people" against legislative tyranny. [2]

Until September, the last month of the convention, most delegates favored a single executive, chosen by Congress for a single term of seven years, whose authority would be limited by the power of Congress to appoint judges and ambassadors and make treaties. This plan for legislative supremacy was then abandoned for the more balanced one that finally was adopted and incorporated in Article II of the Constitution. A president would be chosen by electors for a four-year term without limit as to re-election, and he would have the power to make all appointments subject to confirmation by the Senate and to make treaties subject to approval by a two-thirds vote of the Senate.

A Single Executive

Edmund Randolph, who presented the Virginia Plan, opposed a single executive as "the foetus of monarchy" and proposed three persons, who, George Mason thought, should be chosen from the northern, middle and southern states. But James Wilson foresaw "nothing but uncontrolled, continued and violent animosities" among three persons. A single executive, he said, would give "most energy, dispatch and responsibility to the office." [3] On June 4 the delegates voted for a single executive, seven states to four, and the convention confirmed the decision July 17 without dissent.

The Committee of Detail then proposed that "the Executive Power of the United States shall be vested in a single person" to be called the president and to have the title of "His Excellency." These provisions were adopted Aug. 24 without debate, but in drafting the final document the Committee of Style dropped the title and provided simply that "the Executive Power shall be vested in a President of the United States of America." The omission from the Constitution of any title other than president helped to defeat a proposal in the First Congress that he be addressed as "His Highness." [4]

Method of Election, Term of Office

The method of election and the term of office of the executive were closely related issues. If Congress were to choose the president, most delegates thought he should have a fairly long term and be ineligible for reappointment. For as Randolph put it, "if he should be reappointable by the Legislature, he will be no check on it." [5] But if the president was to be chosen in some other manner, a shorter term with re-eligibility was favored by most of the delegates. Thus the method of election was the key question.

The convention first decided that Congress should choose the president for a single seven-year term. On reflection, however, some delegates thought this would not leave him sufficiently independent. Wilson proposed election by electors chosen by the people, but Elbridge Gerry considered the people "too little informed of personal characters" to choose electors, and the proposal was rejected, eight to two. Gerry proposed that the governors of the states pick the president to avoid the

71

corruption he foresaw in having Congress choose, but this plan also was scratched. [6]

Several other methods were proposed, and at one point the delegates agreed on selection by electors chosen by the state legislatures. But this decision then was reversed. However, when Gouverneur Morris on Aug. 24 renewed Wilson's original proposal for electors chosen by the people only six states were opposed; five voted in favor of it. Three of the latter were smaller states that had opposed an earlier proposal to have the membership of the Senate and the House vote to elect the president, thereby giving the large states (having a greater number of representatives) a bigger voice in the decision.

All of the questions concerning the presidency then were reconsidered by the Special Committee on Postponed Matters, whose report of Sept. 4 recommended most of the provisions that were finally adopted. According to Morris, the committee rejected the choosing of the president by Congress because of "the danger of intrigue and faction" and "the opportunity for cabal." [7] Instead, it proposed that he be chosen by electors equal in number to the senators and representatives from each state, who would be chosen as each state decided. They would vote by ballot for two persons, at least one of whom could not be an inhabitant of their state. The one receiving a majority of the electoral votes would become president, the one with the next largest vote would become vice president. In the event of a tie, or if no one received a majority, the Senate would decide.

The plan provided for a four-year term with no restriction as to re-election; shifted from the Senate to the president the power to appoint ambassadors and judges and to make treaties subject to Senate approval; and gave to the Senate, instead of the Supreme Court, the power to try impeachments. This realignment of powers between the president and the Senate appealed to the small states because it was generally assumed that the Senate (in which each state was to be represented equally) would have the final say in choosing the president in most cases.

For the same reason, however, some delegates now feared that the combination of powers to be vested in the Senate would, in Randolph's words, "convert that body into a real and dangerous aristocracy." [8] Sherman thereupon proposed moving the final election of the president from the Senate to the House, with the proviso that each state have one vote. The change, which preserved the influence of the small states while easing the fears expressed about the Senate, was quickly adopted, as was

The President's Cabinet

In 1787 eight states had a Privy Council to advise the governor, and the idea of providing for a similar body to advise the president was discussed at length at the Constitutional Convention. Elbridge Gerry thought it would "give weight and inspire confidence" in the executive. Benjamin Franklin concurred: "A Council would not only be a check on a bad President, but be a relief to a good one." But Gouverneur Morris disagreed: "Give him an able Council and it will thwart him; a weak one, and he will shelter himself under their sanction." *

On Aug. 22 the Committee of Detail submitted to the convention the following proposal, first offered by Morris and Charles Pinckney:

> The President of the United States shall have a Privy Council which shall consist of the President of the Senate, the Speaker of the House of Representatives, the Chief Justice of the Supreme Court, and the principal officer in the respective departments of Foreign Affairs, Domestic Affairs, War, Marine, and Finance, as such departments of office shall from time to time be established, whose duty it shall be to advise him in matters respecting the execution of his office, which he shall think proper to lay before them; but their advice shall not conclude him, nor affect his responsibility for the measures which he shall adopt. **

The convention did not vote on this proposal. The Sept. 4 report of the Special Committee on Postponed Matters proposed only that the president "may require the Opinion in writing of the principal Officer in each of the executive Departments, upon any Subject relating to the Duties of their respective Offices." This provision — adopted Sept. 7 after the convention had rejected the idea of an executive council to be appointed by Congress — was included among the powers of the president set out in Article II, Section 2.

The word "Cabinet" was not used in the convention or in the Constitution. But as that body developed under Washington and later presidents, it conformed to the limited role that had been envisioned in the Morris-Pinckney proposal for a Privy Council.

* Charles Warren, *The Making of the Constitution* (Boston: Little, Brown & Co., 1928), p. 646.
** Ibid., pp. 646-47.

the rest of the electoral plan and the four-year term without limit as to re-eligibility.

Qualifications

The Committee of Detail first proposed that a president be at least 35 years of age, a citizen and an inhabitant of the United States for 21 years, just as age, citizenship and minimum period of residence were the only qualifications stipulated for senators and representatives. The committee added the qualification that the president had to be a natural-born citizen or a citizen at the time of the adoption of the Constitution, and it reduced the time of residence within the United States to at least 14 years "in the whole." The phrase "in the whole" was dropped in drafting the final provision of Section 1, Article II, which also was adjusted to make it clear that the qualifications for president applied equally to the vice president.

The Vice President

The office of the vice president was not considered by the convention until Sept. 4, when the Special Committee on Postponed Matters proposed that a vice president, chosen for the same term as the president, serve as ex officio president of the Senate. (A vice president or lieutenant governor served in a similar capacity in four of the 13 states.) The proposal was designed to provide a position for the runner-up in the electoral vote and to give the Senate an impartial presiding officer without depriving any state of one of its two votes.

When this proposal was debated Sept. 7, Mason objected that "it mixed too much the Legislative and the Executive." Gerry thought it tantamount to putting the president himself at the head of the Senate because of "the close intimacy that must subsist between the president and the vice president." But Sherman noted that "if the Vice President were not to be President of the Senate, he would be without employment." [9] The convention adopted the proposal of the special committee, with only Massachusetts opposed. The provision that the vice president "shall be president of the Senate, but shall have no Vote unless they be equally divided," was placed in Section 3 of Article I.

In case of the president's impeachment, death, absence, resignation or inability to discharge the powers or duties of his office, the special committee proposed that "the Vice President shall exercise those powers and duties until another President be chosen, or until the inability of the

President be removed." This language was revised slightly in Article II, Section 1: "In case of the removal of the President from office, or of his death, resignation, or inability to discharge the powers and duties of the said office, the same shall devolve on the Vice President." The revised wording left it unclear whether the "said office" or the "powers and duties" were to "devolve" on the vice president. The right of the vice president to assume the office of president was first asserted by John Tyler in 1841. He assumed the presidency on the death of William Henry Harrison and served for the remainder of Harrison's term, thus establishing the practice.[10]

There remained the question of providing for the office in the event both men died or were removed. Randolph proposed that Congress designate an officer to "act accordingly until the time of electing a President shall arrive." Madison objected that this would prevent an earlier election, so it was agreed to substitute "until such disability be removed, or a President shall be elected." The Committee of Style ignored this change, so the convention voted on Sept. 15 to restore it. The final provision, authorizing Congress to designate by law an officer to "act as President" until "a President shall be elected," was joined to the earlier provision in Article II relating to the vice president.[11]

Presidential Powers

Initially, the convention conferred only three powers on the president: "to carry into effect the National laws," "to appoint to offices in cases not otherwise provided for," and to veto bills. The Committee of Detail proposed a number of additional powers drawn from the state constitutions, most of which were adopted with little discussion or change. This was true of provisions placed in Section 3 of Article II for informing Congress "of the State of the Union" and recommending legislation to convene and adjourn Congress, receive ambassadors, and see "that the Laws be faithfully executed."

The convention also agreed without debate that "the President shall be Commander in Chief of the Army and Navy" and of the militia when called into national service. Almost all of the state constitutions vested a similar power in the state executives. The power of the president "to grant reprieves and pardons except in cases of impeachment" likewise was approved, although Mason argued that Congress should have this power and Randolph wanted to bar pardons for treason as "too great a

75

trust" to place in the president.[12] These two provisions were included in Section 2 of Article II.

Power to Appoint. The appointive powers of the president initially were limited by the convention to "cases not otherwise provided for." The Virginia Plan had proposed that judges be appointed by the national legislature, a practice followed in all except three states, but the delegates voted to give the power to the Senate alone as the "less numerous and more select body." In July the delegates considered and rejected alternative proposals that judges be appointed by the president alone, by the president with the advice and consent of the Senate, and by the president unless two-thirds of the Senate disagreed.

By late summer, sentiment had changed. On Sept. 7 the convention adopted the proposal of the special committee that the president appoint ambassadors and other public ministers, justices of the Supreme Court and all other officers of the United States "by and with the Advice and Consent of the Senate." This power, incorporated in Section 2, later was qualified by requiring that offices not otherwise provided for "be established by law" and by authorizing Congress to vest appointment of lower-level officers in the presidency, the courts and the heads of departments. Nothing was said about a presidential power to remove executive branch officials from office once confirmed by the Senate — a power that was to become a much-argued issue.

Treaty Power. The Committee of Detail's recommendation that the Senate alone be given the power to make treaties drew considerable opposition. Mason said it would enable the Senate to "sell the whole country by means of treaties." Madison thought the president, representing the whole people, should have the power. Gouverneur Morris argued for a provision that "no treaty shall be binding . . . which is not ratified by a law." [13] Southern delegates were especially concerned about preventing abandonment by treaty of free navigation of the Mississippi River.

The issue was referred to the Special Committee on Postponed Matters, which recommended vesting the president with the power to make treaties, subject to the advice and consent of two-thirds of the senators present. The latter provision provoked extended debate. On Sept. 7 the convention voted to except peace treaties from the two-thirds rule. Madison then moved to allow two-thirds of the Senate alone to make peace treaties, arguing that the president "would necessarily derive so much power and importance from a state of war that he might be

Two-Thirds Majority Rule

To the men who drafted the Constitution, a major weakness of the Articles of Confederation was the rule that nine (or two-thirds) of the 13 states had to concur in all important decisions. Therefore, they specified that in the two chambers of Congress "a Majority of each shall constitute a Quorum to do Business." (Article I, Section 5) With respect to certain powers, however, the delegates decided to require more than a simple majority vote:

— For conviction through impeachment by the Senate, which requires the concurrence of two-thirds of senators present and voting.

— Approval of treaties with other countries, which requires the concurrence of two-thirds of senators present and voting.

— Expelling a member of Congress, which requires a two-thirds vote of the House or Senate, respectively.

— Enacting a bill over the president's veto, which requires a two-thirds vote of both houses.

— Proposed constitutional amendments, which require a two-thirds vote of both houses before they can be submitted to the states for ratification.

— Selection of the president by the House — the constitutional requirement when no candidate receives a majority of the electoral votes — requiring the presence of a quorum, which must "consist of a Member or Members from two-thirds of the States. . . ." (Once a quorum is established, however, a simple majority is sufficient to elect the president, with each state delegation in the House allowed to cast one vote.)

Of the provisions included in the Constitution, only those relating to the Senate's role in trying impeachments and approving treaties made it clear that the decision rested with two-thirds of the members present and voting, rather than with two-thirds of the entire membership. There is persuasive evidence that the latter interpretation was intended by the delegates for the provisions relating to vetoes, expulsion of members and constitutional amendments. However, in the absence of an explicit requirement to that effect, Congress over the years had established the precedent that two-thirds of members "present" and voting likewise was sufficient for a decision in those cases — an assumption sustained by the Supreme Court in 1919 *(Missouri Pac. R.R. Co. v. Kansas)* and 1920 *(Rhode Island v. Palmer)*.

tempted, if authorized, to impede a treaty of peace." [14] The motion was rejected, but after further debate on the advantages and disadvantages of permitting a majority of the Senate to approve a peace treaty, the convention reversed itself and made all treaties subject to the concurrence of a two-thirds vote of the senators present.

Veto Power. The Virginia Plan had proposed joining the judiciary with the executive in exercising the power to veto acts of the legislature, subject to a vote in the Congress on overriding vetoes. Since it was expected that the judiciary would have to pass on the constitutionality of legislation, most delegates thought it improper to give the judiciary a share of the veto power; the proposal was rejected.

Wilson and Alexander Hamilton favored giving the executive an absolute veto, but on June 4 the delegates voted for Gerry's motion, based on the Massachusetts Constitution, for a veto that could be overridden by two-thirds of each branch of the legislature.

When this provision was reconsidered on Aug. 15, it was in the context of a plan to give Congress the power to elect the president, to impeach him and to appoint judges. Many delegates then agreed with Wilson that such an arrangement did not give "a sufficient self-defensive power either to the Executive or Judiciary Department," and the convention voted to require a vote of three-fourths of each chamber to override a veto.[15] But on Sept. 12, after having adopted the presidential elector plan and other changes proposed by the special committee, the convention restored the earlier two-thirds requirement.

The veto power, incorporated in Section 7 of Article I, established the procedure for the enactment of a bill with or without the president's signature. This section also made provision for the "pocket veto" of a bill when "the Congress by their Adjournment prevent its return, in which Case it shall not become Law." Although some delegates indicated a belief that the two-thirds provision was intended to apply to the entire membership of the House and Senate, a two-thirds vote of those present and voting came to be accepted in practice.

Notes

1. Charles Warren, *The Making of the Constitution* (Boston: Little, Brown & Co., 1928), p. 359.
2. Ibid., pp. 174, 360.
3. Ibid., pp. 174-175.

4. Ibid., p. 525. The Committee of Style (composed of Samuel Johnson of Connecticut, Alexander Hamilton of New York, Gouverneur Morris of Pennsylvania, James Madison of Virginia, and Rufus King of Massachusetts) was named Sept. 8 to revise the style and arrange the articles that had been agreed to by the convention.

5. Ibid., p. 360.

6. Ibid., p. 358.

7. Ibid., pp. 621, 623. The Special Committee on Postponed Matters, whose responsibility it was to work out the method of election of the president, had 11 members: Rufus King of Massachusetts, Roger Sherman of Connecticut, David Brearly of New Jersey, Gouverneur Morris of Pennsylvania, John Dickinson of Delaware, Daniel Carroll of Maryland, James Madison of Virginia, Hugh Williamson of North Carolina, Pierce Butler of South Carolina, Abraham Baldwin of Georgia and Nicholas Gilman of New Hampshire.

8. Ibid., pp. 628-629.

9. James Madison, *Notes of Debates in the Federal Convention of 1787*, with an introduction by Adrienne Koch (Athens, Ohio: Ohio University Press, 1966), p. 596.

10. Warren, *The Making of the Constitution*, pp. 635-638.

11. Ibid., p. 638.

12. Ibid., p. 530.

13. Ibid., pp. 651-652.

14. Ibid., p. 656.

15. Ibid., p. 456.

Chapter 7

THE JUDICIARY

Article III of the Constitution, relating to "the judicial Power of the United States," was developed in the convention with relative ease. The Virginia Plan called for "one or more supreme tribunals" and inferior tribunals to be appointed by the national legislature to try all cases involving crimes at sea, foreigners and citizens of different states, "collection of the National revenue," impeachments and "questions which may involve the national peace and harmony." The convention went on to spell out the jurisdiction of these courts in greater detail, but the only basic changes made in the plan were to vest initially in the Senate and then in the presidency the power to appoint judges, and to transfer the trial of impeachments from the Supreme Court to the Senate.

Lower Courts and Appointment of Judges

Without debate, the delegates agreed to one Supreme Court, but some objected to the establishment of any lower courts. John Rutledge thought the state courts should hear all cases in the first instance, "the right of appeal to the Supreme National Tribunal being sufficient to secure the National rights and uniformity of judgments." Roger Sherman deplored the extra expense. But James Madison argued that without lower courts "dispersed throughout the Republic, with final jurisdiction in many cases, appeals would be multiplied to an oppressive degree." Edmund Randolph said the state courts "cannot be trusted with the administration of the National laws." [1] As a compromise, the convention agreed to permit Congress to decide whether to "ordain and establish" lower courts.

The proposal that the national legislature appoint the judiciary was based on similar provisions in most of the state constitutions. James Wilson, arguing that "intrigue, partiality and concealment" would result from such a method, proposed appointment by the president. Madison urged appointment by the Senate as "a less numerous and more select body," and this plan was approved on June 13.[2] Although a proposal that the president appoint judges "by and with the advice and consent of the Senate" was defeated by a tie vote July 18, it was adopted in September as part of the compromise that moved the trial of impeachments from the Supreme Court to the Senate.

Tenure and Jurisdiction

Both the Virginia Plan and the New Jersey Plan provided that judges would hold office "during good behaviour" — a rule long considered essential to maintaining the independence of the judiciary. When this provision was considered Aug. 27, John Dickinson proposed that judges "may be removed by the Executive on the application by the Senate and the House of Representatives." Others objected strongly, Wilson contending that "the Judges would be in a bad situation if made to depend on every gust of faction which might prevail in two branches of our Government." [3] Only Connecticut voted for the proposal. The convention also agreed to tenure during good behavior.

Section 2 of Article III specified the cases to which "the judicial Power shall extend" and placed these cases under either the original or appellate jurisdiction of the Supreme Court. Most of the provisions embodied in the section were presented in the Aug. 6 report of the Committee of Detail and adopted by the convention on Aug. 27 with little debate. The most important modification was in the committee's first provision — extending jurisdiction to "all cases arising under the laws" of the United States. Here, the convention amended the language to read: "all cases arising under the Constitution and the laws." This change made it clear that the Supreme Court ultimately was to decide all questions of constitutionality, whether arising in state or federal courts.

Article III did not explicitly authorize the court to pass on the constitutionality of acts of Congress, but the convention clearly anticipated the exercise of that power as one of the acknowledged functions of the courts. Several delegates noted that state courts had "set aside" laws in conflict with the state constitutions. The convention debated at great length, and rejected four times, a proposal to link the court with the president in the veto power. Wilson favored it because "laws may be unjust, may be unwise, may be dangerous, may be destructive, and yet may not be so unconstitutional as to justify the judges in refusing to give them effect." George Mason agreed that the court "could declare an unconstitutional law void." [4]

Supremacy Clause

The role of the judiciary in determining the constitutionality of laws also was implicit in the provision, incorporated in Article VI, which asserted that the Constitution, the laws and the treaties of the United States "shall be the supreme Law of the Land." This provision first appeared on July 17 after the convention had reversed itself and voted to deny Congress the proposed power. Anxious to place some restraint on the free-wheeling state legislatures, the convention adopted instead a substitute offered by Luther Martin and drawn directly from the New Jersey Plan of June 14.

The substitute provided that the laws and treaties of the United States "shall be the supreme law of the respective States, as far as those acts or treaties shall relate to the said States, or their citizens and inhabitants — and that the Judiciaries of the several States shall be bound thereby in their decisions, anything in the respective laws of the individual States to the contrary notwithstanding." In its report of Aug. 6, the Committee of Detail dropped the qualifying phrase "as far as those acts or treaties shall relate to the said States," and substituted the word "Judges" for "Judiciaries" in the next clause and the words "Constitutions or laws" for "laws" in the final proviso.

The convention agreed to these and other modifications Aug. 23 and then prefaced the entire provision with the words, "This Constitution." Further revision by the Committee of Style changed "supreme law of the several States" to "supreme law of the land." The effect of the various changes was to make it clear that all judges, state and federal, were bound to uphold the supremacy of the Constitution over all other acts. As finally worded, the "supremacy" clause of Article VI stated:

> This Constitution, and the laws of the United States which shall be made in Pursuance thereof; and all Treaties made, or which shall be made, under the Authority of the United States, shall be the supreme Law of the Land; and the Judges in every State shall be bound thereby, any Thing in the Constitution or Laws of any State to the Contrary notwithstanding.

The supremacy clause was reinforced by a further provision in Article VI stating that all members of Congress and of the state legislatures, as well as all executive and judicial officers of the national and state governments, "shall be bound by Oath or Affirmation to support this Constitution." [5]

Limits on Powers of the States

The supremacy clause was designed to prevent the states from passing laws contrary to the Constitution. Since the framers of the Constitution also intended to specify the powers granted to Congress, those powers by implication were denied to the states. By the same reasoning, however, any powers not specifically granted to Congress remained with the states.

To eliminate any doubt of their intention to put an end to irresponsible acts of the individual states, the delegates decided to specify what the states could not do as well as what the states were required to do. Acts prohibited to the states were placed in Section 10 of Article I, while those required of them were placed in Sections 1 and 2 of Article IV.

Most of these provisions — many of which were taken from the Articles of Confederation — were proposed by the Committee of Detail and adopted by the convention on Aug. 28 with little debate or revision. The committee had proposed that the states be required to use gold or silver as legal tender unless Congress gave its consent to another medium of exchange, but the convention voted for an absolute prohibition on other forms of legal tender, Sherman saying the times presented "a favorable crisis for crushing paper money." [6] The convention also added a provision, drawn from the Northwest Ordinance, aimed at the welter of state laws favoring debtors over creditors: no state was to pass any ex post facto law or law impairing the obligation of contracts.

The provisions of Article IV requiring each state to give "full faith and credit" to the acts of other states, to respect "all Privileges and Immunities" of all citizens, and to deliver up fugitives from justice were derived from the Articles of Confederation. To these the convention, at the suggestion of southerners, added a provision that became known as the "fugitive slave" clause; it required such persons to be "delivered up on Claim of the Party to whom such Service or Labour may be due." As with the rest of the Constitution, the enforcement of these provisions in Article IV was assigned, by the supremacy clause, to the courts.

Notes

1. Charles Warren, *The Making of the Constitution* (Boston: Little, Brown & Co., 1928), pp. 326-327.
2. Ibid., pp. 327-328.
3. James Madison, *Notes of Debates in the Federal Convention of 1787*, with an introduction by Adrienne Koch (Athens, Ohio: Ohio University Press, 1966), pp. 536-537.
4. Warren, *The Making of the Constitution*, pp. 333-334.
5. Ibid., p. 650.
6. Ibid., p. 552.

Chapter 8

AMENDMENT AND RATIFICATION

A major reason for calling the Constitutional Convention had been that the method for amending the Articles of Confederation — requiring the unanimous consent of the states — had proved to be impractical. So there was general agreement that it was better to provide a process for amending the Constitution "in an easy, regular and constitutional way, than to trust to chance and violence," as George Mason put it.[1] But the formula for doing so received little consideration until the final days of the convention.

The Committee of Detail first proposed that the legislatures of two-thirds of the states have the sole power to initiate amendments by petitioning Congress to call a convention for that purpose. Debate on this provision, adopted Aug. 30, was brief; no one supported the argument of Gouverneur Morris that Congress also should have the power to call a convention. But when the convention reconsidered the issue Sept. 10, Alexander Hamilton raised several objections. "The State Legislatures will not apply for alterations but with a view to increase their own powers," he said, arguing that "the National Legislature will be the first to perceive and will be the most sensible to the necessity of amendments." Hamilton proposed that two-thirds of the Senate and House also be given the power to call a convention." [2]

James Wilson moved that amendments to the Constitution be considered adopted when they had been ratified by two-thirds of the states. When that proposal was defeated, six states to five, Wilson moved to substitute ratification by three-fourths of the states, which was approved without dissent. The convention then adopted a new process, providing that Congress shall propose amendments "whenever two-thirds of both Houses shall deem necessary or on the application of two-thirds" of the state legislatures, and that such amendments would become valid when ratified by either the legislatures or conventions of three-fourths of the states depending on which mode of ratification Congress directed.

Under this formula, any constitutional amendment proposed by two-thirds of the states would be submitted directly to the states for ratification. This was modified Sept. 15 on a motion by Gouverneur Morris. His revision gave Congress the authority, on the application of two-thirds of the states, to "call a Convention for proposing Amendments." Thus, as finally drafted, Article V provided that, in proposing amendments, Congress would act directly while the states would act indirectly. In either case, however, amendments would take effect when approved by three-fourths of the states.

While working out these terms, the convention was forced to restrict the amending power. As a concession to the South, the convention already had barred Congress from outlawing the slave trade before 1808 and from levying any direct tax unless it was in proportion to a count of all whites and three-fifths of the black population (Article I, Section 9). But John Rutledge of South Carolina noted that there was nothing in the proposed article on the amending process to prevent adoption of a constitutional amendment outlawing the slave trade before 1808. He said the slave provisions "might be altered by the States not interested in that property and prejudiced against them" and that he could never agree to such an amending power. [3] So on Sept. 10 it was agreed without debate to add to Article V the proviso that no amendment adopted before 1808 "shall in any manner affect" those two provisions of Article I.

Roger Sherman now worried that "three fourths of the States might be brought to do things fatal to particular States, as abolishing them altogether or depriving them of their equality in the Senate." He proposed, as a further proviso to the amending power, that "No state shall without its consent be affected in its internal police, or deprived of its equal suffrage in the Senate." [4] The term "internal police" covered much more than most delegates were prepared to exclude, and only three states supported Sherman. But the more limited proviso that "no State, without its Consent, shall be deprived of its equal suffrage in the Senate" was accepted without debate and added at the end of Article V.

Campaign for Ratification

According to the resolution of Congress, the Philadelphia convention was to meet for the "sole and express purpose of revising the

Articles of Confederation and reporting to Congress and the several legislatures" its recommendations. But the nationalists who organized the convention were determined that the fate of the new Constitution not be entrusted to the state legislatures. The Constitution, they insisted, should be considered "by the supreme authority of the people themselves," as James Madison put it. The legislatures, he pointed out, were in any event without power to consent to changes that "would make essential inroads on the State Constitutions."[5]

By "the people themselves" the nationalists meant special conventions elected for the purpose. Conventions would be more representative than the legislatures, which excluded "many of the ablest men," they argued. The people would be more likely than the state legislatures to favor the Constitution because, according to Rufus King, the legislatures, which would "lose power [under the Constitution] will be most likely to raise objections." Opposing this view were Oliver Ellsworth, who thought conventions were "better fitted to pull down than to build up Constitutions," and Elbridge Gerry, who said the people "would never agree on anything." [6] But the convention rejected Ellsworth's motion for ratification by the legislatures and agreed July 23, by a vote of nine states to one, that the Constitution should be submitted to popularly elected state conventions.

This decision was followed on Aug. 31 by another crucial agreement: the Constitution should enter into force when approved by the conventions of nine of the 13 states. By this time, only a few of the delegates still felt, as Luther Martin did, that "unanimity was necessary to dissolve the existing Confederacy." [7] Seven and ten states also were proposed as minimums, but nine was chosen as the more familiar figure, being the number required to act on important matters under the Articles of Confederation. It also was clearly impractical to require (as the Committee of Detail had proposed) that the Constitution be submitted to the existing Congress "for their approbation," so it was agreed to strike out that provision.

Edmund Randolph and Mason — two of the three delegates who would refuse to sign the Constitution — continued to argue that the document, along with any amendments proposed by the state conventions, should be submitted to another general convention before any final action on it was taken. This proposal to extend the already lengthy constitutional debate generated little enthusiasm among the delegates. Few believed another convention could improve the Constitution significantly. On Sept. 13 Randolph and Mason's proposal was unanimously rejected. As finally drafted, Article VII provided simply that "the Ratification of the Conventions of nine States shall be sufficient for the Establishment of this Constitution between the States so ratifying the Same."

By a separate resolution adopted Sept. 17, it was agreed by the convention that the Constitution should "be laid before the United States in Congress assembled," and that it should then be submitted to "a Convention of Delegates, chosen in each State by the People thereof." As soon as nine states had ratified, the resolution continued, the Congress should set a day for the election of presidential electors, senators and representatives and "the Time and Place for commencing Proceedings under this Constitution." [8]

On Sept. 17, 1787, after nearly four months of debate, the convention adjourned. Ten days later the Congress of the Confederation submitted the Constitution to the states for their consideration, and the struggle for ratification began. Ironically, those who had argued successfully in the convention for a national rather than merely a federal system, and who now took the lead in urging ratification, called themselves Federalists, although there was no reference to anything federal in the Constitution. Those who opposed the Constitution became known as the Anti-Federalists, although the sentiments they espoused had been forming for several years before the fight over ratification.

These two factions, out of which the first political parties in the United States were formed, tended to reflect long-standing divisions among Americans between commercial and agrarian interests, creditors and debtors, men of great or little property, tidewater planters and the small farmers of the interior. But there were important and numerous exceptions to the tendency of Federalists and Anti-Federalists to divide along class, sectional and economic lines. Among the Anti-Federalists were some of the wealthiest and most influential men of the times, including George Mason, Patrick Henry, Richard Henry Lee, George Clinton and James Winthrop.

The Federalists seized the initiative in the ratification process as they had earlier in initiating the convention in Philadelphia. The ensuing campaign of political maneuver, persuasion and propaganda was intense and bitter. Both sides questioned the motives of the other and exaggerated the dire consequences that would ensue if the opposing course was followed. All Anti-Federalists, wrote Ellsworth, were either "men who have lucrative and influential State offices" or "tories, debtors in desperate circumstances, or insurgents." To Luther Martin, the object of the Federalists was "the total abolition of all State Governments and the erection on their ruins of one great and extreme empire." [9]

All of the newspapers of the day published extensive correspondence on the virtues and vices of the new plan of government. The fullest and strongest case for the Constitution was presented in a series of letters written by Madison, Hamilton and Jay under the name of "Publius." Seventy-seven of the letters were published in New York City newspapers between Oct. 27 and April 4, 1788, and in book form (along with eight additional letters) as *The Federalist*, on May 28, 1788. These letters probably had only a small influence on ratification, but *The Federalist* came to be regarded as the classic exposition of the Constitution as well as one of the most important works on political theory ever written.

Political maneuvers were common in both camps. In Pennsylvania, Federalists moved to call a convention before Congress had officially submitted the Constitution. Nineteen Anti-Federalists thereupon withdrew from the assembly, thus depriving it of a quorum, until a mob seized two of them and dragged them back. When the Massachusetts convention met, the Anti-Federalists were in the majority until John Hancock, the president of that state's constitutional convention, was won over to the Federalist side by promises of support for the new post of vice president of the United States.

Many questions were raised about the new Constitution. Why did the convention fail to draft a Bill of Rights? Would an elected president, with no limit on the number of terms he could serve, lean towards monarchy? Would a strong central government lead to the consolidation and destruction of the separate states? Anti-Federalists accused supporters of the Constitution of trying deliberately to end state sovereignty. They also charged that in drafting the Constitution the Federalists hoped to establish a small ruling class that would protect their economic interests.

In response, Federalists quickly pledged to amend the Constitution to include a Bill of Rights. The fear of monarchy was mitigated by a widespread assumption — held also in the convention — that George Washington would become the first president. This assumption, together with the fact that most Americans knew Washington and Benjamin Franklin supported the Constitution, contributed greatly to the success of the ratification campaign.

The Federalist Papers

The Federalist Papers, a collection of 85 letters to the public signed with a pseudonym, Publius, appeared at short intervals in the newspapers of New York City beginning on Oct. 27, 1787. The identity of Publius was a secret until several years after publication. In March 1788 the first 36 letters were issued in a collected edition. A second volume containing numbers 37-85 was published in May 1788.

The idea for *The Federalist* letters came from Alexander Hamilton who wanted to wage a literary campaign to explain the proposed Constitution and build support for it. James Madison and John Jay agreed to work with him.

Of the 85 letters, Hamilton wrote 56; Madison, 21; and Jay, five. Hamilton and Madison collaborated on three. Jay's low productivity was due to a serious illness in the fall of 1787.

The essays probably had only a small impact on the ratification of the Constitution. Even the most widely circulated newspapers did not travel far in 1788. But they gained importance later as a classic exposition of the Constitution.

Professor Clinton Rossiter wrote in an introduction to the papers:

> *The Federalist* is the most important work in political science that has ever been written, or is likely ever to be written, in the United States. It is, indeed, the one product of the American mind that is rightly counted among the classics of political theory. . . . *The Federalist* stands third only to the Declaration of Independence and the Constitution itself among all the sacred writing of American political history. *

---

* *The Federalist Papers*, with an introduction by Clinton Rossiter (New York: Mentor, 1961), p. vii.

The Delaware convention was the first to ratify, unanimously, on Dec. 7, 1787. Then came Pennsylvania, by a 46 to 23 vote, on Dec. 12; New Jersey, unanimously, on Dec. 19; Georgia, unanimously, on Jan. 2, 1788; Connecticut, by a 128 to 40 vote, on Jan. 9, 1788; Massachusetts, 187 to 168, on Feb. 6; Maryland, 63 to 11, on April 26; South Carolina, 149 to 73, on May 23; and New Hampshire, 57 to 46, on June 21. This met the requirement for approval by nine states, but it was clear that without the approval of Virginia and New York the Constitution would stand on shaky ground.

In Virginia, according to Ellsworth, "the opposition wholly originated in two principles: the madness of Mason, and enmity of the Lee faction to Gen. Washington." [10] But Randolph, who had refused with Mason and Gerry to sign the Constitution, eventually was persuaded to support it, and on June 25 the Federalists prevailed by a vote of 89 to 79.

New York finally ratified on July 26 by an even narrower margin of 30 to 27, after Hamilton and Jay had threatened that otherwise New York City would secede and join the Union as a separate state. North Carolina on Aug. 4, 1788, first rejected the Constitution by a vote of 75 to 193. It was not until Nov. 21, 1789, that it reversed its earlier vote and ratified the Constitution. Rhode Island — which had not taken part in the Constitutional Convention — by a vote of 34 to 32 on May 29, 1790, became the last of the 13 original states to ratify.

In accordance with the request of the constitutional convention, the Congress of the Confederation on Sept. 13, 1788, designated New York City as the seat of the new government, the first Wednesday of January 1789 as the day for choosing presidential electors, the first Wednesday of February for the meeting of electors, and the first Wednesday of March for the opening session of the first Congress under the new Constitution.

The First Elections

The Constitution empowered the state legislatures to prescribe the method of choosing their presidential electors as well as the time, place and manner of electing their representatives and senators. Virginia and Maryland put the choice of electors directly to the people; in Massachusetts, two were chosen at large and the other eight were picked by the legislature from 24 names submitted by the voters of the eight congressional districts. In the other states, the electors were chosen by the legislature.

In New York, where the Federalists controlled the state Senate and the Anti-Federalists dominated the Assembly, the two houses became deadlocked on the question of acting by joint or concurrent vote. The legislature adjourned without choosing electors.

Election to the House of Representatives also involved a number of spirited contests between Federalists and Anti-Federalists, although the

91

total vote cast in these first elections, estimated to be between 75,000 and 125,000, was a small fraction of the free population of 3.2 million. In Massachusetts and Connecticut, several elections were required in some districts before a candidate obtained a majority of the popular vote. (In the 19th century, five of the New England states required a majority vote to win election to the House; all such requirements had been phased out by the 1890s.[11]) Elbridge Gerry, who had refused to sign the Constitution, finally beat Nathaniel Gorham, also a delegate to the Philadelphia convention, after saying he no longer opposed it. In New Jersey the law did not fix a time for closing the polls, and they stayed open for three weeks. When the House organized for the First Congress, the elections of all four New Jersey representatives were contested.

On March 4, 1789, the day fixed for the new Congress to begin its work, only 13 of the 59 representatives and eight of the 22 senators had arrived in New York City. (Seats allotted to North Carolina and Rhode Island were not filled until 1790, after those states had ratified the Constitution.) It was not until April 1 that a 30th representative arrived to make a quorum of the House; the Senate attained its quorum of 12 on April 6. The two houses then met jointly for the first time to count the electoral vote.

As everyone had assumed, each of the 69 electors had cast one vote for George Washington, who thus became president by unanimous choice. (Four additional electors — two from Maryland and two from Virginia — failed to show up on Feb. 4 to vote.) Of 11 other men among whom the electors distributed their second vote, John Adams received the highest number — 34 — and was declared vice president.

Adams arrived in New York on April 21, Washington on the 23rd and the inaugural took place on the 30th. Washington took the oath of office prescribed by the Constitution on the balcony of Federal Hall, New York's former City Hall, which housed the president and both houses of Congress until the government moved to Philadelphia in 1790. The president then went to the Senate chamber to deliver a brief inaugural address, in the course of which he declined to accept whatever salary Congress might confer on the office. Thus, by April 30, 1789, the long task of designing and installing a new government for the 13 states had been completed. The Constitution had been, in the words of Gouverneur Morris, "the subject of infinite investigation, diputation and declamation." "While some have boasted it as a work from Heaven," he wrote, "others have given it a less righteous origin. I have many reasons to believe that it is the work of plain, honest men, and such I think it will appear." [12]

Notes

1. Charles Warren, *The Making of the Constitution* (Boston: Little, Brown & Co., 1928), p. 673.
2. Ibid., p. 675.
3. Ibid., p. 679.
4. Ibid., pp. 679-680.
5. Ibid., pp. 348-350.
6. Ibid.
7. Ibid., p. 607.
8. Ibid., p. 717.
9. Ibid., pp. 746, 754.
10. Ibid., p. 749.
11. *Guide to U.S. Elections* (Washington, D.C.: Congressional Quarterly, 1976), p. 520.
12. Warren, *The Making of the Constitution*, p. 739.

Part II

History of the House

Contest for the election of House Speaker, a two-month battle that resulted in the election of Nathaniel Banks (American Party-Mass.) on the 133rd ballot, Feb. 2, 1856.

Chapter 9

FORMATIVE YEARS: 1789-1809

When the 30th of the 59 representatives elected to the First Congress reached New York on April 1, 1789, the assembled quorum promptly chose as speaker of the House Frederick A. C. Muhlenberg of Pennsylvania. The next day Muhlenberg appointed a committee of 11 representatives to draw up the first rules of procedure, which the House adopted within a week. The first standing committee of the House — a seven-member Committee on Elections — was chosen April 13, and its report accepting the credentials of 49 members was approved April 18. By then, the House already was debating its first piece of legislation, a tariff bill.

By contrast, it took five years of study and negotiation to produce agreement in the 91st Congress on a limited revision of House rules. But the House, long before 1970, had become a highly structured institution governed by an elaborate set of rules, precedents and customs, all closely guarded by its most senior and influential members. Since its founding, the House often had adapted its procedures to the political pressures of the times. Its continuing ability to do so seemed to be confirmed, during ing the 1970s alone, by passage of the Legislative Reorganization Act of 1970, the Federal Election Campaign Act of 1971 and subsequent amendments in 1974 and 1976, the Congressional Budget and Impound-ment Control Act of 1974 and various other institutional reforms dealing with members' financial disclosures, ethical standards and public ac-countability.

From the beginning, politics and personalities have influenced the timing and direction of changes in House procedure and organization. But it was the rapid increase in the size of its membership in the 19th century and of its workload in the 20th century that compelled development of what became the major features of the legislative process in the House — strict limitations on floor debate, a heavy reliance on the committee system and the elaboration of techniques for channeling the flow of House business.

In 1890 Speaker Thomas B. Reed told the House that "the object of a parliamentary body is action, and not stoppage of action." [1] But how to ensure the right of a majority to work its will has been a perennial challenge in the House, which was conceived by George Mason in 1787 as the governing body that would become "the grand depository of the democratic principles of the government." [2] The men, parties and events that contributed to the evolution of the House as a legislative body are the focus of Part II.

Most of the representatives elected to the First Congress had served in the Continental Congress or in their state legislatures, and the procedures followed in those bodies — derived in large part from English parliamentary practice — formed the basis for the first rules of the House. Those rules included provisions that:

— The Speaker was to preside over the House, preserve decorum and order, put questions to members, decide all points of order, announce the results of votes and vote on all ballots taken by the House.

— Committees of three or fewer members were to be appointed by the Speaker, while larger ones were to be chosen by ballot.

— Members could not introduce bills or speak more than twice to the same question without leave of the House. They were required to vote if present, unless excused, and were barred from voting if not present or if they had a direct personal interest in the outcome.

The first rules also set forth legislative procedures. As in the Continental Congress, the principal forum for considering and perfecting legislation was to be the Committee of the Whole House on the State of the Union — the House itself under another name. When sitting as the Committee of the Whole, a member other than the Speaker occupied the chair and certain parliamentary motions permitted in the House — such as the "previous question" and the motion to adjourn — were not in order, nor were roll-call votes taken. Amendments rejected in the Committee of the Whole could not be offered again in the House except as part of a motion to recommit the entire bill to the committee that reported the measure. In the Committee of the Whole, as in the House, it took a majority of the House membership to constitute a quorum. (Today, a quorum in the Committee of the Whole is reached when 100 members are present.)

Early House Procedure

In the early years of the House, all major legislative proposals began in the Committee of the Whole, which would deliberate until it reached broad agreement on the main purpose of a measure and then name a select committee to draft a bill. When this committee reported back to the House, the bill itself was referred to the Committee of the Whole for section-by-section debate and approval or amendment. Its work completed, the committee rose, the Speaker resumed the chair and the House either accepted or rejected the amendments agreed to in the Committee of the Whole. This was followed by a third and final reading of the engrossed or completed version of the bill. Only then was the House ready to vote on final passage.

Originally, there were no time limits on members' speeches, but even the small membership of the First and Second Congresses found this procedure cumbersome and inefficient. Rep. James Madison blamed the "delays and perplexities" of the House on "the want of precedents." [3] But Rep. Fisher Ames of Massachusetts saw the problem as an excessive concern with detail in the unwieldy Committee of the Whole: "[A] great, clumsy machine is applied to the slightest and most delicate operations — the hoof of an elephant to the strokes of mezzotinto." [4]

A small time-saver was introduced in 1790, when the House amended its rules to permit the Speaker to appoint all committees unless otherwise specially directed by the House. Similarly, in 1794 the House empowered the Speaker to name the chairman of the Committee of the Whole, who previously had been elected. But the time-consuming practice of reaching a consensus in the Committee of the Whole on the broad terms of major legislative proposals before naming a select committee to draft a bill (more than 350 select committees were formed during the Third Congress) continued into the 1800s.

By entrusting each proposal to a special committee that ceased to exist once the measure was reported, the House kept effective control over all legislation. But as its business multiplied and its membership increased (from 59 to 106 after the census of 1790 and to 142 after that of 1800), the House began to delegate increasing responsibility for initiating legislation to standing or permanent committees. By 1795, four committees had been established; between 1802 and 1809, six more were added. Among the more important were Interstate and Foreign Commerce, created in 1795; Ways and Means, a select committee made permanent in

99

1802; and Public Lands, whose establishment in 1805 was prompted by the Louisiana Purchase.

Emergence of Parties

Neither the Constitution nor the early rules of the House envisioned a role for political parties in the legislative process. The triumph of the Federalists over the Anti-Federalists in winning ratification of the Constitution, the unanimous and non-partisan choice of George Washington as the first president, and the great preponderance of nominal Federalists elected to the First Congress tended to obscure the underlying economic, sectional and philosophic differences existing at the time. But these differences surfaced quickly once Alexander Hamilton took office as the first secretary of the Treasury.

The statute creating the department required the Treasury "to digest and prepare plans for the improvement and management of the revenue and for the support of the public credit." [5] Hamilton, a skilled financier, administrator and political organizer at 34, quickly responded with proposals for paying off the national and state debts at par and for creating a bank of the United States. Designed to establish confidence in the new federal government, these proposals also appealed to the mercantile and moneyed interests to whom Hamilton looked for support in his desire to strengthen central authority. Since most of those elected to the First Congress shared his outlook, and some members stood to profit from his proposals, he soon emerged as the effective leader of a new Federalist party, though it remained a loose alliance of interests. Even the Federalists never considered themselves a political party, although they met frequently in caucus to plan legislative strategy.

James Madison was the first to take issue with the substance of Hamilton's program as well as with executive branch dominance in guiding the decisions of the House. He was joined by his close friend and fellow Virginian, Thomas Jefferson, who became secretary of state in 1790. Jefferson strongly opposed Hamilton from within the Cabinet. In a letter to President Washington, Jefferson criticized his colleague for attempting to exert undue influence upon the Congress. He wrote that Hamilton's "system flowed from principles adverse to liberty, and was calculated to undermine and demolish the republic, by creating an influence of his department over the members of the legislature." [6]

The cleavage was reinforced by the French Revolution and the wars that followed in its wake. Hamilton and the Federalists favored strong commercial ties to England and urged American neutrality, while Jefferson and his followers looked on the French as democratic allies to be helped.

By 1792 Madison and Jefferson were the recognized leaders of a nascent opposition party, rooted in southern fears of Federalist economic policies and rising agrarian antagonism to the aristocratic views of Hamilton, Vice President John Adams and other prominent Federalists. In the Third through the Sixth Congresses (1793-1801), which spanned Washington's second term and Adams' single term as president, the House was closely divided between the so-called Jeffersonians and the Federalists. But in 1800 Jefferson's party emerged with a clear majority, and during his two terms as president his party outnumbered the Federalists in the House by two- and three-to-one.

The Jeffersonians never acquired a nationally accepted name, though many referred to themselves as Republicans. Jeffersonians were labeled by their opponents as Anti-Federalists, disorganizers, Jacobins and Democrats — the latter considered in the early years of the Republic to be an unflattering epithet. To many Americans in the late 18th century a Democrat was considered to be a supporter of mob rule and one identified ideologically with the French Revolution. In some states, the designation Democrat-Republican was used by the Jeffersonians, but it was not widely accepted. Eventually, most historians began to refer to them as Democratic-Republicans to avoid confusion with the unrelated Republican Party created in 1854.

Although politicians by the time of the Jefferson administration had acknowledged the existence of political parties, they did not foresee the development of a two-party system. Instead, they tended to justify the existence of their own party as a reaction to an unacceptable opposition. Jefferson himself justified his party involvement as a struggle between good and evil.

Leadership in the House

With the early emergence of two parties, choice of a Speaker soon fell to the party with a majority in the House. Thus in 1799 Theodore Sedgwick of Massachusetts was elected Speaker over Nathaniel Macon of North Carolina by a vote of 44 to 38, a margin that approximated that of the Federalists over the Jeffersonians in the Sixth Congress. Two years later, in the Seventh Congress, Macon was elected Speaker by a wide margin over the Federalist candidate.

Backed by party support, the early Speakers were eager to use their powers to promote party policies. In 1796, when Jeffersonians in the House mounted an attack on the Jay treaty with Britain, Speaker Jonathan Dayton, a Federalist, twice voted to produce ties that resulted in the defeat of anti-treaty motions. Jeffersonians in the Sixth Congress found the rulings of Sedgwick so partisan that they refused to join in the by-then customary vote of thanks to the Speaker at adjournment.

But the early Speakers were not the actual political or legislative leaders of the House. Until he left the Treasury in 1795, Hamilton, operating through members of his own choice, dominated the Federalist majority. According to one Jeffersonian observer, Hamilton was an "all-powerful" leader, who "fails in nothing he attempts." [7] As the leader of the Jeffersonians in the House until he left Congress in 1797, Madison was seen in much the same light by Federalist Fisher Ames, who wrote: "Virginia moves in a solid column and the discipline of the party is as severe as the Prussian. Deserters are not spared." [8]

The Jeffersonians or Democratic-Republicans were opposed in principle to the concept of executive supremacy embraced by Hamilton and the early Federalists. When he became president in 1801, Jefferson promptly discarded a favored symbol of Federalist theory — the personal appearance of the president before a joint session of Congress to read his annual State of the Union message. Instead he instituted the practice, followed by all presidents until Woodrow Wilson, of sending up the message to be read by a clerk.

Jefferson, however, was not unwilling to assert his own leadership over the new Democratic-Republican majority in the House. His secretary of the Treasury, Swiss-born Albert Gallatin, who had succeeded Madison as leader of the Jeffersonians, soon became as adept as Hamilton had been in guiding administration measures through the party caucus and the House. Moreover, Jefferson picked his own floor leader, who was named chairman of the Ways and Means Committee at the same time. The men who held the posts of floor leader and Ways and Means chairman during Jefferson's tenure were known as the president's spokesmen in establishing party policy. When one of these leaders, the tempestuous John Randolph, broke with Jefferson over a plan to acquire Florida, the president had him deposed as Ways and Means chairman.

Randolph already had affronted some members of the House by his conduct as committee chairman. Rep. James Sloan complained in 1805 that he had tied up committee business "by going to Baltimore or elsewhere, without leave of absence," and by keeping appropriations' estimates "in his pockets or locked up in his drawer." At the end of the session Randolph had rushed out important bills "when many members had gone home." [9] Sloan proposed that members of all standing committees be elected by ballot and that committees be allowed to choose their own chairmen. A rules change in the Eighth Congress gave committees the right to select their own chairmen if they so chose, but at the beginning of the 11th Congress selection of chairmen as well as committee members reverted to the Speaker.

In sum, the first 20 years of the House saw the beginnings of the standing committee system and the emergence of a floor leader and committee chairmen as key men in the legislative process. But that process was dominated largely by the executive branch, and major decisions on legislative issues were reached behind the scenes in closed caucuses of the majority party. As Federalist Josiah Quincy lamented in 1809, the House "acts and reasons and votes, and performs all the operations of an animated being, and yet, judging from my own perceptions, I cannot refrain from concluding that all great political questions are settled somewhere else than on this floor." [10]

Notes

1. George B. Galloway, *History of the House of Representatives* (New York: Thomas Y. Crowell Co., 1969), p. 135.
2. Ibid., p. 2.
3. Ibid., p. 10.
4. Ibid., p. 12.
5. Ibid., p. 18.
6. Paul Leicester Ford, ed., *The Writings of Thomas Jefferson*, 10 vols. (New York: G. P. Putnam's, 1895), VI: 102.
7. Galloway, *History of the House of Representatives*, p. 18.
8. Ibid., p. 129.
9. Ibid., p. 71.
10. Ibid., pp. 129-130.

Chapter 10

CONGRESSIONAL ASCENDANCY: 1809-1829

The era of executive supremacy over Congress came to an end under Jefferson's successor, James Madison, whose strong leadership in the Constitutional Convention of 1787, in the House and as secretary of state for eight years was not matched in his presidency. Although he was nominally backed by Democratic-Republican majorities during his two terms in office, Madison soon lost control of his party to a group of young "war hawks" (as John Randolph called them) first elected to the 12th Congress. These men eventually pushed the president into the War of 1812 against England. Led in the House by Henry Clay and John C. Calhoun, these radicals within Madison's party capitalized on the president's weakness as a leader and on a rising resistance within Congress to executive control. The shift of power to the legislative branch that they brought about was not reversed until Andrew Jackson became president in 1829.

Clay as Speaker

Henry Clay first came to national attention while serving briefly as a Kentucky senator from 1810 to 1811. He then spoke eloquently of the need for "a new race of heroes" to preserve the achievements of America's founders. He proposed the conquest of Canada, asserting that "the militia of Kentucky are alone competent to place Montreal and Upper Canada at your feet."[1] It was as spokesman for a new nationalism, affronted by British interference with American trade and shipping, that Clay entered the House in 1811 and, although only 34 and a newcomer, promptly was elected Speaker by like-minded Democratic-Republicans. Using to the full his power to select committee chairmen and appoint members to committees, Clay put his fellow war hawks in all the key positions. Together they took control of the House.

Clay greatly enhanced the power and prestige of the Speaker. In addition to presiding over the House as his predecessors had done, he assumed leadership of the majority party. This made him the leader of the House in fact as well as name. A forceful presiding officer, Clay also was an accomplished debater who frequently participated in House legislative debates. Gifted with great charm and tact, Clay remained Speaker as long as he was in the House. Although he resigned his seat twice (in 1814, to help negotiate an end to the War of 1812, and in 1820), he was re-elected Speaker as soon as he returned to the House in 1815 and again in 1823.

It was the job of the Speaker, Clay said in his 1823 inaugural speech, to be prompt and impartial in deciding questions of order, to display "patience, good temper, and courtesy" to every member, and to make "the best arrangement and distribution of the talent of the House" for the dispatch of public business. Above all, he said, the Speaker must "remain cool and unshaken amidst all the storms of debate, carefully guarding the preservation of the permanent laws and rules of the House from being sacrificed to temporary passions, prejudices or interests." [2]

This was no easy job in Clay's time. Political passions were strong, the size of the House was increasing rapidly (to 186 members after the census of 1810 and to 213 after that of 1820) and the right of debate was essentially unlimited. It is true that the House (after becoming exasperated with the unyielding tactics of Rep. Barent Gardenier, a New Yorker who once held the floor for 24 hours) decided in 1811 that a majority could shut off further debate on an issue by employing a parliamentary tactic known as the previous question. In time this became the normal and accepted means of closing House debate, but in the early years many representatives, such as John Randolph, regarded this device as a gag rule, and it was not easily invoked. Under the rules then existing, those skilled in parliamentary tactics — as Randolph was — could and frequently did succeed in tying up House proceedings.

Once Clay outwitted Randolph. It was after the House in 1820 finally had passed the hotly disputed Missouri Compromise bill admitting Missouri to the Union as a slave state but barring slavery in any future state north of 36°30' north latitude. When Randolph, who opposed the bill, moved the next day to reconsider the vote, the Speaker held the motion to be out of order pending completion of the prescribed order of business. Clay then proceeded to sign the bill and send it to the Senate before Randolph could renew his motion. The Speaker's action was

105

upheld, in effect, when the House refused, 61-71, to consider Randolph's subsequent motion to censure the clerk for having removed the bill.

Growth of Standing Committees

Efforts to refine House procedures continued during the 11th through 20th Congresses (1809-1829). The first rule to establish a daily order of business was adopted in 1811. In 1812 the Committee on Enrolled Bills was given leave to report measures at any time — a privilege later granted to certain other committees in order to expedite consideration of important legislation. A rule adopted in 1817 enabled the House to protect itself against business it did not wish to consider. In 1820 the House created through its rules the first legislative calendars of the Committee of the Whole. And in 1822 it was decided that no House rule could be suspended except by a two-thirds majority vote.

But the chief development in House procedures during this period was the proliferation of standing committees and their emergence as the principal forums for the initial, most detailed, consideration of proposed legislation — a practice recognized in 1822 by a rule giving standing committees the right to originate and report legislation directly to the House. The number of select (ad hoc) committees created to draft bills had dropped from 350 in the Third Congress (1793-1795) to 70 in the 13th Congress (1813-1815). And the number of standing (permanent) committees grew from 10 in 1809 to 28 in 1825.

Among the standing committees created in this period were the Judiciary Committee, made permanent in 1813, and the Military Affairs, Naval Affairs and Foreign Affairs committees, all created in 1822. Six Committees on Expenditures, one for each of the executive departments then in existence, were established by Clay in 1816 to check up on economy and efficiency in the administration. Between 1816 and 1826 these and other House committees conducted at least 20 major investigations. The inquiries included such matters as the conduct of General Andrew Jackson in the Seminole War, charges against Secretary of the Treasury William Crawford and the conduct of John C. Calhoun as secretary of war.

Decline of King Caucus

During Clay's reign as Speaker, the party caucus still afforded the House majority, the Democratic-Republicans, an important means of reaching legislative decisions. It took Federalist Daniel Webster less than two weeks after being seated in 1813 to conclude that "the time for us to be put on the stage and moved by the wires has not yet come," since "before anything is attempted to be done here, it must be arranged elsewhere." Webster soon noted that the caucus worked "because it was attended with a severe and efficacious discipline, by which those who went astray were to be brought to repentance." [3] But the extent of party unity had already started to decline under Jefferson as a result of sectional rivalries, and while the Federalists continued to lose ground as a national party, factionalism increased among the Democratic-Republicans in Congress.

The change was reflected also in the rise and fall of the congressional caucus as the vehicle for selecting party nominees for president and vice president. The practice began in 1800, when both Federalist and Democratic-Republican members of Congress met secretly to pick running mates for Jefferson and Adams. In 1804 Jefferson was renominated unanimously and openly by a caucus of 108 Democratic-Republican senators and representatives. Four years later, a caucus of 94 party members nominated Madison for president over the protests of others who preferred James Monroe. But only 83 of the 133 Democratic-Republicans in Congress attended the caucus that renominated Madison in 1812, just before he asked Congress for the declaration of war against England that Clay and others had been urging.

The Democratic-Republican's caucus of 1816 drew 119 of the party's 141 members in the House and Senate. Madison favored the nomination of Monroe, then secretary of state, for president, but there was rising opposition to continuation of the Virginia "dynasty" in the White House and Monroe was nominated by only 65 votes to 54 for Secretary of War William Crawford of Georgia. By 1820, however, there was no real opposition in either party to Monroe, who was credited with bringing about an "Era of Good Feelings" — a phrase coined by a Boston paper to describe the brief period of virtual one-party rule in the United States. (During his administration, Monroe had kept clear of the controversy over the Missouri Compromise.) Fewer than 50 members showed up for the caucus since Monroe's candidacy was not contested. The caucus voted unanimously to make no nomination and passed a resolution explaining that it was inexpedient to do so. Monroe subsequently was re-elected with every electoral vote but one.

In 1824 there still was only one party, the Democratic-Republicans. Within that party, however, there were an abundance of candidates who wished to succeed Monroe, including three members of the president's own Cabinet (Crawford, Calhoun and John Quincy Adams), as well as Henry Clay and Andrew Jackson, hero of the Battle of New Orleans during the War of 1812. When it appeared that Crawford would get a majority in the party caucus, supporters of the other candidates began to denounce the caucus system. As a result, only 66 of the 261 senators and representatives then seated in Congress attended the 1824 caucus that nominated Crawford. The election that fall gave Jackson a plurality but not a majority of the electoral or popular vote, and the choice went to the House, which picked Adams.

The presidential contest of 1824 marked the end of the old party system and the congressional nominating caucus. Changes in voting procedures and an expansion of the suffrage contributed to the caucus' demise. Between 1800 and 1824 the number of states in which the electors were chosen by popular vote instead of by the legislature increased from five out of 16 to 18 out of 24. Four years later, in 1828, the electors were popularly chosen in all except two of the 24 states in the Union, and the popular vote jumped from less than 400,000 in 1824 to more than 1.1 million. With the emergence of a mass electorate, aspirants for the presidency were forced to seek a much broader base of support than the congressional caucus.

Notes

1. Bernard Mayo, *Henry Clay: Spokesman of the New West* (Boston: Houghton-Mifflin, 1937), pp. 346-347.
2. U.S., Congress, *Annals of the Congress of the United States*, 18th Cong., 1st sess., Dec. 1, 1823, p. 795.
3. George B. Galloway, *History of the House of Representatives* (New York: Thomas Y. Crowell Co., 1969), p. 130.

Chapter 11

A HOUSE DIVIDED: 1829-1861

National politics entered a period of increasing turmoil that lasted until the Civil War, during the presidency of Andrew Jackson from 1829 to 1837. Jackson made unprecedented use of the presidential veto and of the removal and patronage powers of the executive office to establish its primacy over Congress. Two new parties emerged during his presidency: the Jacksonian Democrats, heirs to the agrarian and states' rights philosophy of the Jeffersonian Democratic-Republicans, and the Whigs, spokesmen for the commercial and industrial interests once represented by the Federalists. But the Democrats now embraced the Federalist principle of strong executive leadership, while the Whigs extolled the Republican doctrine of legislative supremacy and tried thereafter to weaken the presidency.

The power and influence of the House began to decline under Jackson, while House membership increased to 242. Former luminaries of the House, including Henry Clay, Daniel Webster and John C. Calhoun, moved to the Senate, which now became the major arena of debate on national policy. Party control of the presidency, the House and the Senate fluctuated considerably after Jackson. Increasingly, however, both Democrats and Whigs found themselves divided by the issue of slavery and its extension to the new territories and states beyond the Mississippi River. The issue was reflected in the bitter election battles for the Speakership that occurred in 1839, 1849, 1855 and 1859.

Contests to Elect the Speaker

Intra-party contests for Speaker were not new in the House. In 1805, when Democratic-Republicans outnumbered Federalists almost four-to-one, it took four ballots to re-elect Nathaniel Macon, a southerner, over Joseph B. Varnum, the northern candidate for Speaker. Two years later, when there were five candidates, Varnum won on the second ballot after

Macon withdrew. By 1820 — the year of the Missouri Compromise — the issue of slavery was an explicit part of the sectional contest for Speaker. To replace Clay, who had resigned, the House cast 22 ballots before electing John W. Taylor of New York, the anti-slavery candidate, over William Lowndes of South Carolina, a compromiser.

Taylor was one of five candidates in a contest the next year that underscored the breakup of the Democratic-Republicans and foreshadowed the presidential race of 1824. Taylor lost on the 12th ballot to Philip P. Barbour of Virginia, a Crawford supporter. And in 1834, when Andrew Stevenson resigned in his fourth term as Speaker (only to see the Senate reject his nomination as Minister to Great Britain), it took 10 ballots to elect John Bell over his fellow Tennessean, James K. Polk.

Contest of 1839. Democrat Martin Van Buren, Jackson's handpicked successor, was elected president in 1836, but the Democrats barely won control of the House in the 25th Congress (1837-1839). When it adjourned, Whigs deplored the "most partial and unjust rulings" of Speaker Polk, who had succeeded Bell in 1835. Polk then left the House to become governor of Tennessee. At the opening of the 26th Congress on Dec. 2, 1839, the House found itself with 120 Democrats, 118 Whigs and five contested seats in New Jersey. Control of the House rested on the outcome of these contests, but the clerk (who presided under House practice pending election of a Speaker) refused to choose between the claimants or to bring up the question of the contested seats until the House was organized.

After four days of bitter debate, members elected a temporary chairman — the venerable John Quincy Adams, who had returned to the House in 1831 after one term as president. But it was Dec. 14 before the House decided to elect a Speaker without the contested New Jersey votes. There were six candidates initially, and John W. Jones of Virginia led on the first five ballots. Robert M. T. Hunter, also of Virginia, was elected Dec. 16 on the 11th ballot (when there were 13 candidates) because he "finally united all the Whig votes and all the malcontents of the administration," according to Adams. [1]

Contest of 1849. Control of the House passed to the Whigs in the 27th Congress (1841-1843), then to the Democrats in the 28th and 29th, then back to the Whigs in the 30th (1847-1849) during the last two years of the Polk administration. Zachary Taylor, the Whig candidate, was elected president in 1848. But neither party had a majority in the House when the 31st Congress convened on Dec. 3, 1849, because a number of Free-Soil Whigs and Democrats refused to support the leading candidates for Speaker: Robert C. Winthrop of Massachusetts, Whig Speaker in the previous Congress, or Georgia Democrat Howell Cobb. The pending issue was what to do about slavery in the territory won in the war against Mexico, and the Free Soilers were determined to prevent the election of a Speaker who would appoint pro-slavery majorities to the Committees on Territories and the District of Columbia.

Although Cobb, a proponent of slavery, led 11 candidates on the first ballot with 103 votes, neither he nor Winthrop, who alternated in the lead for 60 ballots, could get a majority from the divided House. Five recognized factions vied for control: Whigs, Democrats, Free Soilers, Native Americans and Taylor Democrats. Finally, on Dec. 22, the House voted, 113 to 106, to elect a Speaker by a plurality, so long as it was a majority of a quorum. Cobb was elected on the 63rd ballot when he received 102 votes to 100 for Winthrop, with 20 votes spread among eight other candidates. This decision then was confirmed by a majority vote of the House.

Contest of 1855. Pro-slavery Democrats held firm control of the House in the 32nd and 33rd Congresses (1851-1855), when Linn Boyd of Kentucky was Speaker. But their attempt to extend slavery into the Kansas and Nebraska territories produced a large turnout of anti-slavery forces in the election of 1854 — the first in which a new Republican party, successor to the Whigs, participated. When the 34th Congress convened on Dec. 3, 1855, the House membership was divided among 108 Republicans or Whigs, 83 Democrats and 43 members of minor parties that sprang up in the 1850s. Although the so-called "Anti-Nebraska men" were in the majority, they were unable to unite behind any candidate for Speaker; two months passed and 133 ballots were taken before a choice was made.

The 21 candidates on the first ballot were led by William A. Richardson of Illinois with 74 votes. As in previous contests, various motions to help resolve the deadlock — including one to drop the low man on each ballot until only two remained — were made and tabled as the voting continued. After a series of votes in which Nathaniel P. Banks of Massachusetts fell only a few votes short of a majority, the House finally agreed to follow the plurality rule of 1849. On Feb. 2, 1856, Banks was declared Speaker. On the 133rd ballot he received 103 votes to 100

111

for William Aiken of South Carolina. Banks, who had been elected to the 33rd Congress as a Coalition Democrat and to the 34th as a candidate of the nativist American Party of Know Nothings, fulfilled the expectations of the anti-slavery forces by his committee appointments.

Contest of 1859. Democrats won the presidency in 1856 with James Buchanan, last of the "northern men with southern principles." They also gained control of the House in the 35th Congress (1857-1859). But the 36th opened on Dec. 5, 1859, with no party in control of the House, which was composed of 109 Republicans, 101 Democrats and 27 Know Nothings. (The Know Nothings were a party of secret organizations whose members, when asked about their political activities, professed to "know nothing." Most Know Nothings were anti-Catholics and favored a 25-year citizenship requirement for residency.) In the 36th Congress pro- and anti-slavery blocs were again deadlocked over the choice of a Speaker. With passions running high and debate unchecked by a presiding clerk who refused to decide any points of order, the struggle dragged on for two months.

The Republicans wanted John Sherman of Ohio. Although he led the early balloting with 110 votes (just six short of a majority), he had become anathema to the pro-slavery camp, and the Republicans finally concluded that he could not be elected. So Sherman withdrew on the 39th ballot, and the Republicans switched their support to William Pennington of New Jersey, a new member of the House and a political unknown. Pennington received 115 votes on the 40th ballot (compared to one on the 38th) and was elected on the 44th ballot, on Feb. 1, 1860, by a bare majority of 117 votes out of 233. Pennington's distinction, shared with Clay, of being Speaker in his first term ended there, for he was defeated at the polls the next year and served only the one term in the House.

Changes in House Rules

Agitation over the issue of slavery was not confined to the contests over the choice of a Speaker. In 1836 John Quincy Adams challenged a House practice, begun in 1792, of refusing to receive petitions and memorials on the subject of slavery. Adams offered a petition from citizens of Massachusetts for the abolition of slavery in the District of Columbia. His action led to protracted debate and the adoption of a resolution, by a 117-68 vote, directing that any papers dealing with slavery "shall, without being either printed or referred, be laid upon the table and that no further action whatever shall be had thereon." [2]

Adams, who considered adoption of the resolution to be a violation of the Constitution and of the rules of the House, reopened the issue in 1837 by asking the Speaker how to dispose of a petition he had received from 22 slaves. Southerners moved at once to censure Adams. The move failed, but the House agreed, 163-18, that "slaves do not possess the right of petition secured to the people of the United States by the Constitution." [3] Further agitation led the House in 1840 to rule that no papers "praying the abolition of slavery . . . shall be received by this House or entertained in any way whatever." [4] Four years later, however, the rule was rescinded.

Other rules adopted during this period were more instrumental in the long-range development of House procedures. In 1837 precedence was given to floor consideration of revenue raising and appropriation bills, and the inclusion of legislation in an appropriation bill (which had led the Senate to kill a number of such bills) was barred. In 1841 the House finally agreed to limit to one hour the time allowed any member in a debate — a proposal first made in 1820 after John Randolph held forth for more than four hours against the Missouri Compromise. To prevent indefinite debate in the Committee of the Whole, a rule was adopted providing that the House, by majority vote, could discharge the Committee of the Whole from consideration of a bill after pending amendments had been disposed of without debate.

Objection to the latter provision led to adoption in 1847 of the five-minute rule, giving any member five minutes during floor debate to explain any amendment he had offered. In effect, this rule encouraged the practice of offering but then withdrawing scores of amendments in an effort to delay action on controversial bills. Although the rule was amended in 1850 to prohibit the withdrawal of any amendment without unanimous consent, the House remained at the mercy of a determined minority. During debate on the Kansas-Nebraska bill of 1854, according to Maine Republican Asher Hinds, opponents engaged in "prolonged dilatory operations, such as the alternation of the motions to lay on the table, for a call of the House, to excuse individual members from voting, to adjourn, to reconsider votes whereby individual members were excused from voting, to adjourn, to fix the day to which the House should adjourn, and, after calls of the House had been ordered, to excuse individual absentees" — all of which required 109 roll calls and consumed many days.[5]

In 1858 the House set up a select committee to revise the more than 150 rules on the books. The committee included the Speaker — the first time that officer had served on any committee of the House. Most of the select committee's recommendations were approved by the House in March 1860. Although largely of a technical nature, this first general revision of the rules affected important aspects of the parliamentary process: use of the previous question motion and the motion to strike the enacting clause. On balance, however, the revised rules of 1860 left ample opportunity for a resolute minority to keep a closely divided House tied up in parliamentary knots.

Apart from the first limitations on debate in the 1840s — the one-hour rule and the five-minute rule — House procedures changed little between 1829 and 1861. The standing committee system begun in 1825 was expanded by the addition of eight permanent committees, bringing the total to 34. The Ways and Means Committee continued to handle both appropriations and revenue bills; and its chairman, while not always the designated floor leader of the majority party, was always among the most influential members. The Speaker continued to appoint members to committees and to designate committee chairmen.

Of the 14 men who were elected Speaker between 1825 and 1860, only three — Stevenson, Polk and Boyd — served for more than one Congress. None achieved the stature or influence of Clay. In one respect only was the job of leading the House made, if not easier, at least no more difficult: the size of the House, after increasing to 242 in 1833, remained about the same size for the next 40 years. Otherwise, the rising passions in the country on the slavery issue doomed the House to increasing turmoil as America moved toward internecine conflict.

Notes

1. George B. Galloway, *History of the House of Representatives* (New York: Thomas Y. Crowell Co., 1969), p. 43.
2. Marie B. Hecht, *John Quincy Adams: A Personal History of an Independent Man* (New York: Macmillan, 1972), p. 545.
3. Ibid., p. 547.
4. Asher C. Hinds, *Hinds' Precedents of the House of Representatives*, 5 vols. (Washington, D.C.: U.S. Government Printing Office, 1907), IV: 278.
5. Ibid., V: 354-355.

Chapter 12

NEW COMPLEXITIES: 1861-1890

The Civil War all but eliminated the South from national politics and representation in Congress for eight years. Most of the 66 House seats held by the 11 secessionist states in 1860 remained vacant from 1861 to 1869. The war also greatly weakened the Democratic Party outside the South. The situation was not dissimilar to that prevailing after the War of 1812 when the Federalists were on the defensive because of their pro-British sympathies. In 1865 the Democratic Party suffered from its identification with the southern cause. And Democratic weakness helped the Republicans to retain control of the presidency until 1885, the House until 1875 and the Senate until 1879.

At the same time, the war and its aftermath gave rise to bitter conflict between Congress and the White House, and led to the impeachment of President Andrew Johnson by the House in 1868 and to a prolonged period of legislative dominance thereafter. The years from 1860 to 1890 saw a further expansion of House membership, an intensification of House efforts to control government spending, an increase in the number and power of House committees and a continuing struggle to adapt the rules of the House to that body's legislative goals.

Congress is Paramount

President Abraham Lincoln assumed unprecedented powers during the Civil War, at a time when the Republican Party in Congress was dominated by a bloc known as the Radicals or Radical Republicans, firm believers in the Whig doctrine of legislative supremacy. The conflict between Lincoln and Congress was sharpest over the issue of Reconstruction. Lincoln, who held that the Confederate states had never left the Union, was prepared to restore their political rights as quickly as possible. But the Radicals, who had been extremely militant during the war, opposed Lincoln's Reconstruction program as too soft. They favored punitive action against the Democratic southern states before readmitting them to Congress. And the final decision, they insisted, should rest with Congress.

When President Lincoln set up new governments in Louisiana and Arkansas in 1863, the Radicals passed a bill placing all Reconstruction authority under the direct control of Congress. Lincoln pocket-vetoed the bill after Congress had adjourned in 1864, whereupon the Radicals issued the Wade-Davis Manifesto asserting that "the authority of Congress is paramount and must be respected." If the president wanted their support, said the Radicals, "he must confine himself to his executive duties — to obey and execute, not make the laws — to suppress by arms armed rebellion, and leave political reorganization to Congress." [1]

The clash of wills between the Radicals and the executive branch continued under the administration of Andrew Johnson, the Tennessee Democrat who became president when Lincoln was assassinated in 1865. Johnson's views were openly sympathetic to the established order in the South. Passed over Johnson's veto were numerous bills, the effects of which were to give Congress full control over Reconstruction policy and to strip the president of much of his authority.

One of these measures was the Tenure of Office Act of 1867, passed on the suspicion that Johnson intended to fire Secretary of War Edwin Stanton. The law made it a high misdemeanor to remove without the Senate's approval any government official whose nomination had been confirmed by the Senate. The Radicals' intention was to protect incumbent Republican officeholders from executive retaliation if they did not support Johnson. Johnson declared the law to be unconstitutional and removed Stanton. The House then voted 126-47 to impeach him. Tried by the Senate, Johnson was acquitted May 16, 1868, when a vote of 35-19 for conviction fell one short of the two-thirds majority required by the Constitution.

Power of the Purse

The Civil War led the House to increase efforts to control government expenditures by exercising its power over appropriations more carefully. Federal spending had climbed from $63 million in 1860 to $1.3 billion in 1865. Until then, the Ways and Means Committee had handled all funding and revenue raising bills as well as legislation relating to monetary matters. But in 1865 the House, with little opposition, agreed to transfer some of these responsibilities to two new standing committees — a Committee on Appropriations and a Committee on Banking and Currency. Referring to the duties of Appropriations Committee members, the sponsor of the committee reorganization declared: "We require of this new committee their whole labor in the restraint of extravagant and illegal appropriations." [2]

Congress at this juncture began to tighten controls on spending. Wartime authority to transfer funds from one account to another was repealed, agencies were required to return unexpended funds to the Treasury and obligation of funds in excess of appropriations was prohibited. Although Congress continued to make lump-sum appropriations to the Army and the Navy, it specified in great detail the amounts and purposes for which money could be spent by the civilian departments and agencies. These efforts helped to keep federal expenditures below $300 million in every year except one from 1871 to 1890.

The House's "power of the purse" was exercised to another end during the administration of Rutherford B. Hayes, the Republican successor to Ulysses S. Grant (1869-1877). Democrats were again in the majority in the House in the 45th Congress (1877-1879) and won control of both chambers in the 46th (1879-1881), but by margins too small to be able to override a presidential veto. So in attempting to repeal certain Reconstruction laws, the Democrats revived the practice of adding legislative riders to appropriation bills in the hope of forcing the president to accept them. Hayes vetoed a series of such bills, calling the tactic an attempt at coercive dictation by the House. When they were unable to override his vetoes, the Democrats relented and approved the appropriation bills without the riders.

During the height of the dispute in 1879, Hayes wrote in his diary:

> This is a controversy which cannot and ought not to be compromised. The Revolutionists claim that a bare majority in the House of Representatives shall control all legislation, by tacking the measures they can't pass through the Senate, or over the President's objections, to the appropriation bills which are required to carry on the government.... [I]t is idle to talk of compromises as to the particular measures which are used as riders on the appropriation bills. These measures may be wise or unwise. It is easy enough to say in regard to them, that used as they are to establish a doctrine which overthrows the Constitutional distribution of power between the different departments of the government, and consolidates in the

House of Representatives, the whole lawmaking power of the government ... we will not discuss or consider them when they are so presented. ...

To tack political legislation to appropriations bills and to threaten that no appropriations will be made unless the political measures are approved is not in my judgment constitutional conduct. [3]

Meanwhile, House members of both parties were becoming concerned over the concentration of power in the Appropriations Committee. In 1877 the committee was deprived of its jurisdiction over appropriations for rivers and harbors — the "pork barrel" on which members relied to finance projects of interest to their districts. The agriculture appropriation was taken from the committee in 1880, and in 1885 the panel was stripped of authority over six other funding bills — Army, Navy, Military Academy, Consular and Diplomatic Affairs, Post Office and Post Roads and Indian Affairs — all of which were transferred to the appropriate legislative committees. Three-fourths of the Democrats and the Republicans joined in the 227-70 vote in 1885 stripping the committee of this giant share of its jurisdiction. They were led by the senior members of most of the other important committees, underscoring the inter-committee rivalry that had developed in the House.

The 1885 vote reinforced the decentralization of power in the House and gave added weight to the criticism of Congress voiced by Woodrow Wilson that year in his book *Congressional Government*. According to Wilson, power in the House was scattered among "47 seigniories, in each of which a standing committee is the court-baron and its chairman lord-proprietor." Wilson noted that "by custom, seniority in congressional service determines the bestowal of the principal chairmanships," and that on the House floor "chairman fights against chairman for use of the time of the assembly." [4]

Wilson attributed the lack of strong party control in the House to the bipartisan composition of committees. He believed they should be composed entirely of members of the majority. "The legislation of a session does not represent the policy of either [party]," he wrote; "it is simply an aggregate of the bills recommended by committees composed of members from both sides of the House, and it is known to be usually not the work of the majority men upon the committees, but compromise conclusions ... of the committeemen of both parties." [5]

118

Influential Speakers

If power in the House was not dispersed among the standing committees and their chairmen, it was also true, as Wilson noted, that "he who appoints those committees is an autocrat of the first magnitude." [6] While Speakers had held that authority since the earliest days of the House, its exercise had assumed new importance with the broadening legislative interests of the country and of the Congress.

Schuyler Colfax of Indiana, first elected to the House in 1854, served as Republican Speaker from 1863 to 1869 and then left to become vice president in President Grant's first term. Although Colfax enjoyed as much personal popularity as had Henry Clay, he was not a forceful Speaker and was regarded as a figurehead in a House dominated by Republican Thaddeus Stevens of Pennsylvania, who became chairman of the Ways and Means Committee in 1861 and of the newly created Appropriations Committee in 1865.

Stevens, who engineered the impeachment of President Johnson, was described by fellow Republican George Boutwell as "a tyrant" in his role as the real leader of the House who was "at once able, bold and unscrupulous." [7]

Colfax's successor as Speaker was James G. Blaine of Maine, one of the founders of the Republican Party. As Speaker from 1869 to 1875, Blaine was an avowed partisan of Republican principles and successfully manipulated committee assignments to produce majorities favorable to legislation he desired. Like Clay, Blaine aspired to the presidency. After losing the Republican nomination to Rutherford B. Hayes in 1876 and to James A. Garfield in 1880, he won the party's nomination in 1884, only to lose in a close election to Democrat Grover Cleveland.

Democrats won control of the House in 1875. After the death in 1876 of their first choice for Speaker, Michael C. Kerr of Indiana, they elected Samuel J. Randall of Pennsylvania, who had entered the House with Blaine and Garfield in 1863. Randall, who served as Speaker until 1881, initiated a thorough revision of House rules in 1880 designed "to secure accuracy in business, economy in time, order, uniformity and impartiality." [8] The net effect of these changes was to increase the ability of floor leaders and committee chairmen to expedite legislation on the floor. The Rules Committee, which had been a select committee since 1789 and had been chaired by the Speaker since 1858, was made a standing committee, and it soon began to make systematic use of special orders, also called special rules. When adopted by the House, these rules governed the amount of time allowed for debate on major bills and the extent to which members might offer amendments. Such special orders from the committee also were a convenience in that they could prohibit potential points of order against provisions of bills that violated a particular rule of the House.

The Democrats lost control of the House in the 47th Congress (1881-1883) but regained it in the 48th (1883-1885). They then passed over Randall, because he had opposed the party's low-tariff policy, and elected John G. Carlisle of Kentucky as Speaker. Carlisle, a member since 1877, remained Speaker from 1883 to 1889. By the device of asking "For what purpose does the gentleman rise?" Carlisle was able to withhold recognition from any member.[9] He made notable use of this power of recognition to forestall motions he opposed. But Carlisle did not lead a united party. In 1884, for example, the Democrats lost the fight for tariff reduction through the defection of Randall and 40 other party members.

Blaine, Randall and Carlisle all contributed significantly to the body of precedents by which future Speakers have been guided under the rules of the House. But none was able or willing to prevent determined minorities from obstructing the business of the House. Under Carlisle in particular the House was subjected to numerous filibusters and such dilatory tactics as the "disappearing quorum," which usually resulted in endless roll calls to no purpose except delay. These displays, coupled with a disappointing legislative output, led to increasing public criticism of the House and to demands that the rules be modified "to permit the majority to control the business for which it is responsible," according to the *New York Tribune.* [10]

The Reed Rules

The opportunity for further reform came when Republicans took control of the House in 1889 and picked Thomas B. Reed of Maine as Speaker. First elected in 1876, Reed had been a Republican leader in the House since 1882 when he became a member of the Rules Committee and an increasingly outspoken critic of the rules. "The only way to do business inside the rules is to suspend the rules," he once said.[11]

When the 51st Congress convened on Dec. 2, 1889, the House was composed of 330 members, with the Republicans commanding a small majority. In keeping with longstanding practice, the rules of the 50th Congress were referred to the five-member Rules Committee chaired by the Speaker, while the House proceeded temporarily under general parliamentary procedure. With the previous general election results for several House seats still being contested, it was expected that the Republicans, before adopting new rules, would settle the election disputes in their favor — as party majorities had always done — in order to increase their majority.

On Jan. 29, 1890, the Republicans called up the West Virginia election case of Smith vs. Jackson. Charles F. Crisp of Georgia, the Democratic leader, immediately raised objection to considering the Republican motion, which had to be decided by majority vote. The roll call produced 161 "yeas," two "nays" and 165 not voting — mostly Democrats who, although present, were using the device of the "disappearing quorum" to block action. But when the point of "no quorum" was made, since less than one-half of the members had voted, Speaker Reed ordered the clerk to enter the names of those present who had refused to vote. He then ruled that a quorum was present and that consideration of the question was in order. [12]

In the ensuing uproar, Reed was denounced as a "tyrant" and a "czar," but he held to his position. An appeal from his ruling was tabled (killed) by a majority of the quorum. The next day, in order to again make a quorum, Reed once more counted non-voting Democrats who were present, and he refused to allow another appeal of the ruling on the ground that the House had already decided the question. Reed then declared that he would refuse to recognize any member rising to make a dilatory motion:

> There is no possible way by which the orderly methods of parliamentary procedure can be used to stop legislation. The object of a parliamentary body is action, and not stoppage of action. Hence, if any member or set of members undertakes to oppose the orderly progress of business, even by the use of the ordinarily recognized parliamentary motions, it is the right of the majority to refuse to have those motions entertained. . . . [13]

Reed's rulings on dilatory motions and the counting of a quorum were incorporated in the revised rules reported by the Rules Committee on Feb. 6, 1890, and adopted by the House after four days of debate by a vote of 161-144. Of the rule that "no dilatory motion shall be entertained by the speaker," the committee report said:

> There are no words which can be framed which will limit members to the proper use of proper motions. Any motion the most

conducive to progress in the public business . . . may be used for purposes of unjust and oppressive delay. . . . Why should an assembly be kept from its work by motions made only to delay and to weary, even if the original design of the motion was salutary and sensible? [14]

In addition to these changes in the rules, the revisions of 1890 reduced the size of the quorum required in the Committee of the Whole House from one-half of the membership of the House to 100 members — a change that facilitated floor action, particularly as the size of the House continued to grow. The revised rules also took account of the fact that the House had long since abandoned its original requirement that members obtain leave to introduce bills. The practice of introducing bills simply by filing them with the clerk was made a rule.

Coincidentally, the number of bills introduced, which had first passed the 1,000 mark during the 24th Congress (1835-1837) and had not exceeded 2,000 until the 40th Congress (1867-1869), reached a new peak of more than 19,000 in the 51st Congress (1889-1891). Woodrow Wilson accurately described the fate of most of these bills: "As a rule, a bill committed [to committee] is a bill doomed. When it goes from the clerk's desk to a committee room, it crosses a parliamentary bridge of sighs and dim dungeons of silence whence it will never return." [15]

Under the Reed rules of 1890, the Speaker was enabled to take effective command of the House. By his authority to name the members and chairmen of all committees he had the power to reward or to punish his fellow members. As chairman of the Rules Committee, which by now shared with Ways and Means and Appropriations the right to report legislation at any time and thereby get immediate access to the floor, he could control the timing and content of bills to be brought before the House. And with unlimited power of recognition, he could determine in large measure what business would be taken up on the floor.

Notes

1. George B. Galloway, *History of the House of Representatives* (New York: Thomas Y. Crowell Co., 1969), pp. 245-246.
2. Richard F. Fenno, Jr., *The Power of the Purse: Appropriations Politics in Congress* (Boston: Little, Brown & Co., 1966), p. 8.
3. T. Harry Williams, *Hayes: The Diary of a President, 1875-1881* (New York: David McKay Co., 1964), p. 206.

4. Woodrow Wilson, *Congressional Government* (1885; reprint ed., Cleveland: Meridian Books, 1956), pp. 76, 82.
5. Ibid., p. 80.
6. Ibid., p. 85.
7. Neil McNeil, *Forge of Democracy: The House of Representatives* (New York: David McKay Co., 1963), p. 185.
8. Galloway, *History of the House*, p. 51.
9. MacNeil, *Forge of Democracy*, p. 76.
10. Galloway, *History of the House*, p. 132.
11. Ibid., p. 251.
12. Ibid., p. 52.
13. Ibid., p. 135.
14. U.S., Congress, *Congressional Record*, 51st Cong., 1st sess., Feb. 10, 1890, pp. 1172-1173.
15. Wilson, *Congressional Government*, p. 63.

Chapter 13

TYRANNY AND REACTION: 1890-1919

Although the Democrats dropped the rule against the "disappearing quorum" when they took control of the House in the 52nd Congress, they restored it in the 53rd. Charles F. Crisp of Georgia, the Democratic Speaker in both Congresses (1891-1895), made just as full use of his powers as had his Republican predecessor, Thomas B. Reed. Crisp, who persuaded two party rivals to withdraw from the Speakership contest by promising them the chairmanships of Appropriations and Ways and Means, once refused to entertain an appeal from a ruling by Reed (then minority leader), refused to let Reed speak any further and directed the sergeant at arms to see that he took his seat.

Reed, who served as Speaker again for the next two Congresses (1895-1899), was able by his forceful leadership of House Republicans to restore the concept of party responsibility in the House. His chief aides in the 51st Congress had included Ways and Means Chairman William McKinley, Jr., of Ohio and Appropriations Chairman Joseph G. Cannon of Illinois. McKinley left the House in 1891 to become governor of Ohio and then president in 1897. When Reed resumed the Speakership in 1895 he named a fellow Maine Republican, Nelson Dingley, Jr., to head Ways and Means. Cannon again became chairman of the Appropriations Committee in 1897, the year Reed also named James A. Tawney of Minnesota as the first Republican whip, charged with keeping party members on the floor and voting in favor of the leadership's positions. Under Reed, House Republicans in the 1890s achieved an exceptional degree of party unity, occasionally voting solidly for measures on which they had been sharply divided in caucus.

The centralization of power in the House during this period coincided with another, less visible, change. Until the Civil War, few members had chosen — or had been enabled by the voters — to make service in the House a long-term career. As late as the 1870s, more than

half of the 293 representatives then elected to the House were freshmen, and the mean length of service for all members was barely two
terms. Although Speakers for some time had followed seniority to a
certain extent in appointing members to subcommittees and committees
of their choice and in advancing them to chairmanships, it was not a
matter of great importance to most members if the Speaker failed to
do so.

By 1899, however, the proportion of newcomers among the 357
members entering the House had fallen to 30 percent, while the mean period of service had increased to more than three terms. As more
members sought to stay in the House for longer periods, it became of increasing importance to them that they have the opportunity to gain
political recognition through specialization and rising influence within
the committee structure. There was thus a growing demand among
members of both parties for assurance that their seniority would be
respected in assigning them rank on committees of their choice. These
expectations contributed to the reaction against centralization that began
under Speaker Cannon.

Revolt against 'Cannonism'

Speaker Reed resigned from the House in 1899, having broken with
President McKinley over U.S. intervention in Cuba and the annexation of
Hawaii. The Republican majority in the 56th Congress (1899-1901)
replaced Reed with David B. Henderson of Iowa, who served two
ineffective terms as Speaker (1899-1903) before retiring from the House.
In 1903, when Joseph G. Cannon was finally elected Speaker by the
Republicans (having been an unsuccessful candidate in 1881, 1889 and
1899), he was the oldest representative (67) and had held the longest service record (28 years) of any Speaker of the House.

Like Reed, Cannon set out to rule the House and its Republican
majority through his control of the Rules Committee and the key
committee chairmen. He kept Sereno E. Payne of New York as majority
leader and chairman of the Ways and Means Committee (positions to
which Payne was first appointed by Henderson in 1899). He also retained
Tawney as majority whip until 1905, when he named him chairman of the
Appropriations panel. Cannon turned over Democrats' committee assignments to their leader, John Sharp Williams of Mississippi, subject to his
veto. But Williams used this authority to build party unity among the
Democrats, and Cannon took back the privilege in 1908 when Missouri

Democrat James Beauchamp "Champ" Clark succeeded Williams as minority leader.

As a strong conservative, Cannon was often out of sympathy with President Theodore Roosevelt (1901-1909) and a growing number of liberal Republicans and Democrats in the House who favored progressive legislation. To maintain control, Cannon made increasing use of his powers as Speaker to block legislation that he opposed and to thwart and punish members who opposed him. In a period of rising public interest in political reform, "Cannonism" came to be a synonym for the arbitrary use of the Speaker's powers to obstruct the legislative will, not of the majority party itself, but of a new majority of House members of both parties.

The movement to curb Cannon got under way during the last session of the 60th Congress when, just before final adjournment on March 3, 1909, the House adopted the Calendar Wednesday rule. This rule set aside Wednesday of each week for calling the roll of committees, whose chairman or other authorized members then were permitted to call up bills that their committees had reported but that had not received clearance from the Rules Committee. At the time, progressives considered this a major reform because it seemed to guarantee that the House would have an opportunity to act on measures favored in committee but opposed by the leadership. In practice, however, the procedure proved ineffective, and in later years the House routinely agreed to dispense with Calendar Wednesday by unanimous consent.

When the 61st Congress convened on March 15, 1909, the House was composed of 219 Republicans and 172 Democrats. But the Republicans included about 30 insurgents led by George W. Norris of Nebraska and John M. Nelson of Wisconsin. After helping to elect Cannon to a fourth term as Speaker, these independently-minded Republicans joined with the Democrats to defeat the usually routine motion adopting the rules of the preceding Congress. Champ Clark, the Democratic leader, then offered a resolution to take away the Speaker's authority to appoint the members of all committees. The resolution limited that authority to only five committees, of which the only important one was Ways and Means, removed the Speaker from membership on the Rules Committee, and tripled the size of that body by adding 10 new members.

Although 28 insurgent Republicans supported the Clark resolution, 22 Democrats voted with the majority of Republicans to defeat it. The

House thereupon adopted a compromise solution, offered by Democrat John J. Fitzgerald of New York, that sidestepped the principal abuses complained of and only slightly curtailed the Speaker's authority. The main change was to establish a Consent Calendar for minor bills of particular interest to individual members and to set aside two days each month when bills on this Calendar could be called up without the prior approval of the Speaker (although required unanimous consent). Adoption of this rule led both parties to designate certain members as official "objectors," to prevent passage of bills opposed for any reason by party members. But the Consent Calendar became a useful device for processing minor bills.

Agitation against "Cannonism" continued, and the coalition of Democrats and progressive Republicans finally prevailed in 1910. Taking advantage of a parliamentary opening on March 16, Rep. Norris asked for immediate consideration of a reform resolution modeled on Clark's previous proposal, which had been bottled up in the Rules Committee. When Cannon held the motion to be out of order, the House overruled him by a decisive vote. Debate then began on the Norris resolution, which stripped the Speaker of all authority to appoint committee members and their chairmen, removed him from the Rules Committee and expanded that committee to 10 members, who would choose their own chairman.

Rep. Nelson expressed the insurgents' dissatisfaction with Cannon's autocratic reign:

> Have we not been punished by every means at the disposal of the powerful House organization? Members long chairmen of important committees, others holding high rank — all with records of faithful and efficient party service to their credit — have been ruthlessly removed, deposed and humiliated before their constituents and the country because, forsooth, they would not cringe or crawl before the arbitrary power of the speaker and his House machine. . . . We are fighting with our Democratic brethren for the common right of equal representation in this House, and for the right of way of progressive legislation in Congress. [1]

The House finally adopted the Norris resolution on March 19 by a vote of 191 to 156, after a continuous session of 29 hours during which Cannon had done his best to round up absentees among his supporters. Recognizing the nature of his defeat, Cannon invited a motion to declare the chair vacant so that the House might elect a new Speaker. Rep. A. S.

Burleson (D-Texas) made the motion, but it was quickly tabled. Known to the House as "Uncle Joe," Cannon was personally popular with many members, and the Republican insurgents were unwilling to help elect a Democrat. Cannon stayed on as Speaker until the end of the 61st Congress in March 1911 and remained a member of the House, except during the 63rd Congress, until 1923, by which time he had completed 46 years of service.

The revolt against "Cannonism" was consolidated in 1911, when the Democrats took control of the House, elected Champ Clark as Speaker and adopted a revised body of rules that incorporated most of the changes agreed to in 1909 and 1910. The new rules provided that all members of the standing committees, including the chairmen, would be "elected by the House, at the commencement of each Congress." [2] The rules of 1911 included the Calendar Wednesday and Consent Calendar innovations of 1909 as well as a discharge rule, adopted in 1910, by which a petition signed by a majority of House members could be used to free a bill stalled in committee. Also established at this time was a special calendar for private bills that could be called up on two designated days of each month.

Return of the Caucus

No less important than the rules of 1911 were the procedures adopted by the Democratic majority to solidify their control of the House. At the party caucus of Jan. 19 that nominated Clark for Speaker, Alabama Democrat Oscar W. Underwood was named majority leader and chairman of the Ways and Mean Committee. And it was decided that the Democratic members of Ways and Means would constitute the party's Committee on Committees, whose task it was to draw up the committee assignments of all Democrats. It was left to the Republicans themselves — who established their own Committee on Committees in 1917 — to select their own committee members. In practice, the election of committees and their chairmen now took the form of a perfunctory vote approving the slates drawn up by key members of the majority and minority parties (the Ways and Means Committee Democrats for the Democratic Party) and endorsed by the party caucus.

Underwood rather than Speaker Clark became the recognized leader of House Democrats from 1911 to 1915 (when he moved to the Senate), and he made frequent use of the party caucus to develop unity on legislative issues. Democratic caucus rules at this time provided that "in deciding upon action in the House involving party policy or principle, a two-thirds vote of those present and voting at a caucus meeting shall bind all members of the caucus" so long as the vote represented a majority of the Democrats in the House. But no member could be bound "upon questions involving a construction of the Constitution of the United States or upon which he made contrary pledges to his constituents prior to his election or received contrary instructions by resolution or platform from his nominating authority." A typical caucus resolution of 1911 bound members of the Democratic Party to vote on the House floor for certain bills reported by the Ways and Means Committee and "to vote against all amendments, except formal committee amendments, to said bills and [against] motions to recommit changing their text from the language agreed upon in this conference." [3]

Underwood also used the caucus to develop legislative proposals, which then would be referred to committees for formal approval; to instruct committees as to which bills they might or might not report; and to instruct the Rules Committee on the terms to be included in its special orders governing floor consideration of major bills and proposed amendments.

Thus the power once concentrated in the hands of Speaker Cannon was transferred to the Democratic caucus, which was dominated by Underwood as majority leader. Historian George B. Galloway thus described Underwood's power:

> As floor leader, Underwood was supreme, the Speaker a figurehead. The main cogs in the machine were the caucus, the floor leadership, the Rules Committee, the standing committees, and special rules. Oscar Underwood became the real leader of the House. He dominated the party caucus, influenced the rules and, as chairman of Ways and Means, chose the membership of the committees. Clark was given the shadow, Underwood the substance, of power. As floor leader, he could ask and obtain recognition at any time to make motions, restrict debate or preclude amendments or both. [4]

Wilson and Congress

As president, Woodrow Wilson (1913-1921) revived the custom begun by Washington but abandoned by Jefferson of addressing Congress in person. He worked closely with the Democratic leaders in both houses and conferred frequently with committees and individual members to solicit support for his legislative program. With Wilson's help, Underwood and the Democrats were able to effect House passage of four major pieces of legislation in the 63rd Congress (1913-1915) — the Underwood Tariff Act, the Federal Reserve Act, the Clayton Antitrust Act and the Federal Trade Commission Act.

The Democrats were not as united on foreign policy, however. Both Speaker Clark and Majority Leader Underwood disagreed with Wilson over repeal of the exemption from Panama Canal tolls originally accorded to American coastal shipping. Claude Kitchin of North Carolina, who had become second-ranking Democrat on Ways and Means in 1913 and who succeeded Underwood as committee chairman and majority leader in 1915, openly challenged the president on several issues, notably when Wilson asked for a declaration of war against Germany in 1917. Clark later denounced the president's military conscription program. Despite this, House Democrats supported Wilson's decision. The only vote against the war was cast by Jeannette Rankin (R-Mont.), elected four years before the 19th Amendment gave women the right to vote and the only member of Congress to vote against both world wars.

Reflecting these disagreements, the strong party unity displayed by House Democrats during Wilson's first term began to fracture in his second. By the time the party lost control of the House at the midterm elections of 1918, the binding party caucus had ceased to be an effective instrument in the hands of the leadership. The Republican minority, meanwhile, in 1911 had all but abandoned use of the binding caucus, erecting in its place a non-binding "conference" used for little more than choosing the party's nominee for Speaker and ratifying committee slates. By 1919 the House no longer was willing to accept the centralization of power that had developed under Speakers Reed, Crisp and Cannon and Majority Leader Underwood. Party leaders thus were faced with the task of finding new ways to build and maintain consensus.

Accompanying this change — and helping to account for it — was a hardening of the unwritten rule of seniority that virtually guaranteed succession to committee chairmanships, when such vacancies occurred, by the next-ranking majority members on the committees. Democrats violated the rule three times in 1911 and on a few occasions thereafter, as did the Republicans. But members could now be fairly confident of rising in the ranks of their committees — so long as they were re-elected — upon the retirement or death of the more senior members of those committees. Such assurance gave chairmen and ranking members a degree of independence from dictation that put a new premium on the persuasive skills of party leaders.

Recognition of seniority as the way of advancement on committees still left each party's Committee on Committees with the job of assigning newcomers to committees, particularly important at the beginning of a new Congress when there usually were many slots to be filled, and filling interim vacancies when members died or sought to switch from one committee to another. The task of filling vacancies often was complicated by keen competition among individuals and among state and regional delegations for the right to spots on such choice committees as Ways and Means and Appropriations. (The popularity of many of the committees, and thus the competition for membership on them, varied to some extent with the issues dominating at the time.) In the inevitable bargaining, the political loyalties of the competitors weighed as much as their interests, capabilities and experience. The filling of important committee vacancies was to remain a significant tool in the hands of party leaders.

Notes

1. George B. Galloway, *History of the House of Representatives* (New York: Thomas Y. Crowell Co., 1969), pp. 54-55.
2. Ibid., p. 55.
3. Ibid., pp. 139, 140.
4. Ibid., p. 108.

Chapter 14

REPUBLICAN YEARS: 1919-1931

By the end of World War I in 1918, most American voters already appeared anxious for the return to "normalcy" promised them two years later by Warren G. Harding, the Republican nominee for president. The midterm elections of 1918 replaced Democratic with Republican majorities in both houses of the 66th Congress (1919-1921), during which President Woodrow Wilson lost his historic battle with the Senate over the Treaty of Versailles. With the election of Harding in 1920 there began a decade of undivided GOP control of the executive and legislative branches of the federal government, lasting until Democrats recaptured the House in 1931.

These were not years of presidential leadership or strong party government. Harding's administration was marked by widespread corruption, brought to light by Senate investigators after his death in 1923. As Harding's successor, Calvin Coolidge (1923-1929) did little to push his legislative program through Congress. President Herbert Hoover (1929-1933) was unable to deal effectively with the economic depression that began just a few months after he took office. Meanwhile, Republican control of the Senate was occasionally nominal, and a minority of progressives in the party often held the balance of power. Party conservatives were more successful in keeping control of the House during the 1920s, and legislative conflicts between the Senate and the House were common. A notable case in point involved the Senate-approved "lame duck" amendment to the Constitution, which House leaders managed to block until 1932.

There were some important changes in the organization and procedures employed by the House in this period. Full authority over all money bills funding the operations of the federal departments and agencies was returned to the Appropriations Committee in 1920, and some minor committees were abolished in 1927. Republican leaders introduced, then abandoned, use of a party Steering Committee to guide their legislative program. Under pressure from Republican progressives, some House rules were modified in 1924, but the Rules Committee continued to exercise tight control over the legislative options of members. Meanwhile, the representative nature of the chamber was brought into question by the House's failure to reapportion its seats to reflect the results of the 1920 census. After the census of 1930, House seats were reapportioned.

New Budget System

Until 1920 there was no central system in the government for drawing up the federal budget and, therefore, no procedure for congressional consideration of a national budget covering all programs and expenditures. The secretary of the Treasury did no more than compile the estimates of the various departments. These then were referred to eight different House committees, each of which would report an appropriations bill for the departments and programs under its jurisdiction, with no reference to governmentwide expenditures or revenues.

Nor were all the requests of a single department necessarily considered by the same committee or funded in the same bill. The appropriations for some departments came from more than one bill and were considered by different committees working often at cross-purposes. This process, which was repeated in the Senate, led to rising criticism. As Alvan T. Fuller (R-Mass.) complained in 1918: "The president is asking our business men to economize and become more efficient while we continue to be the most inefficient and expensive barnacle that ever attached itself to the ship of state." [1]

To improve control over expenditures within the executive branch, President Wilson in 1919 proposed a new budget system. Although he vetoed the first bill from Congress embodying his proposal because it placed the comptroller general beyond the president's power of removal, a second bill, signed by President Harding, became the Budget and Accounting Act of 1921. This measure directed the president to prepare and transmit to Congress each year a budget showing federal revenues and expenditures for the previous and current years and the estimated levels for the ensuing year. It set up a Bureau of the Budget within the executive branch to undertake these tasks. The new law also created a General Accounting Office under the comptroller general to assist

Congress in exercising oversight of the administration of federal funds.

Anticipating enactment of this bill, the House on June 1, 1920, voted to restore to the Appropriations Committee jurisdiction over all money bills originally given to it in 1865. Many senior Republicans and Democrats opposed that move, and the House barely agreed, 158-154, to a crucial parliamentary step allowing the recommendation to be brought to the floor. As finally passed, the reorganization of the Appropriation Committee's jurisdiction also increased the size of the panel from 21 to 35 members. At the same time, the House barred its conferees on appropriations bills from accepting Senate amendments that contravened the rules of the House — such as non-germane provisions, or riders — unless specifically authorized by a separate House vote on each such amendment.

Most of the responsibility for reviewing budget estimates now was lodged in 10 five-member subcommittees of the House Appropriations Committee, each of which passed on the requests of one or more agencies. Parallel subcommittees were set up by the Senate Appropriations Committee, and in 1922 it, too, was given exclusive authority over money bills. These steps toward a more systematic approach to federal expenditures came at a time of general concern about economy in government. They helped to hold expenditures to little more than $3 billion a year from 1922 to 1930. With revenues of close to $4 billion each year, the public debt was reduced from $25 billion in 1919 to $16 billion in 1930.

Other House Innovations

When the Republicans regained control of the House in 1919, the leading contender for Speaker was Rep. James R. Mann of Illinois, who had been minority leader since 1911. But Mann had offended some of his party colleagues by objecting to passage of their private bills, and others feared he would centralize power once again in the Speaker's office in the manner of Joseph G. Cannon, his mentor and close friend. So the Republican conference, looking for someone who would be less forceful, nominated the respected Frederick H. Gillett of Massachusetts. Mann refused the office of majority leader, which then was given to Wyoming Rep. Frank W. Mondell, and for the first time this position was separated from the chairmanship of the Ways and Means Committee.

In a further effort to decentralize power, the Republicans created a five-member Steering Committee chaired by the majority leader. Both the Speaker and the chairman of the Rules Committee were barred from sitting on it. Complaints about the narrow range of views and regions represented on the Steering Committee led, in the 67th Congress (1921-1923), to enlarging its membership to eight. Mondell also invited the Speaker, the chairman of the Rules Committee and others to attend meetings of the Steering Committee, which met almost daily and served as the major organ of party leadership from 1919 to 1925.

With a Republican majority of 300 in the 67th Congress, the party's leaders nevertheless came in for growing criticism for blocking action on measures with wide support in the House. Rules Chairman Philip P. Campbell of Kansas, for example, simply refused to report a number of resolutions, approved by a majority of his committee, to authorize certain investigations. He once told the committee: "You can go to hell. It makes no difference what a majority of you decide. If it meets with my disapproval, it shall not be done. I am the committee. In me repose absolute obstructive powers." [2] Campbell's right to pocket resolutions reported by his committee was upheld by Speaker Gillett and, on appeal, by the House.

But Campbell and many other Republicans were defeated in the elections of 1922, and when the 68th Congress met in December of 1923 the House consisted of 225 Republicans and 207 Democrats. Lack of a larger majority enabled the group of about 20 reform-minded Progressives to hold up the election of a Speaker in an effort to bring about some liberalization of the rules. For two days and eight ballots the two party nominees — Speaker Gillett and Minority Leader Finis J. Garrett (D-Tenn.) — received about 195 votes each, while the Progressives cast 17 votes for Rep. Henry A. Cooper (R-Wis.).

Then Ohio Republican Nicholas Longworth, who had succeeded Mondell as majority leader, persuaded the insurgents to support the election of Gillett in return for a promise to allow full debate on revision of the rules in January. Gillett was re-elected Speaker on the ninth ballot. Democrat Henry T. Rainey of Illinois congratulated Longworth for having steered safely between "the Scylla of progressive Republicanism" and "the Charybdis of conservative Republicanism." "There is not a scratch on the ship. The paint is absolutely intact," Rainey declared. [3]

The promised debate on the rules lasted five days and led to a number of changes. One, designed to outlaw the "pocket veto" exercised arbitrarily by Rules Chairman Campbell, required the committee to "present to the House reports concerning rules, joint rules, and order of business within three legislative days of the time when ordered reported by the Committee." [4] The new rule provided also that if the member making the report failed to call it up within nine days, any other member designated by the committee could do so.

The House also agreed to amend the discharge rule first adopted in 1910. The amended rule reduced from 218 (or a majority of the House membership) to 150 the number of members needed to bring to the floor a bill bottled up in committee. Once a discharge petition was signed by the required number of members, however, the legislation could be called up for debate only on the first and third Monday of the month, and it was subject to other constraints. The single attempt, led by Democrats, to use the new rule in the 68th Congress (1923-1925) was successfully thwarted by the Republican Party leadership.

Disciplining the Progressives

President Calvin Coolidge won an easy victory in the election of 1924, receiving 15.7 million votes to 8.4 million for Democrat John W. Davis and 4.8 million for the Progressive candidate, Sen. Robert M. La Follette, Jr., of Wisconsin. In the same election, the Republican majority of 225 in the House was increased to 247. This gain in the 69th Congress wiped out the leverage that Republican Party Progressives had been able to exert at the beginning of the 68th Congress and opened the way for party leaders to discipline those — including most of the Wisconsin delegation — who had supported La Follette in the 1924 campaign.

By the time the new Congress met on Dec. 7, 1925, the Republican Conference had chosen Majority Leader Longworth for Speaker, Gillett having been elected to the Senate. It also decided to oust Progressive leaders John M. Nelson and Florian Lampert, both of Wisconsin, from their chairmanships of the Committee of Elections and the Committee on Patents, respectively, and to let the other insurgents know that their committee assignments would depend on how they voted for Speaker and for a new and tougher discharge rule. The insurgents responded by again nominating and voting for Cooper. As Rep. James A. Frear (R-Wis.) stated:

> The Wisconsin delegation in Congress today finds itself challenged by those assuming to be in control of the Republican Party by threats and intimidation on the one hand and by the offer of

party recognition with its favors and patronage on the other. We refuse to compromise, or to bargain with Mr. Longworth or with any other Member of the House on an issue affecting our rights as Representatives in Congress to vote our convictions.... Neither flattery nor suggestions concerning committee assignments nor threats will cause the Wisconsin delegation in the House to deviate.... [5]

Longworth was easily elected Speaker on the first ballot, receiving 229 votes to 173 for Minority Leader Garrett and 13 for Cooper. By a vote of 210 to 192, the House then agreed to a new discharge rule in place of the 1924 version. It was described by Rep. Charles R. Crisp (D-Ga.), the son of former Speaker Charles F. Crisp, as one that "hermetically seals the door against any bill ever coming out of a committee when the Steering Committee or the majority leaders desire to kill the bill without putting the members of this House on record on the measure." [6]

In order to discharge a recalcitrant committee from a bill under its jurisdiction, the new rule required a majority of the House membership (218), rather than the old rule's 150, to sign the discharge petition. Once the bill was on the floor, the new rule also stipulated that a majority, established by means of a teller vote, was needed to second a motion to consider the measure, a difficult hurdle since members rarely showed up for teller votes. Moreover, the discharge procedure could be used in the House only on the third Monday of the month, and if it failed to be seconded as prescribed, the bill could not be brought up again in the same Congress. (Not surprisingly, the rule was never invoked during its life and was dropped when Democrats revived the old discharge rule in 1931.)

Soon after Longworth was installed as Speaker, the Republicans submitted to the House their slate of committee assignments. Those Progressives who had voted for Cooper and against the new discharge rule found themselves demoted to the bottom of their committees. (Senate Progressives who had supported La Follette also lost their seniority.) Other Republicans had apparently been brought into line by threats of similar action, according to Minority Leader Garrett. "It was demanded that 71 gentlemen who at the beginning of the 68th Congress thought a discharge rule was proper should change their votes," he said, and forced to "eat the bravest word that many of them ever spoke in order to maintain their standing with the party." [7]

These developments at the beginning of the 69th Congress reflected Longworth's determination to play the role of party leader in the House.

He had already stated his belief that it was the duty of the Speaker, "standing squarely on the platform of his party, to assist in so far as he properly can the enactment of legislation in accordance with the declared principles and policies of his party and by the same token resist the enactment of legislation in violation thereof. . . ." [8] As Speaker, Longworth ignored the party Steering Committee and for six years (1925-1931) personally took charge of the House with the aid of Majority Leader John Q. Tilson (R-Conn.) and Rules Committee Chairman Bertrand H. Snell (R-N.Y.).

Norris Amendment Blocked

The power of House Republican leaders during the 1920s was illustrated by their success in blocking an amendment to the Constitution designed to abolish the regular "short" session of every Congress by advancing from March 3 to Jan. 3 the date when the previous Congress would expire and the new one would begin. House leaders liked the short session because its automatic termination on March 3 strengthened their ability to control the legislative output of the House. The constitutional amendment was sponsored by Sen. George W. Norris (Independent Republican-Neb.), the Progressive who had helped to curb the powers of Speaker Cannon in 1910. Norris' proposal to abolish the short session was approved six times by the Senate before the House in 1932 finally consented to what became the 20th Amendment.

The effort to adopt what was popularly called the "lame duck" amendment began in the Senate in 1922. Sen. Thaddeus H. Caraway (D-Ark.) offered a resolution "that all members defeated at the recent polls abstain from voting on any but routine legislation." When his request that the resolution be referred to the Agriculture Committee, chaired by Sen. Norris, was greeted by laughter from his colleagues, he explained:

> I presume that by ordinary parliamentary procedure the concurrent resolution would go to the Committee on the Judiciary, but . . . I have every reason to believe that it will slumber there, as some other resolutions that I introduced found a morgue there; and I should like to have the Senate itself pass upon this one. [9]

The Agriculture Committee reported instead a joint resolution embodying the "lame duck" amendment, and the Senate endorsed it on Feb. 13 by a vote of 63 to 6 — well over the two-thirds majority required by the Constitution.

The Norris resolution was approved a week later by the House Election Committee, and a special rule providing for its consideration by the House was approved by a majority of members on the Rules Committee. But Rules Chairman Philip P. Campbell of Kansas pocketed the rule, refusing to report it. Then, while sitting in for the ailing Speaker during the last few days of the session, Campbell (who was himself a "lame duck," having been defeated at the polls the previous November) refused to recognize members seeking a House vote to reverse Campbell's action.

On March 18, 1924, in the first session of the 68th Congress, the Senate again adopted the Norris proposal. And three days later, the amendment again was approved by the Election Committee. This time, however, it was blocked in the Rules Committee, leading Norris to accuse House leaders of "killing it, not directly but smothering it without giving the House of Representatives an opportunity to vote." Norris charged that his amendment was "being held up because machine politicians can get more out of this [legislative] jam than the people's representatives can get." [10] The amendment died with the adjournment of the 68th Congress on March 3, 1925.

The Senate approved the proposed amendment a third time on Feb. 15, 1926, in the first session of the 69th Congress. On Feb. 24 it once more was reported to the House by a unanimous vote of its Election Committee. The committee's chairman, Hays B. White (R-Kan.), then discussed the problem he faced under the rules:

> Gentlemen, realize how meager is the chance to reach the resolution [proposed amendment] under the Calendar Wednesday rule. That is the logical and proper rule under which it should be considered. . . . I cannot get unanimous consent . . . nor can I hope to pass a measure fundamental as this under a motion to suspend the rules. . . . The last alternative is for the Rules Committee to grant a special rule for its early consideration. [11]

A special rule was not granted, however, before final adjournment of the 69th Congress on March 3, 1927.

The Senate adopted the proposed constitutional amendment a fourth time on Jan. 4, 1928, and this time House supporters were able to bring it to the floor. Rep. Ole J. Kvale (Farmer-Labor-Minn.) said the leaders who had kept the House from voting on it for so long "did not dare block it any longer." [12] Rules Committee Chairman Snell acknowl-

Terms and Sessions of Congress and the . . .

Under the Constitution, representatives were to be elected "every second year," and Congress was to meet at least once each year — "on the first Monday in December, unless they shall by law appoint a different day." But the Continental Congress, which had been asked by the Federal Convention in Philadelphia to fix "the time and place for commencing proceedings" of the new government, told the First Congress to meet on the first Wednesday of March 1789, which happened to be March 4th. Soon afterward, Congress decided that the terms of office of the president, senators and representatives would begin on March 4 of the year following their election and expire, in the case of representatives, exactly two years later.

Out of these early precedents developed the practice of long and short sessions. The Fourth Congress, for example, met for the first time on Dec. 7, 1795, and remained in session until June 1, 1796. A second session, beginning Dec. 5 of that year, lasted until March 3, 1797, when by law the terms of the representatives elected in 1794 expired. Congresses thereafter often were called into special session by the president, and on numerous occasions they fixed earlier dates for meeting.

For more than 140 years, however, Congress stuck closely to the basic pattern of two sessions: the first, a long one of six months or so that began in December of odd-numbered years (more than one year after the election); the second, a short one that met from December to March (a session that did not begin until after the next election had already taken place).

The political consequences of this schedule became apparent in short order. Presidents inaugurated on March 4 were generally free to make recess appointments and take other actions without consulting Congress until the following December. The short sessions became prey to filibusters and other delaying tactics by members determined to block legislation that would die upon the automatic adjournment of Congress on March 3. Moreover, the Congresses that met in short session always included a substantial number of "lame-duck" members who had been defeated at the polls, yet were able in many instances to determine or greatly influence the legislative outcome of the session.

... 20th Amendment to the Constitution

Dissatisfaction with short sessions of Congress began to mount after 1900. During the Wilson administration, each of four second sessions of Congress ended with a Senate filibuster and the loss of important bills including one or more appropriation bills.

Sen. George W. Norris (Independent Republican-Neb.) became the leading advocate of a constitutional amendment to abolish the short session by starting the terms of Congress and the president in January instead of March. The Senate approved the Norris amendment five times during the 1920s, only to see it blocked by the House each time. It was finally approved by both chambers in 1932, and became the 20th Amendment upon ratification by the 36th state in 1933.

The amendment established Jan. 3 of the year following the election as the day on which the terms of senators and representatives would begin and end, and Jan. 20 as the day on which the president and vice president would take office. The 20th Amendment provided also that Congress should meet annually on Jan. 3 "unless they shall by law appoint a different day." The second session of the 73rd Congress was the first to convene on the new date, Jan. 3, 1934, and Franklin D. Roosevelt was the first president inaugurated on Jan. 20, when he began his second term in 1937.

The amendment was intended to permit Congress to extend its first session for as long as necessary and to complete the work of its second session before the next election, thereby obviating legislation by a "lame-duck" body.

Congress met in almost continuous session during World War II, and the exigencies of the Korean War forced the 81st Congress to meet after the elections of 1950. The Senate met after the 1954 elections to act on the censure of Sen. Joseph R. McCarthy (R-Wis.). In 1970 the 91st Congress resumed work after the midterm elections.

There also were lame-duck sessions in 1974, when Congress approved Nelson A. Rockefeller as President Ford's vice president, and in 1980, to deal with a large backlog of controversial legislation. By the mid-1970s, the average Congress was in session for more than 20 months of its 24-month tenure, with most sessions in non-election years running into December.

edged that "if it had not been for the significant application of these two words, lame duck, the propaganda that has been spread throughout this country would never have been one-half as effective as it has been, and if it had not been for that propaganda I doubt whether this proposition would be on the floor at this time." [13] The amendment was endorsed by a majority of the House on March 9, 1928, but the vote of 209 to 157 fell 35 short of the two-thirds required for approval.

The Senate approved the Norris amendment a fifth time on June 7, 1929. A slightly amended version was approved by the House committee on April 8, 1930, but was not debated until Feb. 24, 1931. Speaker Longworth then offered a further amendment providing that the second session of each Congress must expire on May 4; it was adopted by a 230-148 vote before the resolution itself was approved, 290-93. But the measure was locked in conference when Congress adjourned March 3.

When the 72nd Congress convened in December 1931, Democrats had taken control of the House, and after the Senate had adopted the resolution for a sixth time on Jan. 6, 1932, the House on Feb. 16 quickly passed it without amendment by a vote of 335-56. Within less than a year, the 20th Amendment had been ratified by three-fourths of the states.

Struggle Over Reapportionment

By 1920 no state had lost a seat in the House through reapportionment since Maine and New Hampshire were deprived of one each after the census of 1880. The reason was that Congress regularly had agreed to increase the total membership by a sufficient number to prevent such a loss. Thus the House was increased to 357 members after the census of 1890, to 391 after that of 1900 and to 435 after the 1910 census.

The 1920 census showed that unless the size of the House were again increased, 11 states would lose seats through reapportionment while eight would gain seats. One argument against making such a shift in the House was that voiced in 1921 by Rep. John E. Rankin (D-Miss.):

> The census was taken at a time when we were just emerging from the World War, and when so many thousands of people had left the farms and the small towns temporarily and gone to the large cities of the North and East that a reapportionment under that census would necessarily take from Mississippi and other agricultural states their just representation and place it to the credit of the congested centers. [14]

Limit on Size of House. To avoid reducing the representation of any state, the House Census Committee early in 1921 reported a bill to increase the membership to 483, with the additional seats going to 25 states whose population relative to that of the others had grown the most. But the House proceeded to reverse the committee's action, voting 267-76 to keep the membership at 435. Proponents of that limit argued that the great size of the membership already had resulted in serious limitations on the right to debate and an over-concentration of power in the hands of the leadership. Much also was made of the increased costs of a larger House.

The version of the reapportionment legislation passed by the House on Jan. 19, 1921, thus provided for changes in the states' representation on the basis of the existing membership, taking 12 seats from 11 states and dividing them up among those states that had increased their populations by the largest percentage. But the Senate failed to act on the measure before the 66th Congress adjourned on March 3. When the 67th Congress was called into special session a month later, the House Census Committee approved a new bill fixing the membership at 460 and costing only two states — Maine and Missouri — one seat each. But in October the House voted 146-142 to recommit the bill to committee, and no further action was taken.

By 1925 it was clear that the wartime shift of population from rural to urban areas was not a temporary trend. Such rapidly growing cities as Los Angeles and Detroit began to clamor for the increased representation to which they believed they were entitled under the Constitution. When the House Census Committee refused to report another reapportionment bill, Rep. Henry E. Barbour (R-Calif.) on April 8, 1926, offered a motion to discharge the committee from a bill similar to that passed by the House in 1921. Barbour argued that the bill was privileged under the Constitution, while Rules Committee Chairman Snell, raising a point of order, denied that reapportionment was mandatory under the Constitution.

Speaker Longworth found that three of his predecessors — Joseph W. Keifer, Thomas B. Reed and David B. Henderson — had ruled, to the contrary, that Congress was required to order a new apportionment after each census. But Longworth said he doubted that such a ruling was correct, and he put to the House this question: "Is the consideration of the bill called up by the motion of the gentleman from California in order as a question of constitutional privilege, the rule prescribing the order

143

of business to the contrary notwithstanding? " [15] By a vote of 87-265, the House decided the question in the negative.

Coolidge for Reapportionment. In January 1927 President Coolidge made it known that he favored enactment of a reapportionment bill. When the House Census Committee refused to act, its chairman, Rep. E. Hart Fenn (R-Conn.), tried on March 2, the day before adjournment, to suspend the rules and pass his own bill authorizing the secretary of commerce to reapportion the House on the basis of the 1930 census. With only 40 minutes of debate allowed under the rule (which also required a two-thirds vote for passage) and a filibuster under way in the Senate, the House rejected the Fenn motion, 183-197.

The Fenn bill was resubmitted in modified form early in the 70th Congress, but on May 18, 1928, the House voted 186-165 to recommit it to committee. After further revision the measure was passed by voice vote on Jan. 11, 1929. Reported by a Senate committee four days later, it was eventually abandoned by its supporters on Feb. 27 — five days before the end of the session — in the face of a threatened filibuster by senators from states destined to lose seats in the House.

President Herbert Hoover called the 71st Congress into special session on April 15, 1929, and listed provision for the 1930 census and for a corresponding reapportionment as priority matters. On June 13, 1929, the Senate passed a combined census-reapportionment bill that had been approved by voice vote by the House two days earlier.

Automatic Reapportionment. The 1929 law established a permanent system for reapportioning the 435 seats in the House following each census. It provided that immediately after the convening of the regular session of the 71st Congress in December 1930, the president should transmit to Congress a statement providing for the apportionment of representatives to the House by each state according to the existing size of the House. Failing enactment of new apportionment legislation by Congress, that apportionment would go into effect for ensuing elections without further action and would remain in effect until another census had been taken. Reapportionment then would be effected in the same manner after each decennial count of the population.

The reapportionment based on the 1930 census resulted in a major reshuffling of House seats in the 73rd Congress, which was elected in 1932. Twenty-one states lost a total of 27 seats. Missouri alone lost three seats, and Georgia, Iowa, Kentucky and Pennsylvania two each. Among the 11 states to which these seats were transferred, California gained nine, increasing the size of its delegation from 11 to 20. Other states gaining more than one additional seat were Michigan (four), Texas (three) and New Jersey, New York and Ohio (two each).

Notes

1. Paul DeWitt Hasbrouck, *Party Government in the House of Representatives* (New York: Macmillan, 1972), p. 15.
2. Floyd M. Riddick, *The United States Congress: Organization and Procedure* (Manassas, Va.: National Capitol Publishers, 1949), p. 123.
3. Hasbrouck, *Party Government*, p. 20.
4. Ibid., p. 99.
5. *Congressional Record*, 69th Cong., 1st sess., Dec. 7, 1925, p. 380.
6. Hasbrouck, *Party Government*, p. 164.
7. *Congressional Record*, 69th Cong., 1st sess., Dec. 16, 1925, p. 933.
8. Hasbrouck, *Party Government*, p. 23.
9. *Congressional Record*, 67th Cong., 3rd sess., Nov. 22, 1922, p. 26.
10. *Congressional Record*, 68th Cong., 2nd sess., Feb. 18, 1925, pp. 4009-4010.
11. *Congressional Record*, 69th Cong., 1st sess., March 25, 1926, p. 6313.
12. George B. Galloway, *History of the House of Representatives* (New York: Thomas Y. Crowell Co., 1969), p. 145.
13. Ibid.
14. *Congressional Record*, 67th Cong., 1st sess., Oct. 14, 1921, p. 6315.
15. *Congressional Record*, 69th Cong., 1st sess., April 8, 1926, p. 7148.

Chapter 15

DEMOCRATIC YEARS: 1931-1945

The Great Depression that began in 1929 foreshadowed the end of Republican rule in Washington. The party's majority status in the House of 267 members in the 71st Congress (1929-1931) evaporated in the midterm elections of 1930, which gave the Republicans 218 seats, the Democrats 216 seats, and the Independents one seat. By the time the 72nd Congress met on Dec. 7, 1931, however, 14 representatives-elect, including Speaker Nicholas Longworth, had died, and special elections to fill the vacancies had resulted in a crucial net gain of four seats for the Democrats, giving them control of the House.

With 12 million Americans unemployed by 1932, Democrat Franklin D. Roosevelt was elected president along with commanding Democratic majorities in both houses of Congress. A strong party leader, Roosevelt in his first term (1933-1937) won approval of a broad range of New Deal economic and social measures. But during his second term (1937-1941), he was less successful; a conservative coalition in Congress blocked many of his domestic programs. Germany's attack on Poland in 1939, followed by the fall of France in 1940, helped to re-elect Roosevelt to an unprecedented third term (1941-1945) that was largely devoted to waging and winning World War II. Legislative-executive relations deteriorated during the war, and when Roosevelt died in April 1945 at the beginning of his fourth term Congress was in open rebellion against his plans for postwar reconstruction.

The Democrats who led the House during the Roosevelt years worked closely with the president to marshal support for the administration's requests. But their power to shape the legislative output of the House was sharply curtailed after 1937, when a coalition of southern Democrats and Republicans gained control of the Rules Committee, which had been a key arm of House leaders since 1880. The unprecedented four-term presidency of Roosevelt and growing concern about the capacity of Congress to function effectively as a coequal branch of government during wartime increased demands for government reforms. As a result, substantial institutional changes in the way Congress operated were incorporated in the Legislative Reorganization Act of 1946.

Party Leaders

The long period of influence in Congress by conservative southern Democrats began in 1931 when the party took control of the House. John Nance Garner of Texas, who had become minority leader upon the retirement of Finis J. Garrett in 1929, was elected Speaker, and Henry T. Rainey of Illinois was named majority leader. Southern Democrats became chairmen of 28 of the 47 standing committees of the House. Among them were Edward W. Pou (N.C.), Rules; Joseph W. Byrns (Tenn.), Appropriations; James W. Collier (Miss.), Ways and Means; and Sam Rayburn (Texas), Interstate and Foreign Commerce.

When Garner became vice president in 1933, House Democrats elevated Rainey to Speaker and made Byrns the new majority leader. Rainey died in 1934, and Byrns was elected Speaker at the beginning of the 74th Congress in 1935, to be suceeded as majority leader by William B. Bankhead (Ala.). When Byrns died in 1936, Bankhead became Speaker and the Democrats chose Rayburn as majority leader.

Bankhead remained Speaker until his death in 1940, when he was succeeded by Rayburn; a northern Democrat — John W. McCormack of Massachusetts — became majority leader. Rayburn and McCormack remained in these posts until Republicans took control of the House in 1947.

Although Democrats had been in the minority in Congress during the 1920s, southerners had constituted more than one-half of their ranks and there was little occasion for complaint about an unwarranted influence in party councils. But when the party won control in 1931, northern and western Democrats pressed for a larger voice in committee assignments. They proposed entrusting this crucial authority to a new Committee on Committees; since 1911 the Democratic members of the Ways and Means Committee had performed this function. The new committee was to be made up of one member from each state having Democratic representation in the House. The committee also was to select a nine-member Steering Committee that would be in charge of the Democrats' legislative program.

These steps were not agreed to in 1931, although additions to the Ways and Means Committee, including McCormack, brought about a better balance of geographical representation. By 1933, however, the Democratic majority in the House had been increased to 313 members, nearly two-thirds of whom were from states outside the South. As a result, it was agreed to set up a Steering Committee composed of the Speaker, the majority leader, the whip, the chairmen of the Appropriations, Ways and Means and Rules Committees and of the party caucus, plus 15 representatives from as many regions to be chosen by Democratic members within those areas. This Steering Committee operated with some success during the 73rd Congress (1933-1935), but fell into disuse thereafter.

Emergency 100-Day Session

The Rules Committee itself was the major tool of House Democratic leaders during the 73rd Congress. It was this Congress that was called into special session by President Roosevelt on March 9, 1933, and asked to pass a series of emergency economic recovery measures almost sight unseen. Ten of the measures were brought to the House floor under special "closed" rules — drafted by the Rules Committee and adopted by majority vote in the House — that barred all except committee amendments, waived points of order against provisions or procedures violating rules of the House, and sharply limited debate. Among the laws enacted with the help of these "gag" rules during the famous 100-day session were the Emergency Banking Act, the Economic Act, the Emergency Relief Act, the first Agricultural Adjustment Act, the Tennessee Valley Authority Act and the National Industrial Recovery Act.

Faced with mounting opposition to cuts in veterans' benefits and government salaries ordered under Roosevelt's economic recovery program, the Rules Committee at the opening of the second session on Jan. 3, 1934, brought in a rule to bar amendments to any appropriation bill for the remainder of the session that would conflict with the economy program. The purpose, said Rep. Bankhead, was to have the House "deliberately determine for today and hereafter ... whether they are going to follow the President's recommendations or not." [1]

Minority Leader Bertrand H. Snell of New York maintained that he had never been opposed to special rules so long as they were "fairly fair," and called the new proposal "the most vicious, the most far-reaching special rule" ever drafted. No majority, he said, had "ever dared bring in a rule that not only hog-tied and prohibited the members from expressing themselves on the legislation in hand but even extended through the entire session of Congress." The real purpose, said Snell, was that "you think it will be easier to hog-tie your own men today than it will [be] after we have been in session for five months." [2] Snell was joined by all the Republican members, 84 Democrats and five Farmer Laborite members in voting against the rule; but it was narrowly adopted by a 197-192 vote.

The only major change in the standing rules of the House in this period involved the discharge rule. When the Democrats took control of the House in 1931 they replaced the unworkable rule of 1925 with that of 1924, which was altered slightly to reduce from 150 to 145 the number of signatures needed to place a discharge motion on the calendar. But that number was increased to 218 again (the number in force from 1910 to 1924) at the beginning of the 74th Congress in 1935, when Democrats in the House numbered 322 but the leadership was finding it difficult to maintain party unity.

The Conservative Coalition

Party unity was badly shaken at the beginning of the 75th Congress in 1937 when President Roosevelt submitted a plan to reorganize the Supreme Court and the lower courts. His plan, among other changes, allowed the president to appoint up to six additional high court justices whenever a sitting justice age 70 or over refused to retire. Its implied purpose was to increase the likelihood that the Supreme Court could be counted on to uphold the constitutionality of New Deal economic measures, of which six of the most sweeping already had been overturned.

The plan to "pack" the court — which eventually died in the Senate — created a furor in the country and led to a new alignment of conservative Democrats and Republicans in Congress generally and in the House Rules Committee in particular. Ironically, it was a conservative coalition in Congress, rather than in the Supreme Court, that posed the greater threat to the New Deal programs.

The "conservative coalition" first appeared in August 1937, when the Rules Committee voted 10-4 against granting a special rule for floor consideration of an administration bill that eventually became the Fair Labor Standards Act. The committee was chaired by Rep. John J.

O'Connor (D-N.Y.) and was composed of five northern Democrats, five southern Democrats and four Republicans. After the committee's refusal to grant the special rule, House leaders obtained 218 signatures on a discharge petition, but when they brought the bill to the floor in December the House voted 216-198 to recommit it to the Labor Committee.

When the Rules Committee in 1938 again refused to clear the wage-hour bill, House leaders once more resorted to the discharge rule in order to bring the bill to a vote. This time they won House approval by a margin of 314-97. (Although the House occasionally had passed a bill by use of the discharge rule, the Fair Labor Standards Act of 1938 was the first such measure to become law.)

Chairman O'Connor's defection on this bill made him one of the targets of President Roosevelt's attempted purge of anti-New Deal Democrats in the 1938 primaries. At a press conference on Aug. 16, Roosevelt denounced the Rules chairman as "one of the most effective obstructionists in the lower house." [3] O'Connor, unlike other prominent targets of the purge effort, lost his bid for renomination.

O'Connor was succeeded as chairman of the Rules Committee in 1939 by Adolph J. Sabath of Illinois, the senior House Democrat at the time and an ardent New Dealer. But Sabath continued to be outvoted in the committee by a coalition of Republicans and southern Democrats led by Reps. E. E. Cox (D-Ga.) and Howard W. Smith (D-Va.). During the 76th Congress (1939-1941), the committee began the practice of demanding, as the price of sending administration bills to the floor, substantive changes to accord with the views of the conservatives.

Besides blocking or weakening administration measures, the coalition used its power on the Rules Committee to clear measures opposed by Roosevelt. The committee investigated the National Labor Relations Board in 1939, the activities of executive agencies in 1943, and, in 1944, the government's seizure of properties of Montgomery Ward & Co. All three investigations embarrassed the administration. The Rules Committee in 1944 also approved a special rule bringing to the floor a price control bill that had been rejected by the Banking and Currency Committee and never reported by any legislative committee. Speaker Rayburn took the floor to denounce the rule, saying the Rules Committee "was never set up to be a legislative committee," and the House rejected it. [4]

At the beginning of the 79th Congress in 1945, the size of the Rules Committee was reduced from 14 to 12 members, consisting of eight Democrats and four Republicans. Sabath was still chairman, but whenever Reps. Cox and Smith decided to vote with the Republicans they could produce a tie that would block committee action. In 1945, for example, the committee by a six-to-six vote refused a direct appeal from President Harry S Truman for a rule permitting the House to vote on a bill to establish a permanent Fair Employment Practices Commission. The coalition also blocked a rule permitting consideration of an administration bill to raise the minimum wage from 40 cents to 65 cents an hour.

In 1946, when the Rules Committee was asked to clear an administration-backed labor relations bill reported by the House Labor Committee, it reported instead a rule to permit substitution of a more drastic measure sponsored by Francis H. Case (R-S.D.) that had just been introduced. Chairman Sabath denounced the action as arbitrary and undemocratic, but in this case a majority of House members upheld the committee majority by adopting the rule and passing the Case substitute, which Truman later vetoed.

The Rules Committee thus ceased to be a dependable arm of the Democratic leadership after 1937, when the coalition of conservative Democrats and Republicans took control. While the views of members of the coalition on social and economic issues were in conflict with those of most Democrats, they frequently reflected the legislative preferences of a bipartisan majority in the House, and it was the support of this broader conservative coalition that enabled those who controlled the Rules Committee to make the most effective use of its powers.

1946 Legislative Reorganization Act

Momentum for congressional reform mounted during World War II, during which the powers of the executive branch were vastly enlarged. According to a 1945 report by the American Political Science Association, Congress needed to

> . . .modernize its machinery and methods to fit modern conditions if it is to keep pace with a greatly enlarged and active executive branch. This is a better approach than that which seeks to meet the problem by reducing and hamstringing the executive. A strong and more representative legislature, in closer touch with and better informed about the administration, is the antidote to bureaucracy. [5]

Responding to such criticisms, the House and Senate agreed early in 1945 to establish a Joint Committee on the Organization of Congress composed of six members from each house equally divided among Democrats and Republicans. Sen. Robert M. La Follette, Jr., of Wisconsin, was named chairman, with Rep. A. S. Mike Monroney (D-Okla.) vice chairman. From March 13 through June 29, 1945, the group took extensive testimony from more than 100 witnesses, including many members of Congress.

Among the proposals heard were several to restrict the power of the House Rules Committee. Rep. Christian A. Herter (R-Mass.) thought the committee should be required to grant, within a specified time, requests for special rules on bills favorably reported by the legislative committees. Herter said: "The House Committee on Rules should not have the power of deciding which committee reports shall be considered by the whole House, but should be confined merely to determining the order of their consideration. The Rules Committee ought not to be permitted to prevent the submission of favorable committee reports to the whole House." [6] Rep. Sherman Adams (R-N.H.) thought a unanimous report from a legislative committee should automatically give a bill the right of way without reference to the Rules Committee.

In its final report issued March 4, 1946, the La Follette-Monroney committee made no recommendations concerning Rules "because of a lack of agreement within the committee as to workable changes in existing practices." [7] Nor did the committee recommend any of the numerous proposals it had received for appointing committee chairmen on some basis other than seniority, or to make it easier to limit debate in the Senate.

The report did include a broad range of proposals designed to streamline the committee structure, strengthen congressional control over the budget, reduce and redistribute the workload of Congress and improve staff assistance. Most of these reforms were incorporated in the Legislative Reorganization Act enacted on Aug. 2, 1946. The major provisions of the act concerned committees, the federal budget, congressional workload, staff and salaries.

Standing Committees. The 1946 reorganization reduced the number of standing committees from 33 to 15 in the Senate and from 48 to 19 in the House. Many inactive committees were dropped, and some others having related functions were consolidated. As reorganized, the House committees were: Agriculture, Appropriations, Armed Services, Banking and Currency (name changed to Banking, Currency and Housing in 1975 and to Banking, Finance and Urban Affairs in 1977), District of Columbia, Education and Labor, Expenditures in the Executive Departments (name changed to Government Operations in 1952), Foreign Affairs (name changed to International Relations in 1975 and then changed back to Foreign Affairs in 1979), House Administration, Interior and Insular Affairs, Interstate and Foreign Commerce (name changed to Energy and Commerce in 1981), Judiciary, Merchant Marine and Fisheries, Post Office and Civil Service, Public Works (name changed to Public Works and Transportation in 1975), Rules, Un-American Activities (name changed to Internal Security in 1969 and abolished in 1975; a select committee before and during World War II, it was made a standing committee by a 208-186 vote of the House on Jan. 3, 1945), Veterans' Affairs, and Ways and Means.

All standing committees, except Appropriations, were directed to fix regular days for meeting; to keep complete records of committee action, including votes; and to open all sessions to the public except when marking up bills or voting or when the committee by a majority vote ordered a closed session to discuss national security or other sensitive subjects. The act made it the duty of each committee chairman to bring bills to a final vote and to see to it that any measure approved in committee was reported promptly to the House. But no measure was to be reported from any committee unless a majority of the members were present.

Control of the Federal Budget. The act directed the House Ways and Means and Senate Finance committees and the Appropriations committees of both houses, acting as a Joint Budget Committee, to prepare each year a governmentwide budget containing estimates of total receipts and expenditures. The Joint Budget Committee's report was to be accompanied by a concurrent resolution that would be the legislative vehicle for adopting each year's budget and fixing the amount to be appropriated for each federal agency. Congress was prohibited from appropriating more than the estimated receipts without at the same time authorizing an increase in the public debt. The act did not include a proposal that the president be required to reduce all appropriations by a uniform percentage if expenditures later were found to have exceeded receipts.

Workload, Staff, Salaries. The act prohibited private bills from being used for the payment of pensions or tort claims, the construction of bridges, or the correction of military records — categories of legislation that at one time consumed much of the lawmakers' time. But Congress did not accept the Joint Committee's proposal that the District of Columbia be given home rule, a step that would have eliminated the District of Columbia committees in both houses and a considerable amount of legislative work.

Each standing committee was authorized by the act to appoint four professional and six clerical staff members, although no limit was placed on the number that could be hired by the Appropriations committees. The 1946 reorganization act also made the Legislative Reference Service, which provided information for members upon request, a separate department of the Library of Congress and renamed it the Congressional Research Service.

The Joint Committee had recommended the appointment of a director of personnel, with authority to establish the equivalent of a Civil Service for legislative employees, but this proposal was eliminated in the Senate.

The act increased the salaries of senators and representatives from $10,000 to $12,500, effective in 1947, and retained an existing $2,500 nontaxable expense allowance for all members. The salaries of the vice president and the Speaker were raised to $20,000. The act brought members of Congress under the Civil Service Retirement Act and made them eligible for benefits at age 62 after at least six years of service.

The 1946 reorganization also included a section on lobbying (Title III — the Federal Regulation of Lobbying Act) that for the first time required lobbyists to register with and report their expenditures to the clerk of the House. But it did not include a provision, recommended by the La Follette-Monroney committee, that both parties establish seven-member policy committees in each chamber, with the majority policy committees serving as "a formal council to meet regularly with the executive, to facilitate the formulation and carrying out of national policy and to improve relationships between the executive and legislative branches of government." [8] (Republicans and Democrats in the Senate, but not in the House, agreed later in 1946 to set up party Policy Committees.)

Although the 1946 act was regarded at the time as a major achievement, its provisions for budget control as a tool in controlling government spending soon proved to be unworkable and were dropped after three years. And the Regulation of Lobbying Act proved to be too weak to shed much light on the purposes and activities of pressure groups. By reducing the number of standing committees, the act attempted to limit representatives to membership on one committee (two committees for senators) in order to make more efficient use of their time. But in practice this broke down, due in part to the proliferation of subcommittees in later years and the creation of several select committees. The 1946 reorganization skirted the issue of the distribution of power within Congress and did not address the question of the balance of power between the legislative and executive branches; these remained troublesome issues throughout the postwar years.

Notes

1. *Congressional Record,* 73rd Cong., 2nd sess., Jan. 11, 1934, p. 481.
2. Ibid., p. 485.
3. *The Public Papers and Addresses of Franklin D. Roosevelt,* 13 vols. (New York: Macmillan, 1941), VII: 489.
4. Richard Bolling, *Power in the House: A History of the Leadership of the House of Representatives* (New York: E. P. Dutton, 1968), p. 164.
5. *The Reorganization of Congress,* A Report of the Committee of Congress of the American Political Science Association (Washington, D.C.: Public Affairs Press, 1945), pp. 80-81.
6. *Hearings Before the Joint Committee on the Organization of Congress,* 79th Cong., 1st sess., March 19, 1945, p. 109.
7. *Organization of the Congress,* Report of the Joint Committee on the Organization of Congress, 79th Cong., 2nd Session (Washington, D.C.: U.S. Government Printing Office, 1946), p. 35.
8. Ibid., p. 13.

Chapter 16

POSTWAR DEVELOPMENTS: 1945-1969

The Democrats lost control of the House and Senate in the 80th Congress (1947-1949) and the 83rd (1953-1955), but enjoyed majorities in all of the other Congresses from 1949 through 1981. Meanwhile, the presidency passed from Democrat Harry S Truman (1945-1953) to Republican Dwight D. Eisenhower (1953-1961), who was followed by Democrats John F. Kennedy (1961-1963) and Lyndon B. Johnson (1963-1969); Republicans Richard M. Nixon (1969-1974) and Gerald R. Ford (1974-1977) and Democrat Jimmy Carter (1977-1981). With the election of Ronald Reagan in 1980, Republicans won control of the Senate for the first time since 1953, but the House remained in Democratic hands.

These periods of divided government tended to emphasize the partisan aspects of conflicts between the president and Congress over public policy. But none of the postwar presidents was in full command of his own party in Congress, whether it was in the majority or not. All of them were forced to varying degrees to seek bipartisan support to get their programs enacted. In the House, the Democratic Party always included 60 or more southern conservatives who were opposed to much of their party's economic and social programs. And a score of moderate to liberal Republicans frequently were at odds with the party's conservative majority.

Leadership in the House was relatively stable between 1945 and 1969. After World War II, the control of federal expenditures became a central issue, as it had after the Civil War and World War I. Attempts by Congress in general and by the House Appropriations Committee in particular to exercise the power of the purse were matters of controversy. There was continuing agitation over the power of the House Rules Committee to block or reshape major legislation, leading once again to several attempts to restrict the panel's powers. Talk of the need for broad-scale congressional reform increased in the 1960s, and in 1970 the

House finally approved a reorganization bill first passed by the Senate in 1967.

Party Leaders

Sam Rayburn of Texas was the unrivaled leader of House Democrats from 1940 until his death in 1961, serving as Speaker in all but the Republican-controlled 80th and 83rd Congresses, during which he was minority leader. Rayburn was a strong Speaker, whose influence was enhanced by his veneration of the House of Representatives as an institution and his high personal standing with most of his colleagues. Faced with a divided party on many issues, he relied heavily on his personal friendships with key members on both sides of the aisle to attain his legislative objectives. And younger Democrats who followed his advice — "to get along, go along" — could expect to be rewarded with preferment of some kind, especially if they could demonstrate talent and a capacity for hard work. [1]

Rayburn's preferences were controlling when it came to Democratic committee assignments. In 1948 he obtained the removal from the Un-American Activities Committee of three Democrats who had supported Dixiecrat Strom Thurmond in the 1948 presidential campaign. He saw to it that Democrats named to vacancies on the Ways and Means Committee were favorable to reciprocal trade bills and opposed to reductions in the oil depletion allowance. And he turned the predominantly conservative Education and Labor Committee into a liberal body during the 1950s by an infusion of younger Democrats. But Rayburn resisted pressure from party liberals to restructure the Rules Committee until 1961, when he reluctantly agreed to go along.

When Rayburn died late that year after 49 years in the House, he was replaced by John W. McCormack (D-Mass.), who had served as majority leader during Rayburn's 20 years as Speaker. Carl Albert (D-Okla.) was named majority leader at the same time. McCormack's performance as Speaker suffered by comparison with that of Rayburn. Criticism of his weakness as a party leader culminated at the beginning of the 91st Congress in 1969 when 58 Democrats voted for Morris K. Udall (D-Ariz.) for Speaker in the party caucus. Although easily re-elected as Speaker, McCormack decided in 1970 to retire at the end of his term, after 43 years in the House. Albert was designated to succeed him. Hale Boggs (D-La.) became majority leader when Albert moved up. Albert was re-elected Speaker for the 93rd and 94th Congresses. After Boggs was pronounced "missing and presumed dead" following an airplane accident in October 1972, Thomas P. O'Neill, Jr., (D-Mass.) succeeded him as majority leader in January 1973 at the beginning of the 93rd Congress.

House Republicans were led from 1939 to 1959 by Joseph W. Martin, Jr., of Massachusetts. Martin served as Speaker in the 80th and 83rd Congresses, during which Charles A. Halleck (R-Ind.) held the post of majority leader. Martin, a close friend of Rayburn's, was considered by more conservative House Republicans to be too accommodating to the Democratic leadership during the 1950s, and in 1959 he lost his post as minority leader to Halleck, an outspoken partisan. Before long, however, Halleck began to incur the opposition of younger Republicans seeking a more forceful and positive style of leadership, and in January 1965 he himself was ousted when the Republican Conference (the party's caucus), chose Gerald R. Ford, Jr., of Michigan as minority leader on a 73-67 vote.

Efforts to Control Spending

In 1947, pursuant to the requirement of the Legislative Reorganization Act of 1946, the Republican-controlled 80th Congress formed a Joint Committee on the Legislative Budget, which quickly agreed to ceilings on governmentwide appropriations and expenditures that were substantially under the amounts projected in President Truman's federal budget. The House approved the ceilings, but the Senate raised them, insisting that any budget surplus be used to reduce the public debt rather than to provide a tax cut desired by House leaders. As a result, the resolution embodying the federal budget died in a House-Senate conference.

In 1948 both chambers reached quick agreement on a federal budget that projected a surplus of $10 billion — more than double President Truman's estimate — and paved the way for enactment of a tax cut over the president's veto. But Republican leaders expressed doubt about the efficacy of the budget procedure as a device for reducing expenditures. Rep. John Taber of New York, chairman of the House Appropriations Committee, called it "a stab in the dark." His Senate counterpart, H. Styles Bridges of New Hampshire, said that it was "a pregame guess at the final score." [2] In fact, the projected surplus vanished in fiscal 1949, which ended with a deficit of $1.8 billion.

Democrats took control of the 81st Congress in 1949, and the new chairman of the House Appropriations Committee, Clarence A. Cannon of Missouri, proposed suspension of the budget provisions of the 1946 act, saying they were "unworkable and impracticable." He told the House: "We have tried it. We gave it every opportunity. It cannot be made effective. We can no more expect success . . . with this well-meant but hopeless proposal than we can expect a verdict from the jury before it has heard the evidence." [3] Congress put off a decision by voting to postpone until May of that year the deadline for the Joint Committee's recommendations, but these were never forthcoming. The budget provisions of the 1946 act remained a part of the law, but Congress made no further effort to comply with them.

In 1950 Cannon tried another approach to expenditure control by having his committee draft a single omnibus appropriations bill that carried almost $37 billion in spending authority as finally enacted. But this bill was quickly outdated by the Korean War and the need for large supplemental appropriations. More significant, the omnibus approach had the effect of reducing the authority of the Appropriations Committee's subcommittees and their chairmen. Cannon asserted that "every predatory lobbyist, every pressure group seeking to get its hands into the U.S. Treasury, every bureaucrat seeking to extend his empire downtown is opposed to the consolidated bill." [4] In 1951 the committee voted 31-18 to return to the traditional method of separate appropriation bills for each government department.

Cannon and his committee were in full agreement, however, in opposing the concept of a Joint Budget Committee composed of several members of the Senate and House Appropriations committees. Bills to create such a group were passed by the Senate eight times between 1952 and 1967, but they were never accepted by the House. George H. Mahon (D-Texas), who succeeded Cannon as chairman of the Appropriations Committee in 1964, summed up the prevailing House view in 1965 when he said that "every key provision of the [Senate's] bill . . . is, in my judgment, either unsound, unworkable or unnecessary." [5]

Behind Mahon's statement lay a long history of resentment over the Senate's claim to coequal status in the appropriations process, where the House had always asserted its primacy. The issue boiled over in 1962 when the House Appropriations Committee demanded that conference meetings, traditionally held on the Senate side, be rotated between the House and Senate wings of the Capitol. Senate Appropriations countered by proposing that it initiate one-half of all appropriation bills. The ensuing deadlock froze action for months.

At one point the House Appropriations Committee complained that "in the past 10 years the Senate conferees have been able to retain $22 billion of the $32 billion in increases which the Senate added to House appropriations — a 2 to 1 ratio in favor of the body consistently advocating larger appropriations, increased spending, and corresponding deficits."[6] Sen. A. Willis Robertson (D-Va.) called the communication in which this complaint was voiced "the most insulting document that one body has ever sent to another." When the Senate adopted an emergency funding resolution allowing federal agencies to keep on spending at the old rate until appropriations for the new fiscal year had been approved (called a continuing resolution), the House went on record, in a 245-1 roll call, that the Senate action was "an infringement on the privileges" of the House. Incensed, the Senate resolved, in turn, that "the acquiescence of the Senate in permitting the House to first consider appropriation bills cannot change the clear language of the Constitution nor affect the Senate's coequal power to originate any bill not expressly 'raising revenue.' " [7]

The feud was allowed to die without resolution. While it was true that the Senate had consistently voted for larger expenditures than the House, it was also true that Congress had managed generally to authorize less spending than was proposed by the postwar presidents. Yet the amounts authorized grew more or less steadily after 1947, and it became increasingly apparent that the capacity of Congress to control expenditures through its power of the purse was limited. Congress did not pass any further legislation to reform its budget procedures until 1974.

Checking the Rules Committee

The negative power of the Rules Committee was forcefully displayed during the Republican 80th Congress in connection with efforts to enact a major housing bill. The committee insisted that the Banking and Currency Committee delete provisions for public housing and slum clearance before it would agree to release the bill. The Rules panel also refused to allow the House to vote on a new universal military training bill reported by the Armed Services Committee, and it was only under strong pressure from Speaker Martin that the committee cleared a bill to revive the existing Selective Service System.

Liberals dominated the 263-member Democratic majority elected to the House in 1948, but they were again faced with the prospect that the 12-member Rules Committee would be controlled by a conservative coalition of four Republicans and three southern Democrats — E. E. Cox of Georgia, Howard W. Smith of Virginia and William M. Colmer of Mississippi. Thus, with the backing of Speaker Rayburn, the party caucus voted 176-48 for a "21-day rule" proposed by Rules Committee Chairman Adolph J. Sabath of Illinois. The rule authorized the chairman of any legislative committee that had reported a bill favorably, and requested a special rule from the Rules Committee, to bring the matter to the House floor if the committee failed to act within 21 calendar days of the request.

Adopted by the House on Jan. 3, 1949, by a procedural vote of 275-143, the 21-day rule was used eight times during the 81st Congress to obtain House passage of bills blocked in the Rules Committee. These included an anti-poll tax bill and statehood measures for Alaska and Hawaii. An effort to repeal the new rule in 1950, led by Rep. Cox, was rejected by the House by a vote of 183-236.

The Democrats lost 29 seats in the 1950 congressional elections, and when the 82nd Congress convened on Jan. 3, 1951, Cox again moved to drop the rule. It had been adopted in 1949, he claimed, because the Rules Committee had "refused to stampede under the lash of the whip applied by strong unofficial minority groups." Halleck supported repeal because, he said, it was the job of the Rules Committee to screen "unwise, unsound, ill-timed, spendthrift and socialistic measures." Sabath protested that repeal would permit an "unholy alliance" of southern Democrats and Republicans to "tear down the rights of every member of the House." But 91 Democrats joined 152 Republicans to repeal the 21-day rule on a 243-180 vote. [8]

Chairman Smith's Reign. Control of the Rules Committee by a conservative coalition virtually went unchallenged for the next decade. Rep. Howard W. Smith, who became chairman in 1955, made the most of his power to censor the legislative program of the House. The committee had no regular meeting day and could be called together only by the chairman. It often was unable to clear any bills for floor action during the final days of a session as Chairman Smith simply would disappear to his Virginia farm.

In 1958, 283 Democrats were elected to the House, their largest majority since 1936, and party liberals again talked of curbing the Rules Committee. They proposed changing the ratio of Democrats to Republicans on the committee from 8-4 to 9-3 and reinstituting the 21-day rule. Speaker Rayburn was opposed to any changes, however, and the liberals called off their drive when he "offered his personal assurance" that housing, civil rights, labor and other social welfare legislation "would not be bottled up in the committee." [9]

Rayburn was unable to fulfill his pledge during the 86th Congress (1959-1961). When Democrat John F. Kennedy was elected president in 1960 (along with a reduced Democratic majority in the House of 263), it was clear that much of his program might be stymied unless Democrats supportive of administration policies gained control of the Rules Committee at the start of the 87th Congress. Rayburn decided to try to enlarge the committee from 12 to 15 members to make room for the addition of two loyal Democrats and thus create an 8 to 7 majority that would be more likely to act favorably on administration bills. His plan was stoutly opposed by Chairman Smith and Republican leader Halleck, and it took Rayburn and his lieutenants a month of maneuvering and lobbying to round up enough votes to win. The House finally adopted the plan increasing the size of the committee from 12 to 15 members on Jan. 31, 1961, by a vote of 217-212.

The new balance on the Rules Committee proved to be precarious. A major school aid bill was effectively killed by the committee in 1961 when James J. Delaney (D-N.Y.), a Catholic from a heavily Catholic district, joined the conservative coalition in voting against the measure because no provision was made for aid to parochial schools. Two pro-administration southern Democrats on the committee in 1962 helped to kill a bill to create a Cabinet-level urban affairs department after Robert C. Weaver, a black, was designated to become the new secretary.

The 1961 resolution enlarging the size of the committee was limited to the life of the 87th Congress. But the House on Jan. 9, 1963, at the beginning of the 88th Congress, agreed by a vote of 235-196 to make the change permanent.

More Changes in House Rules

Although Democratic leaders continued to have problems with the Rules Committee, the 1964 election of Lyndon B. Johnson as president, together with a Democratic majority of 295 in the House, paved the way for further changes in House rules. Three changes were passed at the beginning of the 89th Congress in 1965, again over the opposition of a conservative coalition.

The new rules were adopted Jan. 4 by voice vote after a key procedural motion, backed by proponents of the rules change, had been adopted by a roll-call vote of 224-202. Only 16 Republicans voted with 208 Democrats for the motion, while 79 Democrats, all except four of them southerners, and 123 Republicans opposed the motion, which had the effect of ending further debate on the issue and bringing the rules changes to a final vote.

The first of the new rules revived, with one change, the 21-day rule that had been in force during the 81st Congress. Under the 1949 rule the Speaker had been required to recognize the chairman or other member of any committee seeking to bring before the House a bill that had been denied a rule by the Rules Committee for 21 days. The 1965 version left the question of recognition to the discretion of the Speaker, thereby ensuring that no bill opposed by the leadership could be brought up under the rule.

The second new rule permitted the Speaker to recognize a member to offer a motion (which would be agreed to if approved by majority vote) allowing the House to send a bill to conference with the Senate, provided such action was approved by the committee with jurisdiction over the bill. Previously, it had been necessary to obtain unanimous consent, or approval of a special rule from the Rules Committee or agreement by the House to suspend the rules (requiring a two-thirds vote) in order to send a bill to a conference committee.

The third change repealed a rule dating from 1789 that had permitted any member to demand the reading in full of the engrossed (final) copy of a House bill. Members opposed to legislation frequently had used this privilege to delay final passage of a bill until it could be printed.

The 21-day rule was employed successfully eight times during the 89th Congress, and the threat of its use persuaded the Rules Committee to send several other controversial measures to the floor. As in 1951, however, Republican gains in the 1966 elections opened the way to repeal of the rule at the beginning of the 90th Congress; this was accomplished on Jan. 10, 1967, by a vote of 233-185. The prevailing coalition included 157 Republicans and 69 southern Democrats. The two other rules adopted in 1965 were retained.

Repeal of the 21-day rule in 1967 proved to be of little consequence during the 90th Congress, largely because of two other developments affecting the Rules Committee. Chairman Smith had been defeated in a primary election in 1966, as had another committee Democrat, and these vacancies were filled by administration supporters. Smith's successor as chairman, Colmer of Mississippi, was no less strong a conservative, but he now was outvoted on the committee. This became apparent on Feb. 28, 1967, when for the first time in its history the committee adopted a set of rules governing its procedures. These rules took away the chairman's exclusive power to set meeting dates, required the consent of a committee majority to table a bill and set limits on proxy voting by members. The net effect of these changes was substantial cooperation with the Democratic leadership in 1967 and 1968 and the end of a decade of agitation for reform of the committee. Cooperation between Rules and the leadership continued in subsequent Congresses.

Pressures for Reform

Efforts to modify the organization and procedures of the House after 1946 were not confined to the protracted struggle for control of the Rules Committee. The leadership of the Senate as well as the House came under pressure in the 1950s to curb the free-wheeling activities of their investigating committees. And in the 1960s the questionable conduct of a few senators and representatives raised concern about the personal and professional ethics of members, forcing both chambers to respond. Mounting criticism of the methods and operations of Congress as a whole led the House and Senate to re-examine congressional procedures and in 1970 pass a second reorganization act.

Fair Play for Committee Witnesses. The efforts of the House Un-American Activities Committee to expose subversion and disloyalty through public hearings stirred up considerable controversy in the early 1950s. The committee's access to television was cut off in 1952, when Speaker Rayburn effectively banned radio, television or film coverage of any House committee hearing by holding that there was no authority for such coverage in the rules of the House.

Criticism of the committee's operations increased in the Republican-controlled 83rd Congress, when Chairman Harold H. Velde (R-Ill.) and Sen. Joseph R. McCarthy (R-Wis.), head of the Senate Permanent Investigations Subcommittee, were accused of conducting one-man witch hunts and mistreating witnesses. McCarthy eventually was censured by the Senate for contemptuous treatment of two Senate committees.

The Rules committees of both chambers held hearings in 1954 on proposals to reform committee procedures. On March 23, 1955, the House adopted 10 rules dealing with the conduct of committee hearings which:

— Required a quorum of not less than two committee members in order to take testimony and receive evidence.

— Allowed witnesses at investigative hearings to be accompanied by counsel for the purpose of advising them on their constitutional rights.

— Stipulated that if a committee found that evidence might tend to defame, degrade or incriminate any person, it would have to receive such evidence in executive (closed) session and allow such persons to appear before the committee as witnesses and request the subpoena of others.

— Barred the release or use in public sessions of evidence or testimony received in executive session without the consent of the committee.

The Senate Rules Committee recommended a similar set of standards in 1955, but the Senate left it to individual committees to draw up their own rules of conduct. Those adopted by the Permanent Investigations Subcommittee in 1955, when Sen. John L. McClellan (D-Ark.) became chairman, incorporated provisions similar to those approved by the House. Although the investigative practices of congressional committees continued to vary considerably thereafter, concern about the fair treatment of witnesses declined in importance as a public issue.

Congressional Scandals. Although members of Congress were never immune to the temptations of using public office for private gain, the ethics of Congress as a whole did not begin to stir broad public interest until after World War II. Contributing to this interest were the rising costs of political campaigns and greater concern about conflicts of interest at all levels of government. The fact that some members continued to engage in private law practice or other business activities, and to hold a financial interest in such government-regulated businesses as banks and television stations, added to that concern.

Pressure to do something about congressional ethics was intensified in the 1960s by scandals in the Senate. One involved Robert G. "Bobby" Baker, secretary of the Senate majority; another focused on Sen. Thomas J. Dodd (D-Conn.). The Baker episode led to the establishment of the Senate Select Committee on Standards and Conduct, which was empowered to investigate allegations of improper conduct by senators and staff and to recommend disciplinary action. The committee's first inquiry led to the censure of Dodd in 1967 for misuse of political campaign contributions. In 1968 the select committee recommended, and the Senate adopted, new rules and standards of conduct aimed at the practices disclosed in the Baker and Dodd cases.

The House, meanwhile, had become embroiled in attempts to discipline one of its members — Adam Clayton Powell, Jr. (D-N.Y.), chairman of the Education and Labor Committee since 1961. Powell, one of the few black members in the House, was indicted for tax evasion in 1958 and eventually paid $28,000 in back taxes and penalties. He was sued for libel in 1960 and held in contempt of court in the case on several occasions. He kept his wife on his congressional payroll at $20,000 a year although she lived in Puerto Rico. However, it was his extensive travels at public expense, his prolonged absences from Congress and his high-handed actions as a committee chairman that eventually turned most of his colleagues against him.

At the beginning of the 90th Congress in 1967, the Democratic Caucus removed Powell from his chairmanship of the Education and Labor Committee, and the House by a vote of 365-65 decided to deny him his seat pending an investigation by a special committee. The committee later recommended that Powell be seated but that he be censured for "gross misconduct," stripped of his seniority and fined $40,000 for misuse of public funds." [10] But on March 1, 1967, the House rejected these proposals and voted instead to exclude Powell from the 90th Congress and declare his seat vacant.

Powell promptly filed suit in federal court to regain his seat on the grounds that he met all of the constitutional qualifications for membership and that the House had no authority to exclude him. A district court dismissed the case for lack of jurisdiction, and the court of appeals affirmed the district court's finding, noting that the case involved a political question that, if decided by the courts, would constitute a violation of the separation of powers. However, on June 16, 1969, the Supreme Court reversed the lower courts by a vote of 7-1. Writing for the majority, Chief Justice Earl Warren held that Powell had been improperly excluded by the House. The Constitution prescribes only three criteria for seating a person elected to the House, he noted, all of which Powell met.

Following his exclusion in 1967, Powell was overwhelmingly reelected in 1968, but he made no effort to take his seat during the remainder of the 90th Congress. He presented himself at the opening of the 91st in 1969. By this time tempers had cooled. The House by a vote of 254-158 adopted a resolution that permitted Powell to take his seat but fined him $25,000 as punishment and "stripped him of his seniority." [11] Powell accepted the judgment, but his career in the House was destroyed. In 1970 he was defeated for renomination in a primary election.

The Powell case, together with the Senate's actions, helped to persuade the House in 1967 to establish its own 12-member, bipartisan Committee on Standards of Official Conduct. In 1968 the House adopted a Code of Official Conduct (Rule 43). The code included provisions that:

— Barred House members or employees from receiving compensation through improper use of their official position.

— Prohibited the acceptance of gifts of substantial value from an individual or group with a direct interest in legislation before Congress.

— Prohibited acceptance of honoraria of more than the usual and customary value for speeches and articles.

— Required representatives to keep campaign funds separate from personal funds and prohibited them from converting campaign funds to personal use.

— Required that, unless some other purpose was made clear in advance, all funds raised at testimonial events had to be treated as campaign contributions subject to the reporting requirements and spending limits of the Corrupt Practices Act of 1925.

— Required employees of a member to perform the work for which they were paid.

The House also adopted a rule (Rule 44) requiring members and officers of the House, their principal assistants, and professional staff members of committees to file annually with the new committee a report disclosing certain financial interests — which were to be made available to the public — and a sealed report on the amount of income received from those interests. As under the Senate rules, the sealed report could be opened by the committee only if it determined that such information was essential to an investigation, while the data that could be made public was extremely limited.

The new rules adopted by the Senate and House in 1968 did not put an end to the concern about congressional ethics. For example, the practice of certain senators in introducing hundreds of private immigration bills for Chinese ship-jumpers came under fire in 1969, and an aide to Speaker McCormack was indicted for influence peddling in 1970. When Supreme Court Justice Abe Fortas resigned in 1969 following disclosures of certain financial activities, Sen. Clifford P. Case (R-N.J.)

asserted that public confidence in government would not be restored until Congress required Supreme Court justices and other members of the federal judiciary, as well as members of Congress and high officials in the executive branch, to make "full, regular and, most importantly, public reports of their income and financial activities." [12] Such comprehensive financial disclosure legislation was not enacted until the 1970s.

Reorganization Bill. The efficiency and equity of congressional procedures also were questioned with increasing frequency in the 1960s. The Senate and the House agreed to set up a Joint Committee on the Organization of Congress modeled on the committee headed by Sen. Robert M. La Follette, Jr., and Democratic Rep. A. S. Mike Monroney that had ushered through Congress the 1946 Legislative Reorganization Act. Monroney was named co-chairman of the new committee along with Rep. Ray J. Madden (D-Ind.). After extensive hearings, the committee in 1966 issued a long list of recommendations, most of which were incorporated in a bill that the Senate passed in 1967. But committee chairmen and other senior members opposed the bill, and it remained bottled up in the Rules Committee until the end of the 90th Congress.

Notes

1. Neil MacNeil, *Forge of Democracy: The House of Representatives* (New York: Macmillan, 1927), p. 129.
2. *Congressional Record,* 80th Cong., 2nd sess., Feb. 27, 1948, p. 1878; Feb. 18, 1948, p. 1400.
3. *Congressional Record,* 81st Cong., 1st sess., Feb. 7, 1949, p. 880.
4. George B. Galloway, *The Legislative Process in Congress* (New York: Thomas Y. Crowell Co., 1953), p. 659.
5. Richard F. Fenno, Jr., *The Power of the Purse: Appropriations Politics in Congress* (Boston: Little, Brown, 1966), p. 629.
6. *Congressional Record,* 87th Cong., 2nd sess., July 9, 1962, p. 12899.
7. Ibid., p. 12900; Oct. 10, 1962, p. 23014; Oct. 13, 1962, p. 23470.
8. *Congressional Record,* 82nd Cong., 1st sess., Jan. 3, 1951, pp. 10-18.
9. James A. Robinson, *The House Rules Committee* (Indianapolis: Bobbs-Merrill Co., 1963), p. 72.
10. *Congress and the Nation,* 5 vols., *Congress and the Nation, 1965-1968,* vol. 2 (Washington, D.C.: Congressional Quarterly, 1969), II: 897.
11. Ibid., p. 900.
12. *Congress and the Nation, 1969-1972,* vol. 3 (Washington, D.C.: Congressional Quarterly, 1973), III: 429.

Chapter 17

INSTITUTIONAL CHANGES: 1969-1981

By the beginning of the 1970s, Americans had been through a tumultuous period during which the nation was torn by a costly and unpopular war in Indochina, by civil disturbances and urban riots and by economic dislocation. Then, in 1974, one of the most extraordinary scandals in U.S. history involving the executive branch — Watergate — culminated in the resignation of President Richard M. Nixon. Congress passed a lot of social legislation during this period, including new civil rights bills directed at minorities and women. But the efforts of the lawmakers did not end the unrest in the country. Rather, they left many Americans convinced that Congress was hamstrung by ancient rules and outdated procedures that prevented it from dealing effectively with the nation's complex social and economic problems.

Congress' legislative and institutional problems, and the resulting calls for major reforms in congressional operations, were not new to the 1970s. However, the urgency of the demands for change cast the public's perception of Congress in a different light than in the past. Congress, it seemed, was losing its influence even in such fundamental areas as the economy and decisions of war and peace. The war in Indochina and the rising costs of operating the federal government were critical factors that compelled Congress to examine the way legislative business was conducted and power distributed within its chambers. That examination, initiated in the 1960s by junior members and aided by some senior colleagues, led to major congressional changes.

The Vietnam War and its heavy costs had an effect on nearly everything that Congress did in the latter half of the 1960s. Until virtually the end of American involvement in the war in 1975, Congress routinely approved the military appropriations requested by the Johnson, Nixon and Ford administrations. This largely was a reflection of the public's willingness to go along with the war. However, from about 1968 on, the war became increasingly unpopular with the general public, a change in attitude that only very gradually came to be reflected in Congress. Frustrated legislators conceded they had no effective way to impose their will in such matters on an administration still bent on prosecuting the war.

At first, President Lyndon B. Johnson believed the nation could both carry out his war policies in Southeast Asia and finance his ambitious Great Society social and economic programs at home — a "guns and butter" policy, as commentators observed — without increasing taxes or disrupting the economy. This proved not to be the case. Inflationary pressures soon developed, and the economy suffered.

Johnson was followed in the White House by Republican Richard M. Nixon, who continued to pursue the war but had a different view of federal spending on the so-called Great Society programs. Much of his first term (1969-1973) was spent battling the Democratic Congress over domestic spending. Unable to prevent Congress from continuing to appropriate money for the various domestic programs inspired by past Democratic administrations, Nixon attempted to cut expenditures by impounding the funds — that is, by simply not spending the money. Legal challenges to this practice had considerable success, and Congress enacted laws circumscribing the ability of the executive branch to refuse to spend the money Congress had appropriated for particular programs.

These disputes over the war and spending demonstrated to lawmakers, particularly junior members, that Congress was poorly equipped to handle the most pressing issues facing the nation or even to run efficiently the daily operation of the legislative branch. Even those members who supported the war and the Nixon administration's proposed cuts in social programs conceded that control of the war-making power and federal spending had slipped away from Congress to such an extent that Congress no longer was a vital partner in these decisions. This realization created a determination among a growing number of members in the 1960s to correct this imbalance and restore to the legislative branch the influence that the Founding Fathers had intended.

War Powers Asserted

Congress was criticized in the late 1960s by opponents of the Vietnam War for being slow to act against U.S. military policies in Southeast Asia, but by 1973 it had enacted, over a presidential veto, the

War Powers Act. For the first time in history, Congress had defined and limited the president's power to make war.

Though aimed at U.S. involvement in Vietnam, the new law emboldened Congress to immerse itself in the nation's subsequent conduct of foreign policy. After the withdrawal of all U.S. combat forces from Indochina, Congress in 1975 denied President Gerald R. Ford's request for additional military aid for South Vietnam and Cambodia. Many in Congress expressed fears that more aid might mean a perpetual U.S. involvement in the region. That same year, Congress also clashed with the Ford administration over the sale of arms to Turkey in the wake of that country's invasion of Cyprus in July 1974. Concerned about further U.S. involvement in Africa, the House in January 1976 joined with the Senate in barring U.S. military aid to non-communist factions involved in a civil war in Angola. During the Carter administration, Congress failed to approve foreign aid appropriations bills for two years running, thus frustrating the president's budgetary priorities for that longstanding military and economic assistance program. And early in the Reagan administration, the House voted to block the sale to Saudi Arabia of sophisticated radar planes and other expensive air defense equipment. But that sale ultimately was approved when the Senate refused, by a two-vote margin, to go along with a House veto of the arms deal. All of these examples from the Ford, Carter and Reagan administrations illustrate Congress' determination to exercise its prerogatives in the conduct of America's foreign policy.

Watergate and Impeachment

The Watergate scandal began with the burglary June 17, 1972, of the Democratic Party's national headquarters located in the Watergate Hotel in Washington, D.C. It ended Aug. 9, 1974, when President Nixon resigned in the face of certain impeachment by the House. Along the way it dealt a serious blow to the prestige of the American presidency and heightened congressional influence over virtually every aspect of the daily conduct of government activities. Only once before in American history had the House set in motion the machinery of impeachment of a president of the United States. The impeachment power — the most drastic check on the chief executive possessed by Congress — had been used against President Andrew Johnson more than a century earlier.

Resolutions of impeachment against President Nixon were introduced after he fired special prosecutor Archibald L. Cox in October 1973.

Nixon had secretly tape-recorded for posterity certain conversations that occurred in his presidential office. The president's struggle to deny Cox access to these tapes led to Cox's dismissal. Attorney General Elliot Richardson resigned rather than carry out the White House order to dismiss Cox; and Deputy Attorney General William D. Ruckelshaus was fired after he refused to execute the order. Because the tapes constituted such importance evidence in the case, they were to play a central role in the unfolding Watergate drama.

In November the House voted $1 million for a preliminary investigation, and the House Judicicary Committee, chaired by Rep. Peter W. Rodino, Jr. (D-N.J.) began assembling an investigative staff that soon numbered 100 persons, including 45 attorneys. The House on Feb. 6, 1974, formally charged the Judiciary Committee with determining whether there were grounds to impeach Nixon. The vote to begin the formal investigation was 410-4.

For many weeks, the committee took testimony from witnesses and clashed with the president over access to the White House recordings. Nixon, who had promised to cooperate with the impeachment inquiry, in May refused to honor two Judiciary Committee subpoenas for tapes, adding he would not surrender any more Watergate evidence to the committee. That prompted Chairman Rodino to add the president's defiance to the list of possible grounds for impeachment.

At the end of July, a nationwide television audience looked on as Chairman Rodino read aloud to the committee the first draft article of impeachment, which alleged that "Richard M. Nixon has prevented, obstructed, and impeded the administration of justice, . . . has acted in a manner contrary to his trust as president and subversive of constitutional government, to the great prejudice of the cause of law and justice, and to the manifest injury of the people of the United States . . . [and] warrants impeachment and trial and removal from office." Following a series of emotional statements by individual committee members, the panel voted three articles of impeachment against Nixon — obstruction of justice, abuse of presidential powers and contempt of Congress.

On Aug. 2, 1974, under Supreme Court order, Nixon surrendered to U.S. District Court Judge John J. Sirica tapes of three conversations that had been recorded in the president's office on June 23, 1972, six days after the burglary of the Democrats' national headquarters. On Aug. 5 Nixon released transcripts of those conversations to the press. The transcripts showed Nixon's participation in the Watergate cover-up and approval of CIA involvement as a means of obstructing the FBI investigation of the Watergate break-in. What support Nixon still had in Congress quickly evaporated. He resigned Aug. 9, 1974, nine days before the House was to begin debate on the impeachment articles. [1]

Budget Control

For years the House and Senate were plagued by a disjointed appropriations process that gave no overall control of the federal budget and spending priorities to any congressional unit or even to Congress itself. Before 1974 Congress generally had been content to rely on the administration for budgetary direction. But the Nixon presidency undermined the cordial working relationship that previously had prevailed between the legislative and executive branches. Nixon had sought to dominate the budgetary process through a vastly expanded Office of Management and Budget. He particularly irritated Congress with his policy of refusing to spend funds that had been previously appropriated.

To help remedy the atmosphere of chaos and distrust, Congress in 1974 enacted the Congressional Budget and Impoundment Control Act, which set up House and Senate Budget Committees and a Congressional Budget Office. The act's goals were to focus congressional attention in a systematic way on two broad budgetary concerns: national fiscal policy and national priorities.

The sweeping changes realized in 1974 required Congress for the first time to vote on proposed budget deficits. The process forced Congress to set out in a single measure total spending and total receipts, instead of treating appropriations and tax measures as mutually exclusive budget items. In doing so, Congress was required to confront such fiscal policy issues as the effect of the budget on inflation, unemployment and economic growth. Congress also had to decide on budget priorities. For example, if Congress called for more spending on health, it had to either increase government revenues through higher taxes, accept a larger deficit or balance the added funds for health by cutting money for other programs.

The law also created a complicated set of deadlines for congressional action on the budget. By May 15 of each year, Congress was to complete action on the first of two budget resolutions, setting out preliminary funding targets to guide the various legislative committees as they considered new authorizations for programs under their jurisdiction. By Sept. 15 Congress was to replace the targets through a second budget resolution establishing binding spending ceilings and a floor on revenues. If the revenue and spending figures adopted in the fall differed from those adopted in the spring, Congress had to reconcile the amounts before adjourning by agreeing on specific program changes that either would provide any additional revenues needed or reduce the level of spending.

To give itself more time to work on each year's new budget, Congress moved back the beginning of the federal government's fiscal year from July 1 to Oct. 1. But the process turned out to be even more time-consuming than congressional leaders had predicted. In its first year under the new budget act, Congress did not complete action on the second resolution until three months after the Sept. 15 deadline.

A Younger House

The crisis in Americans' confidence in their government caused by Watergate, and the growing pressure on Congress to change its way of doing business, came at a time of substantial turnover in the membership of the House. At the beginning of the 1970s, about one-half of the House had been elected during the previous decade. By the start of the 94th Congress in 1975, 82 percent of the members had been elected since 1960 and almost one-third — 61 percent — had entered Congress since 1967.

This meant that a substantial majority of the House in the first half of the decade was relatively new to the system and had less interest in maintaining the congressional status quo than the more senior members. In fact, a sizable number of the younger lawmakers — especially those elected in the late 1960s and early 1970s — had a personal interest in changing the way the House operated. Excluded from exercising much influence by the rules and folkways that dominated Congress when they first became members, they welcomed institutional changes. The principal custom that relegated junior members to the lowly status of backbenchers was the inflexible seniority system.

Underlying the junior members' discontent with the congressional power structure was the fact that they were predominantly liberal in their political outlook, while the hierarchy of senior members who controlled the committee system was dominated by southern conservatives. The junior members' lack of influence, despite their greater numbers, made them look to structural changes as a way to achieve positions of power in

Congress. Thus by 1970 the political climate in the House was ripe for the most significant internal reforms in half a century.

New Leadership

Their ranks dominated by Democratic liberals, the House reformers hoped the retirement of 79-year-old Speaker John W. McCormack of Massachusetts in 1971 would result in a new leadership team supportive of their cause. In Carl B. Albert of Oklahoma they found a helpful and cooperative friend, though hardly an outspoken reformer. Albert had served as majority leader since 1962. During his 24 years in the House, he had steered a careful political course along which he had made few enemies. He was acceptable to most factions of the Democratic Party and was elected Speaker with only token, last-minute opposition.

By contrast, Hale Boggs of Louisiana had to overcome strong reformist opposition to advance in 1971 from Democratic whip to majority leader. Boggs rankled the liberals because he made no commitment during the leadership race to change procedures or revise the distribution of power. But traditionalists prevailed in the Democratic Caucus and Boggs was elected. After Boggs' death in a 1972 plane crash in Alaska, the Democrats chose Thomas P. O'Neill, Jr., of Massachusetts as majority leader in January 1973.

Because of his low-key style, Speaker Albert did little to help the liberals or impede their reform efforts, but his passive manner soon drew criticism, especially after House Democrats won a two-to-one majority through the election of 75 freshmen in 1974. That largely liberal class, disdaining the backbencher role expected of freshmen, was particularly vociferous in its outcry against the leadership's inability to muster the two-thirds votes needed to override President Ford's vetoes of numerous Democratic bills. Albert retired from the House at the end of the 94th Congress, clearing the way for O'Neill to assume the Speakership at the start of the Carter administration in January 1977.

Before entering the leadership, O'Neill had been more interested in the pure politics of the House than in the content of legislation. As a former Speaker of the Massachusetts House and later as a member of the House Rules Committee, his specialty had been to count votes, twist arms and broker deals rather than to write bills or fine tune legislative compromises. His background had instilled him with the importance of constituent service and party loyalty rather than with the reformer's zeal.

175

As Speaker of the House, O'Neill reflected these same skills and biases. He fought hard for the legislative programs advanced by the Carter administration, though he showed little enthusiasm for their specific content. He was instrumental, in particular, in getting Carter's energy programs through the House, though he scarcely concealed his disdain for the Carter team's lack of skill in dealing with Congress.

O'Neill generally was supportive of liberal Democrats' demands. But he also emphasized that he was the Speaker of all House Democrats, be they conservative, moderate or liberal. In the final year of the Carter presidency and early in the Reagan administration, O'Neill was criticized by the younger and generally more liberal Democrats for failing to crack down on those conservative members who voted against positions supported by a majority of the party. But O'Neill maintained that the party's diversity left him powerless to discipline or even threaten to discipline disloyal members.

Elected Majority Leader at the time O'Neill became Speaker was Jim Wright of Texas, a moderate who beat out three opponents by the margin of a single vote. Wright's leadership role displayed his polished oratorical skills, almost patronizing friendliness, southern origins and loyal Democratic voting record.

On the Republican side, John J. Rhodes of Arizona was elected minority leader in December 1973 when Gerald Ford was appointed vice president by Nixon. The conservative Rhodes generally supported Republican White House foreign and domestic policies, and he enjoyed siding with the conservative coalition in sustaining many presidential vetoes. [2] His colorless style and passive approach to the top GOP leadership job, however, rankled the younger and more militant conservatives.

While Rhodes sought to work in concert with the Democratic leadership, most younger House Republicans sought a confrontational role for their party. Soon Rhodes was the Republican leader in name only, relegating legislative priorities and floor strategy to the party's militant wing. At the end of the 96th Congress, Rhodes resigned his leadership post though he remained a member of the House for one additional term.

Elected in 1980 to succeed Rhodes as minority leader was Robert H. Michel of Illinois. A low-key but indefatigable individual, Michel worked tirelessly behind the scenes on behalf of President Reagan's economic program. His personal popularity and formidable powers of persuasion were to play a key role in the Republicans' ability to assemble a winning coalition in the Democratically-controlled House during the first session of the 97th Congress.

Democratic Caucus

The pressure for organizational change in Congress touched both chambers, but it began in the House where it had its most important impact. Although the demands for changes came from House Republicans as well as Democrats, many of the reforms took place in the House Democratic Caucus, the formal organization of all House Democrats, which was dominated by the party's liberal wing. Changes in caucus rules often had the same impact on the House as changes in House rules because the Democrats' majority status in the House gave them procedural control of the chamber.

Once a powerful instrument in implementing Woodrow Wilson's domestic program, the caucus had fallen into disuse, meeting only at the beginning of a new Congress for the pro forma election of the Democratic leadership. The move to revitalize the caucus was led by the House Democratic Study Group (DSG), an organization of moderate and liberal Democrats forming the largest reform bloc in the House. The opening came in 1969 when Speaker McCormack agreed to regular monthly meetings of the caucus in a move to appease the reformers.

The membership of the DSG was dominated by the younger, more liberal representatives who had little seniority and therefore little influence in House affairs. Because of their growing numerical advantage within the party, they saw the caucus as a particularly advantageous arena to attack what they considered the imbalance in power between junior and senior members and make changes in House procedures.

The reform effort was directed principally at altering the institutional structure that determined how Congress conducted its business, but it grew out of the younger members' dissatisfaction with how Congress had treated a handful of specific legislative matters, such as domestic spending policy and the conduct of the Vietnam War. On occasion, the caucus became involved in substantive matters, but many of these forays into legislative areas aroused such controversy within the Democratic Party as to ultimately cause leaders of the caucus to back away from using the organization as a major force determining party policy on substantive issues. In 1975, for example, liberal Democrats engineered passage of a "sense of the caucus" resolution opposing further U.S. military aid to Indochina as well as of a measure instructing Democrats on the Rules Committee to bring to the House floor two amendments relating to the oil depletion allowance.

Conservatives, who felt the caucus was usurping the powers of the committees, raised a furor over these actions. Later that same year, however, many conservatives asked the caucus to consider a substantive matter. They proposed a resolution ordering the Judiciary Committee to report a constitutional amendment preventing court-ordered school busing to achieve racial integration. To increase public pressure on the liberals to go along with their anti-busing measure, the conservatives persuaded the caucus to open its meetings and votes to the public. Though the anti-busing proposal was rejected, the new open-meeting rule ironically helped restrain the caucus' bent for legislative activism. "We don't really like sunshine for the caucus, but we've got to stop this damn caucus from legislating," explained Joe D. Waggonner, Jr. (D-La.), a leader of the conservative faction who favored open caucus meetings. [3]

In ensuing years the caucus rarely acted on issues of legislative substance. After the 1980 elections, when the Democrats' margin of control in the House was substantially reduced and their ranks divided, the caucus began once more to routinely close its doors to the public.

Targets for Change

The reform effort was neither instantaneous nor all-encompassing. Many proposals were rejected outright, and most underwent significant modification before gaining final approval. The changes occurred in dribs and drabs over the entire decade of the 1970s, although most of them were made by the time Jimmy Carter was sworn in as president in January 1977, giving the Democrats control of the White House as well as both houses of Congress.

The changes made in House operations were tied together by certain common threads. Reformers attempted to link advancement in the House hierarchy to a member's party loyalty and job skills rather than to seniority alone. They tried to open to the public and the press the inner workings of Congress. And they sought to increase members' accountability for their official actions to their colleagues as well as to their constituents.

The rigid seniority system in Congress had guaranteed a member's rise to a position of authority, particularly the chairmanship of a committee, if he or she remained in Congress long enough and belonged to the majority party. Longevity of service — not legislative skills and leadership ability — was the only qualification. Once having attained power, committee chairmen could carry out their official duties behind closed doors and without much regard for the wishes of their colleagues or the voters outside their own districts. The ability of chairmen to run their committees as their own private preserves diminished the power of the elected House leaders and the national political parties as well as of the committees' junior members.

Legislative Process. The reforms of the decade began with passage of the Legislative Reorganization Act of 1970 — the first major congressional reorganization measure to be enacted since 1946. Four years earlier, a joint committee chaired by Sen. Mike Monroney (D-Okla.) and Rep. Ray Madden (D-Ind.) had recommended similar legislation, but the joint committee's plan had died in the House Rules Committee. A more modest version of that proposal was revived in the final weeks of the 91st Congress; the House passed its bill Sept. 17, 1970, and the Senate approved it Oct. 6.

The 1970 reorganization act was designed to give the House and Senate more information on government finances, guarantee certain rights for minority party members and maintain a continuing review of the legislative machinery through a Joint Committee on Congressional Operations. (The Senate abolished the joint committee in 1977, but its work was continued in the House until 1979 under the House Select Committee on Congressional Operations.) The act also required committees for the first time to have written rules, to make public all roll-call votes taken in closed committee sessions and to make committee reports on bills available to the public and the members at least three days before the bill was brought to the floor. [4] One of the act's most significant provisions was a change in the voting rule in the House. For the first time members were forced to disclose their positions on all major legislative issues. Previously, non-recorded "teller votes" enabled members to cast their votes on amendments without being recorded. The reorganization act authorized use of recorded teller votes upon the request of a sufficient number of members. These votes were similar to roll calls in that the individual member's positions would be recorded and published in the *Congressional Record.* This change put the House on a par with the Senate, where important floor votes almost always were taken by roll call.

179

In January 1973 another voting change replaced the recorded teller vote. The House installed an electronic tallying system making it faster and easier for the House to take recorded votes and quorum calls. Members were given 15 minutes in which to cast their votes. As members voted, large lighted panels installed on the chamber's walls provided a running breakdown of the votes as they were cast and indicated how each individual member had voted.

Seniority System. Although institutional changes were taking place at a rapid pace, committee chairmen were presiding over the same committees in 1974 as at the beginning of the decade, except for those who had retired, died or been defeated. So the Democratic Caucus in 1974 required that each Democratic committee chairmanship be filled by secret ballot at the beginning of each Congress.

The new rule had little impact in the first year as the caucus awarded all chairmanships to the same members who would have received them had secret votes not been required. But when the 94th Congress convened in January 1975, the caucus included a large class of newly elected freshmen who owed no favors to the chamber's senior establishment. By the time the caucus had finished its work, three chairmen had been deposed: Wright Patman (Texas), Banking, Currency and Housing Committee; F. Edward Hébert (La.), Armed Services Committee; and W. R. Poage (Texas), the Agriculture Committee.

Various reasons were given for the three men's ouster, but there was little doubt the trio had made a poor impression on the freshmen Democrats who interviewed all three before deciding whom to support in the caucus. Each of the three had been accused of dominating the operation of their committees and denying equitable treatment to their fellow committee members. Because of the freshmen's strong liberal bent, ideology also was thought to have played a role, though not a major one. The conservative Hébert gave unflinching support to the military and voted with Republicans on many issues. Patman, on the other hand, was a southern populist with a long record of support for many liberal proposals. But at age 82 he had had trouble controlling his fractious committee colleagues.

The removal of the three chairmen jarred the system that for decades had governed representatives' progression to power. The last time a chairman had been removed had been in 1967 when Adam Clayton Powell, Jr., (D-N.Y.) was relieved as head of the Education and

Labor Committee following allegations of misconduct, including payroll padding, excessive junketeering at public expense and tax evasion. Before the Powell case, the House had not ousted a chairman since 1925.

Ways and Means Committee. Other reform efforts adopted by the House or its Democratic Caucus at about the same time further eroded the authority of the House committee chairmen. One of the principal targets of these efforts was Wilbur D. Mills (D-Ark.), chairman of the powerful Ways and Means Committee. Mills had for years run his committee with an iron hand and had been successful in bringing his legislation to the House floor under a "closed rule," barring floor amendments. A skilled parliamentarian and an authoritarian chairman, Mills had argued successfully that tax legislation was so complex that amendments by individual members, offered from the floor without prior committee consideration, would twist the bills out of shape. To curb Mills' power, the caucus adopted this new rule: if a minimum of 50 Democrats proposed an amendment to the caucus and a caucus majority approved the amendment, Democrats on the Rules Committee would be required to write a rule allowing the amendment to be offered on the floor.

Disclosure in late 1974 of a series of bizarre incidents involving Mills and striptease dancer Fanne Fox further eroded Mills' power. The caucus moved rapidly to diminish the authority of the Ways and Means chairmanship. Since 1911 the Ways and Means Committee had been responsible for assigning House Democrats to committees, but in December 1974 the caucus transferred this authority to the party's Steering and Policy Committee, subject to confirmation by the caucus. The committee, created by the caucus in 1973 to assist the Speaker in developing party and legislative priorities, was composed of House leaders, their appointees and members elected by the caucus on a regional basis.

Subcommittees. By increasing the autonomy of the House's numerous subcommittees, the Democratic Caucus further weakened the power of committee chairmen. In changes adopted gradually between 1971 and 1975, the caucus limited the number of subcommittee chairmanships that a single member could hold and gave these subcommittee chairmen their own staffs and budgets as well as significant freedom from the chairmen of the full committees.

In the House Appropriations Committee, caucus reformers faced a different problem. There, senior conservative Democrats had dominated the important subcommittees handling the funding for defense, agriculture, health, education and welfare, leaving the less influential subcommittee slots to the junior members. In the Appropriations Committee, unlike the legislative committees, the subcommittees traditionally wielded great power. In a move designed to make the subcommittee chairmen more accountable, the caucus required that, starting in 1975, each of the Appropriations Committee's 13 subcommittee chairmen had to be approved by the caucus at the beginning of each new Congress.

Congress in the 'Sunshine'

In other moves aimed at a more open legislative branch, the House by the mid-1970s had required all committees and subcommittees to open most of their bill-drafting or "markup" sessions and other business meetings to the public, unless a majority voted at an open session to close a particular hearing. House-Senate conference committee meetings, called to resolve differences in each chamber's version of a bill, also were opened up. Previously, hearings had been open, but conference meetings and the markup sessions where bills were considered and amended usually were closed.

Although the Senate had a long tradition of permitting television and radio coverage of its committee hearings, the House did not amend its rules to permit broadcast coverage of hearings until 1970. Even then, the House rules imposed severe restrictions on broadcasters. Television and radio coverage could not distort the purpose of a hearing or cast discredit upon the House, a committee or any member, and legislative markup sessions still were off-limits to the television cameras and radio microphones. Even with these limitations, some committees (such as Armed Services, Ways and Means and Rules) continued to bar broadcast coverage of their sessions altogether.

Public interest in the 1974 televised broadcasts of the House Judiciary Committee's impeachment proceedings against President Nixon went far toward making other House committees and the membership more receptive to the presence of TV cameras in their midst. To allow television into the Judiciary Committee sessions on impeachment, the House had to amend its rules once more because the proceedings were in fact markup sessions, during which discussion and votes on the articles of impeachment took place.

Less than a year after the historic Judiciary Committee sessions, the House Appropriations Committee, which in the past had permitted telecasting only of its formal budget hearings at the beginning of each year, opened its doors for broadcast coverage of testimony by Defense Secretary James R. Schlesinger and Director of Central Intelligence William E. Colby on controversial CIA activities.

Gavel-to-gavel broadcast coverage of congressional floor proceedings had been proposed as early as 1944, but it took more than 30 years for the idea to come to fruition. The House took its first steps toward broadcast coverage of its proceedings with a 90-day experiment of closed-circuit black-and-white telecasts in March 1977. Though the quality of the picture was poor, the idea caught on and the House approved a permanent, high-quality color broadcast system. Operated by House employees, it began providing full coverage of House proceedings in March 1979. The signal produced by the House system was distributed throughout the Capitol and House office buildings as well as to radio and television stations and cable television systems for nationwide broadcast.

Committee Jurisdictions

Not all the reforms urged upon Congress were adopted during this period. Two major efforts to reorganize the House committee system more or less fell on their face. Committee jurisdictions at the time were a jumble of contradictions, legislative conflicts and outmoded and overlapping divisions. They were still based on the 1946 Legislative Reorganization Act — a plan drawn up when many of the problems experienced during the 1970s, such as energy use and environmental protection, were unknown. Yet attempts to modernize the committee structure seemed doomed to failure.

The most comprehensive reorganization effort occurred in 1974 when a special committee headed by Richard Bolling (D-Mo.) suggested wholesale changes in the committee structure. Largely because of its ambitious scope and sweeping nature, the plan failed. Proposals to realign committee jurisdictions and limit each member to one major committee assignment alienated younger members, with interests that spanned several committees, as well as chairmen and senior members, whose power bases would have been diminished or eliminated. By proposing to split the Education and Labor Committee, the plan alienated the nation's labor unions. By suggesting that the Merchant Marine Committee be abolished, the plan angered the maritime industry.

183

In place of the comprehensive reorganization package drafted by the Bolling committee, the House adopted a far less drastic scheme that left committee jurisdictions largely intact. Some of the Bolling proposals were adopted, but generally they were toned down in redrafting carried out by the Democratic Committee on Organization, Study and Review.

The second major reorganization attempt ended in total failure in early 1980 when the House Select Committee on Committees closed its doors with almost nothing to show for its year-long effort. The committee, chaired by Jerry M. Patterson (D-Calif.), had been established by the House in March 1979 with a broad mandate to improve the House's internal organization and operations. Its principal recommendation was to form a new House energy committee. But the House ignored that recommendation by simply designating the House Commerce Committee as the leading committee on energy matters and renaming it Energy and Commerce.

Earlier in the decade, the Democratic Caucus had voted to abolish the House Internal Security Committee, which before 1969 was known as the House Committee on Un-American Activities. The caucus decision in 1975 ended 30 years of controversy during which the committee zealously pursued subversives in every segment of American society. [5]

Campaign Financing

Congress in the 1970s passed a series of measures aimed at tightening federal laws regulating federal election campaigns. Generally, the changes held candidates for federal office more accountable to the public for their campaign fund raising and spending, and they limited the role wealthy individuals could play in campaigns. The new laws, however, created problems of their own.

The Federal Election Act of 1971, the first campaign law of the decade, was signed in 1972. It placed a ceiling on political campaign expenditures, required the disclosure of campaign contributions and other income and defined more strictly the roles unions and corporations could play in political campaigns. Almost immediately after enactment, the law proved to be an important tool in helping government investigators break open the Watergate scandal.

Prompted by the campaign abuses turned up during Watergate, Congress in 1974 approved legislation providing federal financing of presidential election campaigns from tax dollars, set campaign contribution and spending limits for candidates in federal elections and required disclosure of all sources of contributions and the purposes of expenditures above $100. It also established a Federal Election Commission to enforce the law and distribute the federal funds to the presidential candidates.

In January 1976, however, the Supreme Court declared unconstitutional sections of the law imposing limits on spending by candidates on their own behalf (except where presidential candidates accepted federal funds), and on independent spending by individuals. The court said it found those limits to be unconstitutional infringements on the First Amendment's freedom of expression. The court also declared unconstitutional the composition of the Federal Election Commission, ruling that the law violated the Constitution's separation-of-powers requirement; some of the commission's members were both named by congressional leaders and subject to confirmation by the Senate.

To remedy the 1974 law in the wake of the court decision, and thereby restart the flow of federal funds to presidential candidates in time for the 1976 election campaign, Congress in May 1976 sent to the White House new legislation re-establishing the commission. The new law gave the president the power to name all commission members. Unable to limit independent spending, Congress wrote into the 1976 bill a tight definition of such outlays to prevent collusion between a candidate and an individual desiring to make independent contributions.

Taken as a package, the three election laws went a long way toward opening the federal election process to the eyes of the press and the public. But there were unintended side effects. Perhaps the most significant was the explosive growth of political action committees (PACs), which enabled corporations and unions to become deeply involved in the federal election process. Because the new laws restricted the amount of money candidates could raise from individual donors, congressional incumbents in particular soon found it easier to seek campaign money from PACs than from individuals. Critics charged that corporate and labor union PACs magnified the influence of outside special interests in the legislative process. But Congress repeatedly turned back attempts to limit the role of PACs in federal campaigns or to provide public financing for congressional races.

The availability of ample amounts of campaign money from PACs also diminished the influence of the major political parties in Congress. Incumbents no longer had to rely on their party organizations to provide the backbone of their campaigns; it freed them from the obligation to re-

185

spond to their party's leadership on organizational matters as well as on substantive issues. [6]

Ethics Code

After enactment of the new campaign finance laws, a series of congressional conflict-of-interest cases in the mid-1970s prompted both the House and Senate to adopt new ethics codes. The House code of conduct, adopted in March 1977, was drafted by a bipartisan 15-member Commission on Administrative Review, chaired by Democrat David R. Obey of Wisconsin. Although the commission's draft was toned down during House debate, it significantly toughened existing House rules governing financial disclosure and conflicts of interest. The new code required the disclosure of substantial data on the financial status of members and their top aides, imposed new restrictions on members' outside earned income, ended unofficial office accounts that many members had used to supplement their official allowances and tightened the standards on use of Congress' free mailing privilege.

Perhaps the most controversial code provision limited House members' outside earnings to 15 percent per year of their official salaries. Because the code did not affect unearned income such as interest payments, dividends and rent from properties, members with few holdings maintained the code discriminated in favor of the rich. To remedy the disparity, the House in December 1981 doubled — to 30 percent of a member's salary — the amount allowed for outside earned income. [7]

Depite the new code of conduct, the House's record on disciplinary matters in the 1970s was at best spotty. Only when pressed by the most serious circumstances did the House spend much time policing the ethical conduct of its members or staff. From 1967 through 1975, the House Committee on Standards of Official Conduct, which had been created following the Adam Clayton Powell scandal of the 1960s, made no formal investigations of any House member, although several representatives were convicted of crimes during the period. But in 1976 the ethics committee, as the panel was commonly called, was forced into action by several cases it could not ignore.

The most spectacular centered on a sex and payroll scandal that erupted after a woman employee of the House Administration Committee, Elizabeth Ray, asserted she had been put on the payroll solely to be the mistress of the committee's chairman, Wayne L. Hays (D-Ohio). Ray said she had done no work for the panel and possessed no office skills. Hays subsequently admitted a "relationship" with her but denied she was paid with public funds simply to be his mistress.

The resulting brouhaha forced Hays to resign as committee chairman and as head of the Democratic Congressional Campaign Committee, the group that raised and distributed campaign donations to the party's House candidates. On Sept. 1, 1976, Hays resigned from Congress.

As chairman of the House Administration Committee, Hays had used his authority to enhance his own power and influence in the House. As a result, the scandal set in motion efforts to limit the power of the Administration Committee chairman as well as to revise many of the prerogatives benefiting members that had been handed out by the committee during Hays' chairmanship, such as additional stationery funds and mailing allowances and travel privileges.

In another case that came to light the same year, Robert L. F. Sikes (D-Fla.) was reprimanded by the House after being accused of conflicts of interest, including charges he voted on legislation affecting firms in which he held a financial interest. The following year, the Democratic Caucus ousted Sikes from his chairmanship of the House Appropriations Subcommittee on Military Construction.

South Korea, Abscam Probes

In 1978 the House wrapped up a lengthy investigation of alleged South Korean influence peddling in Congress with only minor disciplinary action taken against members linked to the scandal. The House investigation had begun in 1977 after it was reported that as many as 115 members of Congress had taken illegal gifts from South Korean agents. But after an 18-month probe, the House ended up voting its mildest form of punishment — a "reprimand" — for three California Democrats: John J. McFall, Edward R. Roybal and Charles H. Wilson.

Two years later, however, the House vigorously pursued a congressional scandal that grew out of an undercover FBI corruption investigation. Dubbed "Abscam" for "Arab scam," the FBI probe employed agents who masqueraded as wealthy Arabs and businessmen in order to entice members of Congress and others into accepting bribes in return for promises of legislative help. Because the FBI appeared to rely heavily on government-created "crimes" in Abscam, the entire undercover operation was heavily criticized by civil libertarians and many members of

Congress. But six representatives were convicted as a result of the corruption probe, and by the end of 1981 none was still a member of the House. Michael "Ozzie" Myers (D-Pa.) was expelled; John W. Jenrette, Jr. (D-S.C.) and Raymond F. Lederer (D-Pa.) resigned to halt expulsion proceedings; and Richard Kelly (R-Fla.), John M. Murphy (D-N.Y.) and Frank Thompson, Jr. (D-N.J.) were defeated for re-election before the House could begin disciplinary proceedings against them.

Republican Rule

As the decade of the 1970s wore on, many of the ambitious young Democrats who had helped usher in the unprecedented string of procedural and structural changes in Congress came to rue the day some of those "reforms" had been instituted. Within a few years of their approval, many of the reforms were shown to be more conducive to disorder than to order or more useful to militant conservative Republicans than to the liberals who had rammed them through the House.

The presence in the House chamber of television cameras tended to encourage lengthier speeches, more amendments, and general "grandstanding" by members more interested in how well they performed for their constituents back home than in shaping the legislative process. The prevalence of open rules permitted militant conservatives to overwhelm the House with dilatory parliamentary tactics and endless amendments aimed at making the liberals' legislative goals appear flawed or frivolous. The ability of incumbents to obtain their campaign funds from political action committees isolated party leaders from their party members and weakened their influence and procedural control over House affairs.

As the end of the decade neared, the Democratic leadership's position of authority over Democrats in the House had so eroded that many basic majority party functions had become heavy burdens rather than exercises of power. In perhaps the most extraordinary example of their weakened position, the Democratic leadership discovered in 1980 that it simply could not muster enough votes to pass a budget resolution even though that budget had been proposed by President Carter. Rather than schedule a vote on the budget and face almost certain defeat, the Democratic leaders decided to postpone action on the matter until after the election by scheduling a lame-duck session.

The leadership's admission that a lame-duck session would be needed to get the budget through the House reinforced the Democrats' image as a faltering and ineffective party and contributed to their devastating losses in the 1980 elections. These losses in turn enabled the Republicans in January 1981 to control the Senate for the first time since the 83rd Congress (1953-1955) during Dwight D. Eisenhower's first term as president.

The House remained, at least technically, under Democratic control although the Democrats suffered a net loss of 33 seats. When the 97th Congress convened on Jan. 5, 1981, they held 243 seats compared to 192 for the Republicans. But the party during the first year of Ronald Reagan's administration was so dispirited by the Republican victories that its leaders found themselves powerless to stop the GOP's legislative programs. The time for retrenchment had begun. [8]

Notes

1. *Congressional Quarterly Almanac, 1973* (Washington, D.C.: Congressional Quarterly, 1974), pp. 905-917, 1007-1010; *Congressional Quarterly Almanac, 1974* (Washington, D.C.: Congressional Quarterly, 1975), pp. 867-902; *Congressional Quarterly Almanac, 1975* (Washington, D.C.: Congressional Quarterly, 1976), pp. 327-331, 801, 885-887.

2. *Congressional Quarterly Almanac, 1971* (Washington, D.C.: Congressional Quarterly, 1972), pp. 9-11; *1975 Almanac*, pp. 3-5.

3. *Inside Congress* (Washington, D.C.: Congressional Quarterly, 1976), pp. 1-16, 67-70, 74-91, 99-112, 127-133; *1971 Almanac*, pp. 723-724; *1974 Almanac*, p. 612.

4. *Congress and the Nation*, 5 vols., *Congress and the Nation, 1969-1972*, vol. 3 (Washington, D.C.: Congressional Quarterly, 1973), III: 382-396.

5. *Inside Congress*, pp. 6-7; *1974 Almanac*, pp. 634-640.

6. *Dollar Politics*, 3d ed. (Washington, D.C.: Congressional Quarterly, 1982), pp. 1-27.

7. *Congressional Quarterly Almanac, 1977* (Washington, D.C.: Congressional Quarterly, 1978), pp. 767-770.

8. *Congressional Quarterly Almanac, 1981* (Washington, D.C.: Congressional Quarterly, 1982), pp. 14-16.

Part III

History of the Senate

Rep. Preston Brooks (States Rights Dem.-S.C.) canes Sen.
Charles Sumner (R-Mass.) on the Senate floor for his views
on slavery during debate on the Kansas statehood bill,
May 22, 1856.

Chapter 18

FORMATIVE YEARS: 1789-1809

To English Prime Minister William Gladstone it was "the most remarkable of all the inventions of modern politics." To Viscount James Bryce, a former British ambassador to the United States and well-known historian, it was the "masterpiece of the constitution makers." Prominent British historian Walter Bagehot disagreed. "It may be necessary to have the blemish, but it is a blemish just as much," he wrote.[1]

Whether effusively praised or vigorously condemned, the United States Senate ranks as the most powerful upper legislative chamber in the world. It is not, however, precisely what its creators had in mind. Edmund Randolph said its purpose was to provide a cure for the "turbulence and follies of democracy," and James Madison asserted that "the use of the Senate is to consist in its proceeding with more coolness, with more system, and with more wisdom, than the popular branch." Madison was concerned about the "fickleness and passion" of a numerous body of representatives. "A necessary fence against this danger," he argued, "would be to select a portion of enlightened citizens whose limited number and firmness might seasonably interpose against impetuous councils." Madison envisioned the Senate as "a firm, wise and impartial body" that would give "stability to the General Government." Gouverneur Morris hoped simply "that the Senate will show us the might of aristocracy." But opponents feared it might become an American House of Lords.[2]

Compromise of 1787

Under the "Great Compromise" reached at the Constitutional Convention in 1787, the House of Representatives was to represent the "national principle," while the Senate was to be an expression of the "federal principle." Not only would each state have two votes in the Senate, but the election of senators by the state legislatures was thought to be a means of making the states a component of the national governing system. Although the basis of representation ensured each state an equal voice, senators voted as individuals, their salaries were paid by the federal government rather than by the states and the legislatures that elected them had no power to recall them. Thus it is not surprising that most senators, even in the early years, refused to consider themselves mere agents of the state governments. Efforts by various state legislatures in the 19th century to instruct their senators met with mixed success, although the practice did not die out entirely until 1913 when adoption of the 17th Amendment to the Constitution took the election of senators out of the legislators' hands.

The framers of the Constitution left unsettled many questions concerning the relationships among the three branches of government, and it remained for the Senate — born of compromise and fashioned after no serviceable model — to seek its own place in the governmental structure. In the unending competition for a meaningful share of power, the Senate has been trying for nearly two centuries to define its role, and the history of the Senate is in large part the story of this quest.

Early Views of Senate's Role

It had been confidently predicted that the popularly elected House of Representatives would be the predominant chamber in the national legislature, with the Senate acting chiefly as a revisory body, checking and moderating actions taken by the House. At first the House did overshadow the Senate both in power and prestige, but within a few decades the Senate — endowed with executive functions that the House did not share and blessed with a smaller and more stable membership — had achieved primacy over the directly elected chamber. Although the balance of power shifted from time to time, the Senate never followed the British House of Lords into decline.

As the nation's population expanded, the size of the House mushroomed, but the Senate, in which the large and small states were equally represented, remained a comparatively small body. The nation's growth compelled the House to impose stringent limitations on floor debate, to rely heavily on its committee system and to develop elaborate techniques to channel the flow of legislation — all steps that diminished the power of individual representatives. Such restrictions were not considered necessary in the Senate, where members tended to view themselves as ambassadors of sovereign states even though they exhibited independence in casting their votes. And in the upper chamber, the right of unlimited debate became the most cherished tradition. To the House, action was the primary object; in the Senate, deliberation was paramount.

The delegates at the convention also expected the Senate to serve as an advisory council to the president, but natural friction between the two, aggravated by the rise of the party system, made such a relationship impracticable. As time passed, the Senate was far more likely to try to manage the president than to advise him. In the 19th century the Senate often was the dominant force in the government, but the rapid expansion of presidential power in the 20th century was accompanied by a corresponding decline in the power of the legislative branch. As a result, the Senate increasingly felt that its existence as a viable legislative institution was threatened.

Insulation from Popular Pressure

The delegates had expressed their distrust of democracy by providing for election of senators by the state legislatures rather than by the people directly. In "refining the popular appointment by successive filtrations," they hoped to assure excellence, guard against "mutability" and, incidentally, protect the interests of the propertied classes.[3] Under this system, which Madison described in *The Federalist* as "probably the most congenial with public opinion," the Senate enjoyed its period of greatest prestige.[4] But as the trend toward democratization in government and expansion of suffrage developed early in the 20th century, public opinion began to favor popular election of senators. Eventually, the Senate was forced to participate in its own reform: in 1912 Congress approved a proposed constitutional amendment providing for direct election of the Senate. The 17th Amendment, ratified in 1913, curtailed many of the abuses associated with election by the legislatures, but its other effects were difficult to measure. At any rate, no revolutionary change in the overall character of the institution was discerned.

So successful were the delegates in insulating the Senate from popular pressure that the body often seemed to care more for what Bryce called its "collective self-esteem" than it did for public opinion.[5] Sometimes it could be forced to act, as in the case of the 17th Amendment and the adoption of the cloture rule in 1917, but its resistance to impetuous action was, for the most part, all that its creators could have wished.

Only eight senators had reached New York City by March 4, 1789, the date fixed for the first meeting of Congress, and a quorum of the 22-member Senate — two of the 13 original states had not yet ratified the Constitution — did not appear until April 6, five days after the House had organized. Crucial questions concerning the nature of the Senate and its proper role in the new government remained to be worked out.

Was the upper chamber to be principally a council to revise and review House measures, or a fully co-equal legislative body? And should it also serve in a quasi-executive capacity as an advisory council to the president, particularly with respect to appointments and treaties? Was the Senate primarily the bastion of state sovereignty, the defender of propertied interests, a necessary check on the popularly elected House, or was it, as its opponents charged, a threat to republican principles and an incipient American House of Lords? Even the method of electing senators was in dispute: Were the members to be chosen by joint or concurrent vote in bicameral state legislatures? This issue, which was not resolved until 1866, cost New York state its Senate representation during most of the first session of Congress.

The terms of individual senators also were in doubt. Under the Constitution, the first senators were to be divided into three classes — with terms of two, four and six years respectively — so that one-third of the Senate might be chosen every second year. To avoid charges of favoritism, the Senate resorted to choice by lot in making the division.

The first Senate, preoccupied with questions of form and precedence, was quick to claim for itself superiority over the House, but the lower chamber initially was the more important legislative body. James Madison stated in a letter to Virginia Governor Edmund Randolph that he would rather serve in the House than in the Senate, "chiefly because, if I can render any service there, it can only be to the public, and, not even in imputation, to myself." [6] (Madison subsequently was elected to the House in the First Congress after being defeated for a Senate seat.)

In the earliest days of the first session, while the House was focusing on the financial problems of the infant nation, the Senate devoted three weeks to the consuming problem of an appropriate title for the president. The debate apparently was instigated by Vice President John Adams, whose penchant for ceremony earned him the mocking title of "His Rotundity."

The Senate's early insistence on form and its claim to deference from the House led to disputes over such matters as the method of trans-

The Early Senate

Among the Thirty Senators of that day there was observed constantly during the debate the most delightful silence, the most beautiful order, gravity, and personal dignity of manner. They all appeared every morning full-powdered and dressed, as age or fancy might suggest, in the richest material. The very atmosphere of the place seemed to inspire wisdom, mildness, and condescension. Should any of them so far forget for a moment as to be the cause of a protracted whisper while another was addressing the Vice President, three gentle taps with his silver pencilcase upon the table by Mr. Adams immediately restored everything to repose and the most respectful attention, presenting in their courtesy a most striking contrast to the independent loquacity of the Representatives below stairs, some few of whom persisted in wearing, while in their seats and during the debate, their ample *cocked* hats, placed "fore and aft" upon their heads.

Source: This eyewitness description of the Senate in session about 1796 was offered by William McKoy in a series of articles that appeared in *Poulson's American Daily Advertiser* in 1828 and 1829.

mitting communications between the two chambers, the wording of the enacting clause in proposed legislation, and proposals (briefly accepted) for higher pay for senators. With a mixture of resentment and amusement, the House rebuffed most Senate efforts to enhance its own prestige. The Senate soon abandoned its aristocratic claims, and relations between the two chambers became more cordial.

Between 1789 and 1809, 78 percent of the bills in Congress originated in the House, with the Senate occupied primarily in reviewing and revising House-passed legislation. During the first session of the First Congress only five bills were initiated in the Senate, of which four — including the important Judiciary Act establishing the framework of the American judicial system — were passed. During the same period, the House originated and passed 26 bills. Two of these were rejected by the Senate, one was turned down in conference and the Senate modified at least 20 of the remaining 23.[7]

Relations with the President

The concept of the Senate as an advisory council to the president never materialized. President Washington took informal advice, not from the Senate as a body, but from Alexander Hamilton, Madison (then a House member) and others. The constitutional role of the Senate in the appointment process also fell short of the consultative role that some framers of the Constitution had envisioned. Washington's exercise of the appointment power carefully stressed the separate natures of the nomination and confirmation processes, a point underscored by his decision to submit nominations to the Senate in writing rather than in person. The Senate's role as an advisory council was further restricted in the first session, when the Senate narrowly accepted House-passed language vesting in the president alone the power to remove executive officers. Under Washington's successors, members of Congress had greater influence over appointments, but the principle of executive initiative remained firmly established.

In 1789 Washington attempted to put into practice his early view that the executive should consult with the Senate on all matters concerning treaties. On Aug. 22 and 24 he made a personal appearance in the Senate to discuss a treaty with southern Indians. His presence during Senate proceedings, however, created a "tense" atmosphere that was uncomfortable for the senators and for the president. It was an experience he did not wish to repeat. The result was that Senate participation in the early stages of treaty-making declined. This development made possible greater freedom of action when the time came for senators to vote on treaties.

Indeed, when the treaty with Great Britain negotiated in 1794 by Chief Justice John Jay was brought before the Senate for its approval, a bitter dispute arose. The controversial treaty secured American frontier posts in the Northwest but permitted Britain to search American merchant ships and confiscate provisions destined for Britain's enemy, France. Ultimately, the treaty was approved by a bare two-thirds majority June 24, 1795, but not before the Senate deleted a clause restricting U.S. trading rights in the British West Indies.

Relations with the States

The concept of senators as agents of state sovereignty led to repeated, but largely unsuccessful, efforts to make senators accountable to their state legislatures. Some members of Congress felt an obligation

Washington in the Senate

President Washington believed that "in all matters respecting treaties, oral communications [with the Senate] seem indispensably necessary." * Accordingly, on Aug. 22, 1789, he and his secretary of war, Gen. Henry Knox, appeared in the Senate chamber to consult with the Senate about a treaty with southern Indians. Sen. William Maclay of Pennsylvania gave an account of the proceedings in his *Journal*.

A paper containing the president's proposal was hurriedly read to the Senate by the vice president, but members were not able to hear because of the noise of carriages passing in the street outside. The windows were closed and the proposals read again. In the silence that followed, the vice president began to put the first question, but Maclay, fearing "that we should have these advices and consents ravished in a degree from us," rose and called for reading of the treaties and supporting documents alluded to in the president's paper. The president "wore an aspect of stern displeasure." Maclay "saw no chance of a fair investigation of subjects while the President of the United States sat there, with his Secretary of War, to support his opinions and over-awe the timid and neutral part of the Senate." Therefore, he backed a move to refer the entire subject to a committee. At this suggestion, the president "started up in a violent fret," exclaiming: "This defeats every purpose of my coming here." After he had "cooled down, by degrees," the president agreed to a two-day postponement, then withdrew from the chamber "with a discontented air."

On his return to the Senate two days later, Washington was "placid and serene, and manifested a spirit of accommodation," but the atmosphere was still tense, and "a shamefacedness, or I know not what, flowing from the presence of the President, kept everybody silent." ** At length, the business was concluded, and the president departed. The experience was not one that he cared to repeat.

* George H. Haynes, *The Senate of the United States: Its History and Practice*, 2 vols. (Boston: Houghton-Mifflin, 1938), I: 62.
** Ibid., pp. 63, 68.

to make periodic reports on their activities to the state governments, and a continuing controversy raged over the right of state legislatures to instruct their senators. Instruction was more general in the South than in the North, but there was no unanimity of opinion on the question. However, with the emergence of political parties, party loyalty gradually took the place of allegiance to state legislatures even in those states where the concept received some acceptance.

Early Senate Procedures

Courtesy, dignity and informality marked the proceedings of the Senate in the early days of the Republic. A body that on a chill morning might leave its seats to gather around the fireplace had no need for an elaborate system of procedures and rules. At the first session in 1789 the Senate adopted only 20 short rules, a number deemed sufficient to control the proceedings of a Senate no larger than some modern-day congressional committees. *(See box, pp. 202-203.)* In 1806 the number of rules rose to 40, with most of the additions dealing with nominations and treaties.[8]

The rules left a wide area of discretion to the Senate president, particularly Rule 16 which gave him sole authority to decide points of order. Vice President Adams presided over the Senate between 1789 and 1797 with no specific guidelines on procedures, but his successor as vice president, Thomas Jefferson (1797-1801), felt the need of referring "to some known system of rules, that he may neither leave himself free to indulge caprice or passion nor open to the imputation of them." [9] The result was Jefferson's *Manual of Parliamentary Procedure*, adopted by the House in 1837.

Closed Sessions

Following the practice of the Congress under the Confederation, the Senate originally met behind closed doors. Total secrecy was not maintained, however, since senators often discussed their activities outside the chamber, and the Senate *Journal* as well as sketchy reports of Senate action appeared in print from time to time. The principal result of the closed-door policy was to focus public attention on the widely reported debates of the House and to encourage suspicion of the aristocratic Senate. Beginning in 1790, various state legislatures began to press for open sessions of the Senate as a way of making their senators more accountable.

After four defeats in four years, the Senate finally agreed in 1794 to open its sessions "after the end of the present session of Congress, and so soon as suitable galleries shall be provided for the Senate chamber." [10] Almost two years went by before the galleries were erected and the rule put into effect, but at the beginning of the first session of the Fourth Congress in December 1795, the Senate's doors were opened to the public. The immediate effects of this action were not great, since the Senate sessions were too decorous to attract widespread attention, and the more spirited House remained the center of public interest. Furthermore, there were no official reporters of debates. No accommodation for newspaper reporters was made in the Senate until 1802, after the government had moved to Washington.

Light Workload

The demands upon senators in the early Congresses do not appear to have been unduly burdensome. Ordinarily, the Senate met at 11 a.m., except near the end of the session when the press of business was greater, and 3 p.m. adjournments were common. Sen. William Maclay of Pennsylvania, whose *Journal* provides a prejudiced but invaluable record of the Senate in the First Congress, frequently noted that the Senate adjourned its own tedious sessions so that members could go and listen to the livelier floor debates in the House. Absenteeism, a continuing problem, was only partially attributable to the difficulties of travel in this period. Accordingly, in 1798 the Senate finally added enforcement machinery to Rule 19 prohibiting absence without leave.

Because most legislation initially originated in the House, the Senate had little to do early in a session. Under the so-called *de novo* rule of 1790, all bills died at the end of each session of Congress, so the Senate did not have House-passed bills from a previous session on which to work. The House scornfully rejected Senate proposals that the two chambers jointly prepare a legislative program for an entire session. However, joint committees often were appointed near the end of sessions to determine what business had to be completed before adjournment. Not unlike today, much of the legislative output of each session was pushed through at the last minute. In the second session of the Sixth Congress, for example, the Senate passed 35 bills, one-third of them on the final day.

Presidential messages provided a partial agenda for each session. Washington and Adams delivered their messages in person annually, and

Official Rules and Procedures...

I. The President having taken the chair, and a quorum being present, the journal of the preceding day shall be read, to the end that any mistakes may be corrected that shall have been made in the entries.

II. No member shall speak to another, or otherwise interrupt the business of the Senate, or read any printed paper while the journals or public papers are reading, or when any member is speaking in any debate.

III. Every member, when he speaks shall address the chair, standing in his place, and when he has finished shall sit down.

IV. No member shall speak more than twice in any one debate on the same day, without leave of the Senate.

V. When two members shall rise at the same time, the President shall name the person to speak; but in all cases the person first rising shall speak first.

VI. No motion shall be debated until ... seconded.

VII. When a motion shall be made and seconded, it shall be reduced to writing, if desired by the President, or any member, delivered in at the table, and ready by the President before the same shall be debated.

VIII. While a question is before the Senate, no motion shall be received unless for an amendment, for the previous question, or for postponing the main question, or to commit, or to adjourn.

IX. The previous question being moved and seconded, the question for the chair shall be: "Shall the main question now be put?" and if the nays prevail, the main question shall not then be put.

X. If a question in a debate include several points, any member may have the same divided.

XI. When the yeas and nays shall be called for by one-fifth of the members present, each member called upon shall, unless for special reasons he be excused by the Senate, declare, openly and without debate, his assent or dissent to the question. In taking the yeas and nays, and upon the call of the House, the names of the members shall be taken alphabetically.

. . . of the First United States Senate

XII. One day's notice at least shall be given of an intended motion for leave to bring in a bill.

XIII. Every bill shall receive three readings previous to its being passed; and the President shall give notice at each, whether it be the first, second, or third; which readings shall be on three different days, unless the Senate unanimously direct otherwise.

XIV. No bill shall be committed or amended until it shall have been twice read, after which it may be referred to a committee.

XV. All committees shall be elected by ballot, and a plurality of votes shall make a choice.

XVI. When a member shall be called to order, he shall sit down until the President shall have determined whether he is in order or not; and every question or order shall be decided by the President, without debate; but, if there be a doubt in his mind, he may call for the sense of the Senate.

XVII. If a member be called to order for words spoken, the exceptionable words shall be immediately taken down in writing, that the President may be better enabled to judge the matter.

XVIII. When a blank is to be filled, and different sums shall be proposed, the question shall be taken on the highest sum first.

XIX. No member shall absent himself from the service of the Senate without leave of the Senate first obtained.

XX. Before any petition or memorial, addressed to the Senate, shall be received and read at the table, whether the same shall be introduced by the President or a member, a brief statement of the contents of the petition or memorial shall verbally be made by the introducer.

Source: Roy Swanstom, *The United States Senate, 1787-1801,* Senate Document No. 64, 87th Cong., 1st sess. (Washington, D.C.: U.S. Government Printing Office, 1962).

each chamber prepared a reply that was delivered orally with great ceremony. Since these replies were debated and amended carefully, they provided a valuable opportunity for consideration of the overall legislative program. But Jefferson abandoned his predecessors' practice and delivered his messages in writing, and such messages were not thought by Congress to require a reply.

Rules on Debate

The absence of restrictions on debate in the Senate opened the door to delaying tactics as well as illuminating discussions. But dilatory actions appeared only occasionally in the early Senate and apparently did not present a serious problem.

Only three of the rules adopted by the first Senate in 1789 had any direct bearing on limitation of debate: Rule 4 (no member should speak more than twice in any one debate on the same day without permission of the Senate), Rule 6 (no motion should be debated until seconded) and Rule 16 (every question of order should be decided by the president of the Senate without debate).

The so-called "previous question" motion that was authorized under Rule 9 was not then used for the purpose of halting debate on a measure, but rather it was invoked to remove a particular question from further consideration by reverting to a previous question. This procedural motion was dropped when the Senate rules and procedures were revised in 1806. At the same time, debate was prohibited on a motion to adjourn.

Although bills could be introduced by individual members with the permission of a Senate majority after one day's notice, the more common practice was to request the appointment of a committee to consider and report a bill. Thus only a limited number of bills were introduced, and most of those introduced were passed.

Committee System and Membership Turnover

Standing committees as they are known today did not exist in the early sessions of the Senate. Legislation was handled by ad hoc committees, appointed to consider a particular issue and disbanded once their work was finished. The full Senate maintained firm control over their activities. Membership was flexible, although the same senators frequently were assigned to committees dealing with a particular field of legislation. Following British precedent, opponents of a measure were excluded from membership on the committee that considered it, and the

Federalist majority frequently excluded Republicans from committees appointed to consider legislation involving party issues.

In terms of previous experience, members of the early Senate were well qualified to serve in the national legislature. Of the 94 men in the Senate between 1789 and 1801, 18 had participated in the Constitutional Convention of 1787, 42 in the Continental Congress or the Congress of the Confederation and 84 in their state or provincial legislatures. Only one or two were without some experience in government. A majority were men of wealth and social prominence, but they were a young "council of elders" — the average age in 1799 was only 45 years.[11]

Experience did not bear out the warnings of those who feared that senators would entrench themselves in office for life. Of the 94 senators who served between 1789 and 1801, 33 resigned within that period before completing their terms, and only six did so in order to take other federal posts. Frequent resignations continued for many years — 35 in the period 1801-1813 — and the rate of re-election also was low.[12]

Emergence of Parties

Political parties had no place in the constitutional framework. Early Senate voting reflected geographic or economic divisions within the chamber. The presentation of Alexander Hamilton's controversial financial measures, however, elicited a spirit of partisanship in the Senate and House. Supporters of a strong central government, chiefly representatives of mercantile and financial interests, banded together as Federalists under the leadership of Hamilton, while exponents of agrarian democracy, led by Madison and Jefferson, became known as Republicans (and later as Democratic-Republicans to distinguish them from the Republican Party established in 1854).

Party alignments, still quite fluid in 1791, gradually solidified in the next two years in the face of the excesses of the French Revolution and troubled relations with Great Britain. As Sen. John Taylor of Virginia observed in 1794:

> The existence of two parties in Congress is apparent. The fact is disclosed almost upon every important question. Whether the subject be foreign or domestic — relative to war or peace — navigation or commerce — the magnetism of opposite views draws them wide as the poles asunder.[13]

The Federalists held the Senate until 1801, but in 1794 the Democratic-Republicans came close to overturning that control. The

Federalists succeeded in unseating Swiss-born Albert Gallatin on the charge that he had not been a United States citizen for the requisite nine years under the Constitution. He was deprived of his Senate seat on a 14-12 party-line vote, but on six other occasions during the session they needed the vote of Vice President Adams to sustain their program.

Approval of the Jay Treaty in 1795 united the Federalists and strengthened their influence in the Senate. From that time on, both Federalists and Democratic-Republicans voted with a high degree of party regularity. During the Fourth, Fifth and Sixth Congresses (1795-1801), the Federalists enjoyed roughly a two-to-one edge over the Democratic-Republicans in the Senate, while the House remained closely divided. But the rapprochement with France, engineered by then President John Adams, deprived the Federalists of their principal issue, and this development, combined with the influx of senators from newly admitted southern and western states, broke the power of the Federalists in the Senate. In the elections of 1800, Jefferson's Democratic-Republicans won the presidency and both houses of Congress. When the Seventh Congress convened in December 1801, the Jeffersonians held a narrow Senate majority. Federalist strength in the Senate continued to decline throughout Jefferson's two terms in office.

Leadership in the Senate

The Constitution solved the problem of a job for the vice president by making him president of the Senate, and it directed the Senate to choose a president pro tempore to act in the vice president's absence. There were good reasons, however, why neither of these officers could supply effective legislative leadership.

The vice president was not chosen by the Senate but imposed upon it from outside, and there was no necessity for him to be sympathetic to its aims. Precedent was set by Federalist John Adams. Although clearly in general agreement with the majority of the Senate during his term as vice president, he perceived his role as simply that of presiding officer and made little effort to guide Senate action. His successor, Thomas Jefferson, could not have steered the Federalist-controlled Senate even if he had wanted to, although Jefferson did maintain a watchful eye on the interests of the Democratic-Republicans in the upper chamber.

The president pro tempore was elected by the Senate from among its own members, but he could not supply legislative leadership because his term was too temporary. By custom, a president pro tempore was elected only during the immediate absence of the vice president, and his duties as such ended with the reappearance of the vice president. From the First through the Sixth Congresses (1789-1801), 15 senators served as president pro tempore.[14] Thus the mantle of legislative leadership soon fell upon individual senators — in the beginning these included Oliver Ellsworth and Rufus King, among others — and, more importantly, upon the executive branch. Presidents Washington and Adams shared a strong belief in the separation of powers. Neither was willing to take upon himself the role of legislative leader, but Alexander Hamilton had no such qualms. As secretary of the Treasury until 1795, and even after his retirement to private life, Hamilton not only developed a broad legislative program but functioned, in the words of one historian, "as a sort of absentee floor leader," in almost daily contact with his friends in the Senate.[15]

Under Jefferson and Albert Gallatin, who had become secretary of the Treasury, legislative leadership continued to emanate from the executive branch. Jefferson, wrote Sen. Timothy Pickering of Massachusetts, tried "to screen himself from all responsibility by calling upon Congress for advice and direction. . . . Yet with affected modesty and deference he secretly dictates every measure which is seriously proposed." [16]

By the end of Jefferson's presidency in 1809, the Senate had established internal procedures and exercized many of its prerogatives under the Constitution. It had initiated and revised proposed legislation, given its advice and consent to treaties and nominations, conducted its first investigations and held two impeachment trials: the first resulting in the removal from office of a federal judge and the second in the acquittal of Supreme Court Justice Samuel Chase. But the breadth of its powers was not yet clear; relations with the executive branch, the House and the state governments still were only tentatively charted and awaited further tests.

Notes

1. For the Gladstone quote, see George H. Haynes, *The Senate of the United States: Its History and Practice*, 2 vols. (Boston: Houghton-Mifflin, 1938), I: vii; for the Bryce and Bagehot quotes, see Lindsay Rogers, *The American Senate* (New York: Alfred A. Knopf, 1926), pp. 9, 90.
2. For the Randolph quote, see James Madison, *Notes on Debates in the Federal Convention of 1787*, with an introduction by Adrienne Koch (Athens, Ohio:

Ohio University Press, 1966), p. 42; for the Madison quotes, see Charles Warren, *The Making of the Constitution* (Boston: Little, Brown & Co., 1928), p. 195; for the Morris quote, see Rogers, *The American Senate*, p. 18.

3. Haynes, *The Senate of the United States*, I: 11.
4. Alexander Hamilton, James Madison, and John Jay, *The Federalist Papers*, with an introduction by Clinton Rossiter (New York: Mentor, 1961), p. 377.
5. Rogers, *The American Senate*, p. 21.
6. Gaillard Hunt, ed., *The Writings of James Madison, 1787-1790*, vol. 5 (New York: G. P. Putnam's Sons, 1904), p. 276.
7. Roy Swanstrom, *The United States Senate, 1787-1801*, Senate Document No. 64, 87th Cong., 1st sess. (Washington, D.C.: U.S. Government Printing Office, 1962), p. 86.
8. Haynes, *The Senate of the United States*, pp. 192-194.
9. Swanstrom, *The United States Senate, 1787-1801*, pp. 192-194.
10. Ibid., p. 247.
11. Ibid., pp. 36-37.
12. Ibid., p. 80.
13. Ibid., p. 283.
14. *Members of Congress Since 1789*, 2d ed. (Washington, D.C.: Congressional Quarterly, 1981), p. 167.
15. Swanstrom, *The United States Senate*, p. 271.
16. W. E. Binkley, *The Powers of the President* (New York: Russell & Russell, 1973), p. 52.

Chapter 19

EMERGING SENATE: 1809-1829

Two decades of legislative supremacy began with the administration of Thomas Jefferson's successor, James Madison; the "Father of the Constitution" proved himself incapable of presidential leadership during his two terms in office (1809-1817). He lost control of his party to the young "war hawks" in the House, who succeeded in forcing him into the War of 1812, and for the remainder of his presidency Madison suffered defeats at the hands of Congress. President James Monroe was no more fortunate in his relations with Congress than Madison had been. At the time of Monroe's second inauguration in 1821, Henry Clay of Kentucky commented: "Mr. Monroe has just been re-elected with apparent unanimity, but he had not the slightest influence on Congress." [1]

Neither Madison nor Monroe was temperamentally fit for legislative leadership, and both were further handicapped by their obligation to the congressional caucus that had nominated them for the presidency. The situation of President John Quincy Adams, who served from 1825 to 1829, was even more difficult, since he owed his very election to the members of the House of Representatives.

Rising Senate Influence

Although the House took a commanding role in government during Clay's Speakership (1811-1820, 1823-1825), the influence of the Senate was on the rise. The trend toward Senate dictation of executive appointments, which had begun late in Jefferson's presidency, continued and increased under Madison. When he sought to make Albert Gallatin secretary of state, the Senate blocked his choice and forced him to accept a secretary of its own choosing.

The importance of the Senate's treaty and appointment powers, in which the House had no share, was only one factor in the Senate's growing influence. The rapidly expanding size of the House soon suggested the advantages of serving in a smaller body (in 1820 there still were only 46 senators).[2] The Senate's longer term of office and more stable membership also made it seem a more desirable place in which to serve. Henry Clay moved from the Senate to the House in 1811, but by 1823 Martin Van Buren was able to claim that the Senate, more than any other branch, controlled all the important power of government. Clay returned to the Senate in 1831.

The Senate's legislative importance increased gradually. In the early years, the great debates, such as those surrounding the War of 1812, occurred in the House. But the Senate took a leading role in the struggle over the Missouri Compromise of 1820 and succeeded in imposing upon the House an amendment barring slavery in any future state north of 36°30' north latitude. Since this was the region in which the country's population was expanding most rapidly, proponents of slavery could no longer hope to uphold indefinitely the cause of states' rights in the House. The Senate — where the two sides on the issue were more evenly matched — became the forum for the great anti-slavery debates of the following decades.

Changes in Party Alignment

Party alignments changed between 1809 and 1829. The withering Federalist Party ceased to be a factor in national politics after the election of 1816, but Democratic-Republican supremacy was marred by increasing factionalism. Interestingly, all of the candidates in the 1824 presidential election — Adams, Clay, Andrew Jackson and William H. Crawford — represented different factions of the Democratic-Republican Party. Suffrage had expanded, and the newly enfranchised small farmers of the South and West had little in common with the landed aristocracy that was the backbone of the party. Thus the democratic masses turned from the slaveholding planters to the leadership of Andrew Jackson of Tennessee, an exponent of their fiercely egalitarian philosophy. In 1825 when the House made Adams president — although Jackson had led in the popular vote — the Democratic-Republican Party split and a new Democratic Party was organized by Jackson's lieutenants. In 1826 the Democratic Party won control of both houses of Congress, and in 1828 supporters of the new party elected Andrew Jackson as president — the office they thought he had been wrongly denied four years earlier.

Growth of Standing Committees

The Senate lagged behind the House in establishing a formal committee structure. In its first quarter century it created only four standing committees, all chiefly administrative in nature: the Joint Standing Committee on Enrolled Bills, the Senate Committee on Engrossed Bills, the Joint Standing Committee for the Library, and the Senate Committee to Audit and Control the Contingent Expenses of the Senate.

During this period most of the legislative committee work fell to ad hoc select committees, usually of three members, appointed as the occasion demanded. Eventually continual appointment of these committees (between 90 and 100 in the 1815-1816 session) exhausted the patience of the Senate, and in 1816 it established 11 additional standing committees, each with a legislative jurisdiction: Foreign Relations, Finance, Commerce and Manufactures, Military Affairs, the Militia, Naval Affairs, Public Lands, Claims, the Judiciary, the Post Office and Post Roads, and Pensions. Most of the new committees were parallel in function to House committees already in existence. The usual membership on Senate committees was five, rising to seven by mid-century and to nine by 1900.[3]

A general revision of the Senate rules in 1820, increasing the total number of rules from 20 to 45, incorporated the provisions relating to standing committees that the Senate had adopted four years earlier. As in the case of other general revisions of Senate rules, the 1820 revision represented chiefly an attempt to codify changes that had accumulated over a number of years; no great spirit of reform was involved.

Membership on Senate committees was chosen by ballot until 1823, when the Senate amended its rules to give the presiding officer authority to appoint committee members, unless otherwise ordered by the Senate. At first this power was exercised by the president pro tempore, an officer of the Senate's own choosing, but early in the 19th Congress (1825-1827) Vice President John C. Calhoun assumed the appointment power and used it to place Jackson supporters in key committee positions. In the face of this patent effort to embarrass the administration of John Quincy Adams, the Senate quickly returned to the ballot as the method of filling committee slots. In 1828 the rule was changed again, this time to give appointment power to the president pro tempore, but in 1833 the Senate once more reverted to selection by ballot.

'A Senate of Equals'

Sen. Daniel Webster described the upper chamber in 1830 as a "Senate of equals, of men and individual honor and personal character, and of absolute independence," who knew no master and acknowledged no dictation. [4] In such a body it is not surprising that no single leader emerged to parallel the rise of Henry Clay in the House.

Statesmen of prominence served in the Senate during the 1809-1829 period that spanned the 11th through 20th Congresses. The roster included four future presidents — Andrew Jackson, Martin Van Buren, William Henry Harrison and John Tyler — and a number of presidential hopefuls. And by the close of the period, the great figures of the ensuing "Golden Age" were beginning to gather in the chamber: Thomas Hart Benton of Missouri arrived in 1821, Robert Y. Hayne of South Carolina in 1823 and Daniel Webster of Massachusetts in 1827. Clay, after a brief stint in the Senate from 1810 to 1811, went to the House, then returned to the Senate in 1831. Calhoun resigned as vice president in 1832 to succeed Hayne as senator from South Carolina.

Until Calhoun assumed office in 1825, the vice presidents of the period wielded little influence. Madison's first vice president, George Clinton, was old and feeble and died in office, as did his successor, Elbridge Gerry. Monroe's vice president, Daniel D. Tompkins, hardly ever entered the Senate chamber. Vice President Calhoun, hostile to the Adams administration and harboring presidential ambitions of his own, had no desire to alienate the Senate by exercising undue authority, but he was a commanding figure and his influence was felt. Sen. Hayne generally served as his spokesman on the floor.

Calhoun took advantage of his position to make obviously biased committee appointments, but in other respects he exercized as little outward authority as possible. Although all of his predecessors in the chair had assumed direct authority to call senators to order who were out of line, Calhoun contended that his power was appellate only and refused to act unless an offending senator first was called to order by another senator. He would not "for ten thousand worlds look like a usurper," Calhoun declared. [5] Calhoun's refusal to act on his own initiative led the Senate in 1828 to amend its rules. Henceforth, the chair would have the power to call a senator to order, but for the first time in the Senate's history the rule permitted an appeal from the chair's decision on a question of order.

Between 1809 and 1829, greater continuity of service developed in the office of president pro tempore. John Gaillard of South Carolina occupied the post for ten years (1814-1818, 1819-1825), his service interrupted only once when James Barbour of Virginia served during the second session of the 15th Congress. Elected by the Senate and thus considering himself entitled to its support, Gaillard enforced the rules rigidly but did not exercise a true leadership role.

Notes

1. W. E. Binkley, *The Powers of the President* (New York: Russell & Russell, 1973), pp. 60-61.
2. Lauros G. McConachie, *Congressional Committees: A Study of the Origins and Development of Our National and Local Legislative Methods* (New York: Burt Franklin Reprints, 1973), p. 312.
3. George H. Haynes, *The Senate of the United States: Its History and Practice*, 2 vols. (Boston: Houghton-Mifflin, 1938), I: 272-278.
4. Ibid., II: 1003.
5. Ibid., I: 212-214.

Chapter 20

THE GOLDEN AGE: 1829-1861

The pre-eminent national issue in the period between the Missouri Compromise of 1820 and the outbreak of war in 1861 was the struggle between North and South over slavery. The Senate, where the two sides were equally matched due to the system of representation, became the principal battleground.

Sectional interests were more important than party loyalty during this period, and divisions between the major parties often were blurred. The Jacksonian Democrats had adopted the agrarian and states' rights philosophy of the Jeffersonians, but their concept of strong executive leadership was at odds with the Jeffersonian view. Meanwhile, the Whig Party was formed through a coalition of eastern financial interests that once had constituted the strength of the Federalists, but the Whigs were committed to a doctrine of legislative supremacy that was alien to Federalist thought.

The slavery question split the Democratic Party, and many southern Democrats allied themselves with the Whigs in the hope of protecting states' rights and the institution of slavery. However, in the 1850s the Whig Party gave way to the new Republican Party — an alliance of northern interests dedicated to preventing the spread of slavery into the territories. Mounting southern defiance of abolitionist sentiment led to a North-South split in the Democratic Party, and secession and war soon followed.

In this age of giants three men dominated the Senate chamber. All were former members of the House, and all aspired to the presidency. Daniel Webster of Massachusetts — Whig, spokesman for eastern business interests, sectionalist turned nationalist, supreme orator — entered the Senate in 1827 and served there for 19 years. Henry Clay of Kentucky — Whig, westerner, brilliant tactician and compromiser — returned to the Senate to serve between 1831 and 1842 and again between

1849 and 1852. (His career in Congress began in the Senate in 1806.) John C. Calhoun of South Carolina — outstanding logician, devoted son of the South and champion of the right of secession — stepped down from the vice presidency in 1832 to defend his nullification doctrine on the Senate floor and remained a senator for most of the period until his death in 1850. (Nullification was the refusal of a state to recognize or enforce a federal law it regarded as an infringement on its rights.)

French historian and politician Alexis de Tocqueville in 1834 contrasted the "vulgarity" of the House with the nobility of the Senate, where "scarcely an individual is to be found . . . who does not recall the idea of an active and illustrious career." The Senate "is composed of eloquent advocates, distinguished generals, wise magistrates, and statesmen of note, whose language would, at all times, do honor to the most remarkable parliamentary debates of Europe." [1]

Senate's Pre-eminence over House

De Tocqueville could think of only one explanation for the Senate's superiority over the House: election of its members by elected bodies instead of directly by the people. Sen. Thomas Hart Benton pointed to the Senate's smaller membership, longer terms and greater experience on the part of its members. "Composed of the pick of the House of Representatives," he said, the Senate "gains doubly — by brilliant accession to itself and abstraction from the other." [2]

Undoubtedly the Senate's greater stability of membership contributed to its pre-eminence over the House, where the Jacksonian concept of rotation in office led to greater turnover. Perhaps even more significant was the introduction of the spoils system and the Senate's increasing domination of the nomination and confirmation process. Finally, national expansion had strengthened the Senate by turning it from a small, intimate body into a large forum for the exercise of brilliant oratorical and parliamentary skills.

With the addition of two senators from every new state, the Senate increased from 48 members at the beginning of Andrew Jackson's administration to 66 in James Buchanan's. Its roster included such luminaries as Benton of Missouri, Lewis Cass of Michigan, Sam Houston of Texas, Jefferson Davis and Henry S. Foote of Mississippi, William H. Seward of New York, Stephen A. Douglas of Illinois and Charles Sumner of Massachusetts.

Webster Replies to Hayne

A resolution to inquire into the expediency of limiting the sale of public lands, introduced in December 1829, touched off a debate in which the Senate addressed itself to the problems of sectional rivalry and constitutional interpretation. The principal speakers were Robert Y. Hayne of South Carolina and Daniel Webster of Massachusetts. In his second reply to Hayne, delivered Jan. 26-27, 1830, Webster attacked the doctrine of state sovereignty and nullification advanced by Hayne and affirmed the sovereignty of the Constitution and the federal government over the states. Webster's closing remarks contain some of the most eloquent oratory ever delivered in the Senate.

I have not allowed myself, sir, to look beyond the Union, to see what might lie hidden in the dark recess behind. I have not cooly weighed the chances of preserving liberty when the bonds that unite us together shall be broken asunder. I have not accustomed myself to hang over the precipice of disunion, to see whether, with my short sight, I can fathom the depth of the abyss below; nor could I regard him as a safe counselor in the affairs in this government whose thoughts should be mainly bent on considering, not how the Union may be best preserved but how tolerable might be the condition of the people when it should be broken up and destroyed. While the Union lasts, we have high, exciting, gratifying prospects spread out before us, for us and our children. Beyond that I seek not to penetrate the veil.

God grant that in my day, at least, that curtain may not rise! God grant that on my vision never may be opened what lies behind! When my eyes shall be turned to behold for the last time the sun in heaven, may I not see him shining on the broken and dishonored fragments of a once glorious Union; on states dissevered, discordant, belligerent; on a land rent with civil feuds, or drenched, it may be, in fraternal blood! Let their last feeble and lingering glance rather behold the gorgeous ensign of the republic, now known and honored throughout the earth, still full high advanced, its arms and trophies streaming in their original luster, not a stripe erased or polluted, nor a single star obscured, bearing for its motto, no such miserable interrogatory as "What is all this worth?" nor those other words of delusion and folly, "Liberty first and Union afterwards"; but everywhere, spread all over in characters of living light, blazing on all its ample folds, as they float over the sea and over the land ... that other sentiment, dear to every true American heart — Liberty *and* Union, now and forever, one and inseparable!

Quarrel with President Jackson

The eclipse of presidential power that had begun under James Madison ended when Andrew Jackson became president in 1829. Backed by strong popular majorities and skilled in the use of patronage, Jackson was able to dominate the House, but in the Senate he met vigorous opposition from the new Whig Party made up of commercial and industrial interests and dedicated to the principle of legislative supremacy. The Whigs were quick to challenge the president on questions of policy and executive prerogative, and Jackson's term was marked by numerous acrimonious struggles with the Senate over legislation and executive appointments.

These disputes reached a peak in 1834 when Jackson removed deposits from the Bank of the United States and refused to hand over to the Senate personal communications to his Cabinet relating to that issue. Outraged by Jackson's actions, the Senate adopted a resolution, pushed through by Clay, charging "that the President, in the late executive proceedings in relation to the public revenue, has assumed upon himself authority and power not conferred by the Constitution and laws and in derogation of both." [3] Jackson countered with a message, which the Senate refused to receive, declaring that so serious a charge as that contained in the censure resolution called for impeachment. Because impeachment had to originate in the House, he protested the Senate's action as a violation of the Constitution.

Benton, Jackson's leader in the Senate, promptly undertook a successful campaign to vindicate Jackson by expunging the censure resolution from the Senate *Journal*. Under pressure from the president, some state legislatures instructed their senators to support Benton's efforts, while others forced anti-Jackson senators to retire. By the time Jackson's second term was drawing to a close in 1837, the Jacksonian Democrats had gained control of the Senate and had won adoption, 24-19, of an extraordinary motion expunging the censure resolution. In one of the most dramatic scenes in Senate history, the terms of the resolution were carried out:

> [T]he Secretary of the Senate . . . shall bring the manuscript journal of the session of 1833-34 into the Senate, and, in the presence of the Senate, draw black lines round the said resolve, and write across the face thereof, in strong letters, the following words: "Expunged by order of the Senate, the 16th day of January, in the year of our Lord 1837." [4]

Whigs vs. President Tyler

The hopes of the Whig Party soared with the election of Whig President William Henry Harrison in 1841; Daniel Webster was named secretary of state, Clay supporters were put in other Cabinet positions and Harrison's inaugural address, revised by Webster, was a model statement of the Whig doctrine of legislative supremacy. But Harrison died after only one month in office, to be succeeded by John Tyler, a states' rights Virginian and former Democrat who had been chosen as vice president to give the Whig ticket factional and geographic balance.

At first Clay, as the leading Whig member of Congress, thought he could assume effective leadership of the government, and he even introduced a set of resolutions that were designed to become the party's legislative program. But Tyler, it turned out, was determined to be president in fact as well as in name, and the two men soon clashed head-on. Tyler's vetoes of Whig legislation led to threats of impeachment and to abortive efforts to force his resignation, but Clay was unable to push through his own legislative program. Although most presidents during this period confronted some Senate opposition to their appointments, Tyler was particularly unfortunate. Many of his nominations, including four to the Cabinet, were rejected by the Senate.

After Tyler's lackluster presidency the Whigs were never again able to muster a majority in the Senate that would permit them to put their doctrine of legislative supremacy to a test. Difficulties with nominations continued, for this was the height of the spoils system, but a succession of strong presidents established a pattern of executive leadership that even the weak leadership of Presidents Franklin Pierce (1853-1857) and James Buchanan (1857-1861) could not entirely destroy.

Great Debates over Slavery

Oratory in the Senate reached its peak on the eve of the Civil War, and visitors often thronged the galleries to hear the great debates over slavery. Never had the Senate seemed so splendid as in this period when it served as the chief forum for the discussion of national policy. But the courtesy and decorum of the early Senate began to crumble under the mounting pressures of the time. Although most debates were still brief, passions ran high and legislative obstruction became increasingly common. Filibusters often were threatened and occasionally undertaken, but they were not yet fully exploited as a means of paralyzing the Senate. Senators seldom admitted they were employing dilatory tactics.

The first notable Senate filibuster occurred in 1841, when senators opposed to a bill to remove the Senate printers held the floor for 10 days. Later in the same year a Whig move to re-establish the Bank of the United States was subject to an unsuccessful two-week filibuster. Henry Clay said the tactics of the minority would "lead to the inference that embarrassment and delay were the objects aimed at," and he threatened to introduce a rule to limit debate. Unabashed, the filibusterers invited Clay to "make his arrangements at his boarding house for the winter" and warned that they would resort to "any possible extremity" to prevent restriction of their debate. Unable to obtain majority support for his "gag rule," Clay never carried out his threat. The bank bill eventually was passed, only to be vetoed by President Tyler. [5]

In 1846 a bill providing for U.S.-British joint occupancy of Oregon was filibustered for two months. The measure finally was brought to a vote through use of a unanimous consent agreement, apparently for the first time. This device is still employed today to speed action in the Senate. Later in 1846 the Wilmot Proviso was talked to death in the closing hours of the session. That measure, which the House had attached as a rider to an appropriation bill in the early months of the Mexican War, stipulated that slavery was to be excluded from any territory acquired from Mexico.

The extension of slavery in the territories was again the issue in the extended debates over the Compromise of 1850, Clay's valiant attempt to resolve the sectional controversies that were tearing the nation apart. In a crowded chamber, the great triumvirate — Webster, Clay and Calhoun — made their last joint appearance in the Senate. The dying Calhoun dragged himself into the chamber to hear his final speech read by his colleague James Murray Mason of Virginia. Violence threatened when Sen. Harry S. "Hangman" Foote of Mississippi brandished a pistol at Missouri's Benton, who was well known as a deadly duelist. Only the intervention of other senators prevented bloodshed.

Greater violence marked the 1856 debate on the Kansas statehood bill. Rep. Preston Brooks, a southern Democrat, attacked Sen. Charles Sumner, a Republican from Massachusetts, and beat him senseless with a cane on the Senate floor for his views on slavery in the territories.

As the nation drifted toward war, debates continued to reflect the rancor of the period. Oratory had little place in a chamber where all members were said to carry arms, and by the time the Senate moved into its present quarters in 1859 the great epoch of Senate debate was at an end. Oratory had flourished in the intimate grandeur of the old hall; in the new chamber — vast and acoustically poor — a new style of debate emerged.

The Committee System

The most important procedural development of the 1829-1861 period occurred in 1846 when the Senate ended its policy of determining committee assignments by ballot and gave this responsibility to the party organizations in the chamber. As long as committee assignments were determined by Senate ballot, majority party control of the committees could not be assured. Although by 1829 the majority usually controlled the working committees, the opposition party still held important chairmanships.

When the second session of the 29th Congress met in December 1846, the Senate rejected a proposal to let the vice president name the committees and then, in accordance with the existing rule, began balloting for chairmen. Midway through this process the balloting rule was suspended, and the Senate proceeded to elect on one ballot a list of candidates for all of the remaining committee vacancies that had been agreed upon by the majority and minority. From that time on, the choice of committees usually has amounted to a routine acceptance by the Senate of lists drawn up by committees acting as representatives of the caucus or conference of the two major parties.

The fact that party organizations did not become the standard instrument of committee selection until 1846 gives some indication of the limited extent of party discipline in the early years of the Senate. Party authority usually was confined to organizational questions. When it came to substantive issues, senators voted as individuals rather than as Democrats or Whigs.

Party influence in the Senate was enhanced by the new method of committee selection, but rank within committees was increasingly determined by seniority, thus making chairmanships less subject to party control. Experience always had played a major role in making committee assignments, but as long as appointments to committees were made by ballot, rigid adherence to seniority was impossible. However, with the introduction of party lists in 1846 strict compliance with seniority began to be enforced. The bitter sectional disputes leading up to the Civil War may well have encouraged the use of seniority to avoid fierce inter-party struggles for committee control.

The system was not, of course, impartial in distributing its favors. In 1859 a northern Democrat called the use of seniority "intolerably bad" and complained that it had "operated to give to senators from slaveholding states the chairmanship of every single committee that controls the public business of this government. There is not one exception." [6] There had been one exception earlier that year, however; Stephen A. Douglas of Illinois chaired the Committee on Territories. But the Democratic Caucus took away his chairmanship, in spite of his seniority, because he refused to go along with President James Buchanan and the southern wing of the party on the question of allowing slavery in the territories.

By the time of the Civil War, the Senate's committee system had been transformed from a loose aggregation of ad hoc committees appointed for specific legislative purposes to a formal system of standing committees, whose members owed their appointments to the party organization and their advancement within committees to the seniority system.

Notes

1. Alexis de Tocqueville, *Democracy in America*, 2 vols. (New York: Shocken Books, 1967), I: 233-234.
2. George H. Haynes, *The Senate of the United States: Its History and Practice*, 2 vols. (Boston: Houghton-Mifflin, 1938), II: 1002.
3. W. E. Binkley, *The Powers of the President* (New York: Russell & Russell, 1973), p. 81.
4. Ibid., p. 86.
5. Franklin L. Burdette, *Filibustering in the Senate* (New York: Russell & Russell, 1965), pp. 22-25.
6. Haynes, *The Senate of the United States*, I: 298.

Chapter 21

PARTY GOVERNMENT: 1861-1901

From the 37th to the 43rd Congress (1861-1875), Republicans controlled the White House, the Senate and the House. Not only did the Democrats lose their southern seats in Congress, but many northern Democrats defected to the Republicans rather than remain in a party so closely identified with the southern cause. Republican hegemony during the Civil War and Reconstruction period was marked by a power struggle between Congress and the executive branch. Through such mechanisms as the Joint Committee on the Conduct of the War, consisting of three senators and four representatives, Congress sought to exercize its authority in the prosecution of the war. Yet President Abraham Lincoln managed not only to retain his independence from the legislative branch, but also to increase the armed forces, call for volunteers, spend money on defense, issue a code of regulations for the military, suspend the writ of habeas corpus, and even emancipate the slaves in the rebellious states — all without waiting for a go-ahead from Congress.

When the president in December 1863 announced to the newly convened 38th Congress his own reconstruction program, it promptly put together a sterner plan in the form of the Wade-Davis bill, which transferred Reconstruction powers to itself. Lincoln then pocket-vetoed the bill, an act that incensed the Radical Republicans dominating Congress. In response they issued the Wade-Davis Manifesto, which declared:

> [T]he authority of Congress is paramount and must be respected; that the body of Union men in Congress will not submit to be impeached by him [Lincoln] of rash and unconstitutional legislation; and if he wishes our support he must confine himself to his executive duties — to obey and execute, not to make the laws — to suppress by arms any armed rebellion, and leave political reorganization to Congress. [1]

Radical Republicanism

After Lincoln was assassinated, the Radical Republicans achieved their aims. They passed their own Reconstruction Act, overrode President Andrew Johnson's veto of a civil rights bill and set up Gen. Ulysses S. Grant as General of the Army in Washington, requiring all Army orders to be issued through him — thus bypassing the president as commander in chief — and forbidding the president to remove or transfer the general without prior consent of the Senate. Over Johnson's veto, Congress passed the Tenure of Office Act requiring Senate assent before the president could remove any government official appointed through its advice and consent power. When Johnson dismissed his secretary of war to test the constitutionality of the act in the courts, the House voted to impeach him. The Senate subsequently came within one vote of removing Johnson from office. Congress had broken the authority of the chief executive. Under a compliant President Ulysses S. Grant, the Republican Congress reigned supreme.

In this period of one-party government, the House, led by Radical Republican Thaddeus Stevens of Pennsylvania, overshadowed the Senate. But after the failure of the Republican effort to impeach Johnson, and Stevens' death in August 1868, House prestige declined, and the Senate became the dominant arm of the national legislature. During the remainder of the 19th century, while control of the House shifted back and forth between the two parties, the Republicans managed to maintain control of the Senate in all but two Congresses. It was in this era of relative stability that modern party government developed in the upper chamber.

Meanwhile, later presidents were able to recoup some of the power lost under Grant. With public support, Rutherford B. Hayes refused to let the Republican Senate dictate his Cabinet and customs appointments, and Grover Cleveland's defense of the presidential appointment power led to repeal of the Tenure of Office Act. On the whole, however, the Senate remained the most powerful force in the government. When William McKinley became president in 1897, Congress and the White House entered a period of almost unprecedented harmony. "We never had a president who had more influence with Congress than McKinley," said Sen. Shelby M. Cullom (R-Ill). "I have never heard of even the slightest friction between him and the party leaders in the Senate and House." [2]

Power of Party Bosses

The character of the Senate changed markedly in the post-Civil War era. Senate membership grew from 74 in 1871 to 90 in 1901, and, as state politics became more centralized, a new breed of senator entered the chamber. The great constitutional orators of the prewar period were succeeded by "party bosses" — professional politicians who had risen through the ranks of their state party organizations and who came to Washington only after they had consolidated their power over the state party structure. As long as they maintained state control, they were immune from external political reprisal, but their party loyalty and acceptance of the need for discipline made them good "party senators," willing to compromise their differences in order to maintain harmony within the party. To these men the Senate was a career, and a striking increase in average length of service occurred during this period.

The public viewed the Senate's changing character with suspicion, and the growing power of party organizations was widely attributed to the "trusts." In 1902 political analyst Moisei Ostrogorski charged that the economic interests "equipped and kept up political organizations for their own use, and ran them as they pleased, like their trains." [3] Other observers held that political centralization and business concentration were parallel developments, not directly related, but they agreed that the corporations contributed to the power of the party chiefs.

Lobbying by business groups became a vital element in government during the final decades of the 19th century, but business itself was not unified and its efforts were too haphazard for it to attain great political control. Still, some of the lobbying practices of the period — ranging from wholesale distribution of railroad passes to loans and sales of stock at attractive prices to members of Congress — fostered concern about corruption in the Senate.

The Senate's "usurpation" of executive power, its failure to limit debate by its members and internal corruption all contributed to a loss of public esteem in the institution. By the close of the 19th century, the Senate was derided as a "Millionaires' Club," and it was without question the most unpopular branch of the national government.

Dissatisfaction with the Senate led to demands for the direct election of senators, through which reformers hoped to curtail both the power of political parties and the political influence of the corporations. By 1900 it had become clear that a constitutional amendment providing for direct election eventually would be enacted.

Development of Party Leadership

Political parties already had assumed responsibility for organizational matters in the pre-Civil War Senate, and party authority was extended during the war to substantive questions as well. However, the Senate had no strong tradition of leadership, and party discipline was expected to lapse after the war ended. Indeed, the Republican and Democratic parties themselves were expected to disintegrate, as other parties had done before them, once the issues that had brought them together faded or were resolved.

Although the parties failed to dissolve, party influence in the upper chamber declined. When Grant's administration began in 1869, political parties compelled unity only on organizational questions. Disputes over committee assignments were settled in the caucus where pressing issues were discussed, but caucus decisions could hardly be considered binding as long as there was no leader to enforce discipline or exact reprisals. The Republican caucus did remove Charles Sumner of Massachusetts from the chairmanship of the Foreign Relations Committee in 1871 when his differences with President Grant had become so extreme that he refused to communicate with either the president or the secretary of state.

The possibilities of party leadership first became apparent in the Senate career of Republican Roscoe Conkling of New York. Conkling gathered around him a loyal following, and after 1873 his faction usually controlled the Committee on Committees and thus was able to reward his supporters with valuable committee posts. But the Conkling forces stood together only on organizational questions. Their influence on substantive legislation was minimal. When Conkling resigned his Senate seat in 1881, following an altercation with President James A. Garfield over executive appointments, the Senate reverted to its old independent ways. "No one," wrote Woodrow Wilson in 1885, "is *the* Senator. No one may speak for his party as well as for himself; no one exercises the special trust of acknowledged leadership. The Senate is merely a body of individual critics. . . ." [4]

Modern Party Discipline

Modern party discipline made its appearance in the Senate in the 1890s under the leadership of Repubican Sens. William B. Allison of Iowa, Nelson W. Aldrich of Rhode Island and their fellow members of the School of Philosophy Club, an informal group that met regularly for poker at the home of Michigan Sen. James McMillan. In March 1897 Allison, as the member of his party with the longest Senate service, was elected chairman of the Republican Caucus, a group that soon assumed control of the Senate. Previous caucus chairmen had not taken advantage of the office to solidify the party's control, but Allison was quick to see the possibilities of his new position. "Both in the committees and in the offices," he declared, "we should use the machinery for our own benefit and not let other men have it." [5]

A Republican Steering Committee had been appointed biennially since the mid-1880s to help schedule legislation. Unlike previous caucus leaders, Allison determined to chair this committee himself, and he filled it with like-minded members. Under Allison's guidance, the Steering Committee arranged the order of business in minute detail and managed proceedings on the floor. The Committee on Committees, which made committee assignments, also was controlled by Allison, who staffed it with a majority that would be receptive to his wishes.

Committee chairmanships were by this time invariably filled through seniority, and Allison and Aldrich made no attempt to overturn the seniority rule, to which they owed their own committee chairmanships (Allison on Appropriations and Aldrich on Finance). But seniority did not apply to the filling of committee vacancies, and here the party leaders found an opportunity to reward their supporters and punish dissidents. Access to positions of influence soon depended on the favor and support of the party leaders. When Albert J. Beveridge of Indiana entered the Senate in 1899, he directed his appeal for committee preferment to Allison, in shrewd recognition of the existing order. "I feel that the greatest single point is gained in the possession of your friendship," he told Allison. "I will labor very hard, strive very earnestly to deserve your consideration." [6]

Caucus approval of the committee slates and order of business became a mere formality, but the caucus still met to consider important issues. Compromises on divisive questions were forged in private caucus meetings, enabling the party to speak with a unified voice on the Senate floor. Caucus decisions were not formally binding —"We can get along without that," Allison remarked — but once the party leadership was capable of enforcing discipline on those who broke ranks, party solidarity became the norm. "Senators willing to abandon the opportunity to increase their authority could act freely, following their own inclinations," historian David Rothman noted. "The country might honor their names, but the Senate barely felt their presence." [7]

Under the leadership of Arthur P. Gorman of Maryland, Senate Democrats developed a power structure similar to that devised by the Republicans. As chairman of the Democratic Caucus in the 1890s, Gorman chaired both the Steering Committee and the Committee on Committees, but he never attained the power and influence wielded by Aldrich, his Republican counterpart. The Democrats were in the minority during most of this period, and they often split on substantive issues. The disharmony within Democratic ranks led to adoption in 1903 of a rule making the decisions of the Democratic Caucus binding on members upon a two-thirds vote. Allison considered such a rule unnecessary for the Republicans, but Gorman enthusiastically supported it.

Attitude Toward Party Control

The growth of party government was viewed with grave misgivings by the general public and was by no means welcomed unreservedly in the Senate itself. As early as 1872 the Liberal Republicans (dissidents opposed to the Grant administration) had protested efforts by "a few members of the Senate" to use the party organization to "control first a majority of the members belonging to that organization and then of the Senate." [8] Similar complaints of party coercion came in the 1880s from the Mugwumps (Republicans opposed to the party's leadership) and from the Populist Party in the 1890s.

The Senate in 1899 took one step to disperse authority within the chamber when it transferred responsibility for considering major appropriations bills from the Appropriations Committee to the various legislative committees. The change was promoted not in the party caucus but on the floor, where dissidents within both parties were able to prevail over the combined opposition of the Republican and Democratic leaders.

By the end of the 19th century, political parties had assumed a decisive role in the legislative process. The parties named the committees that made the initial decisions on proposed legislation, and they also determined what bills would be considered on the floor. When divisive issues arose, party members resolved their differences within the caucus and went forth in disciplined ranks to ratify caucus decisions on the floor, often acting without debate or the formality of a roll-call vote.

The Republicans had a plurality but not a majority in the Senate when a controversial tariff bill proposed by Rep. Nelson Dingley, Jr. (R-Maine) came from the House in April 1897. Allison, with the help of only the Republicans on the Senate Finance Committee, drafted new tariff schedules, which all but three of the panel's Republicans had agreed in advance to support. After limited debate in the caucus, the bill went to the Senate, where it was passed over solid Democratic opposition. The rigid party discipline maintained by Allison angered some Democrats. The Republicans, said Sen. Benjamin R. Tillman of South Carolina, "under the stress of party orders, I suppose, given by the caucus, sit by quietly and vote. They say nothing . . . and every schedule prepared by the party caucus is voted by them unanimously." [9] Tillman was wrong in only one particular: he credited the caucus with more influence than it actually had.

Election Law of 1866

For more than 75 years after the adoption of the Constitution, Congress took no advantage of its power to regulate congressional elections. The method of electing senators was left to the states. At first, senators generally were chosen by concurrent vote of the two houses of the state's legislature; a majority in each house had to agree on the candidates in order for them to be elected. Later, in about half the states it became common for the two houses, sitting together, to elect senators by joint ballot.

The election system had serious flaws. Insistence on a majority vote in each house caused frequent deadlocks that not only kept the legislature from considering other business but also caused the state to lose its representation in the Senate. Irregular practices abounded, and the Senate itself was forced to decide many election contests because of the lack of a uniform election law.

Accordingly, Congress in 1866 enacted legislation designed to correct these problems. The new law provided that the first ballot for senator was to be taken by the two houses of a state's legislature voting separately. If no candidate received a majority of the vote in both houses, then the two houses were to meet and ballot jointly until a majority choice emerged. The law also contained provisions for roll-call votes in the state legislatures (secret ballots had been the custom in some states) and for an election timetable requiring a minimum of one ballot on every legislative day until someone was elected. [10]

Senatorial elections were regulated by this law for almost half a century — until the adoption of the 17th Amendment in 1913 — but the measure was not a success. Historian George H. Haynes described many of the pitfalls of election by state legislatures that led to the direct election movement:

> ... not a few, but nearly half the states of the Union suffered from serious deadlocks. These contests, the outcome of which was often as much a matter of chance as would be the throw of dice, aroused men's worst passions and gave rise now to insistent charges of bribery, now to riot, to assault and to threats of bloodshed, such that legislative sessions had to be held under protection of martial law.
>
> Fourteen contests lasted throughout an entire session of the legislature without affecting an election. Four states submitted to the heavy cost and inconvenience of special sessions to select senators. Six states preferred to accept vacancies, thus losing their "equal suffrage in the Senate" while the country was deprived of a Senate constituted as the fathers had intended. At times legislative election led to positive and flagrant misrepresentation of the state in the Senate. To the individual state it brought a domination of state and local politics by the fierce fight for a single federal office, and interference with the work of lawmaking, ranging all the way from the exaction of a few hours of the legislators' time to the virtual annihilation of the legislature, which had been constituted to care for the interests of the state. [11]

Rise of the Filibuster

With the settlement of the slavery question, the oratorical splendor that had brought renown to the Senate in the years preceding the Civil War disappeared. For the remainder of the 19th century, Senate debate was not noted for its brilliance. Crucial legislative decisions were reached in party councils, and few floor speeches were made to sway votes. Attendance at formal Senate sessions became a tedious duty. "It would be a capital thing," wrote Republican Sen. George F. Hoar of Massachusetts in 1897, "to attend Unitarian conventions if there were not Unitarians there, so too it would be a delightful thing to be a United States Senator if you did not have to attend the sessions of the Senate." [12]

Filibusters, increasingly common as the century advanced, became a virtual epidemic in the 1880s and 1890s. Because of its failure to impose stringent curbs on debate, the Senate suffered a marked loss of public confidence. Proposals to limit filibusters were introduced periodically, but the Senate held fast to its cherished tradition of unlimited speech.

Wartime pressures had produced two notable filibusters during the 1860s. One in 1863 was sparked by a measure to protect the president against loss in any action brought against him for having suspended the writ of habeus corpus. But the talkathon in the closing hours of the session failed when the presiding officer, in the face of obvious obstructionism, called for a vote and refused to entertain an appeal. Sen. Lyman Trumbull (R-Ill.) thus described the tactics of the bill's opponents: "Motion after motion was made here last night to lay on the table, to postpone indefinitely, to adjourn, to adjourn, to adjourn and to adjourn again, and the yeas and nays called on each occasion." [13] Similar tactics were employed by Sen. Sumner in 1865 against a move to readmit Louisiana into the Union. He felt so strongly about the issue that he declared himself "justified in employing all the instruments that I find in the arsenal of parliamentary warfare." [14]

Proposals by Democrats to suspend or repeal statutes authorizing the use of federal troops to supervise state elections were the subject of the next great filibusters in 1876 and 1879. In the 1879 filibuster, Republicans relied on dilatory motions, roll-call votes and refusal to answer quorum calls, whereupon the Senate's president pro tempore ruled that he could determine whether enough senators were present to constitute a quorum.

In a famous filibuster in 1881, the Democratic minority prevented the Republicans from organizing the Senate until the resignations of two senators — Roscoe Conkling and Thomas C. Platt of New York — had given the Democrats numerical control. The filibuster made it impossible for the upper chamber to take action on any legislation from March 24 to May 16 of that year.

In 1890 a bill to provide federal aid to education, sponsored by Sen. Henry W. Blair (R-N.H.), was filibustered for more than 20 days by Blair himself. Believing he had won sufficient support for passage, Blair finally permitted the bill to come to a vote, but two senators at the last minute decided to vote against it. The bill was defeated, 31-37, with Blair voting nay in order to be eligible under Senate rules to move to reconsider the bill, but the measure was never revived.

A filibuster against the so-called "Force Bill" — authorizing federal supervision at polling places during national elections to prevent exclusion of black voters in southern states — lasted from Dec. 2, 1890, to Jan. 26, 1891. After seven weeks of debate, the bill's supporters tried to put through a Senate rule providing for majority cloture (allowing a majority of the Senate to end a filibuster). When that strategy failed, the Senate was held in continuous session for four days and nights in an effort to exhaust the filibusterers. After 33 days of obstruction, the bill was dropped to permit the enactment of vital appropriation bills before the 51st Congress expired in March 1891. During the filibuster, West Virginia Democrat C. J. Faulkner nominally held the floor for 11 and a half hours, although for nearly eight hours of that time he was relieved of the necessity of speaking because a quorum was not present to conduct business.

In 1893 a filibuster against repeal of the 1890 Silver Purchase Act lasted from Aug. 29 to Oct. 24. After 46 days of filibustering, including a period of 13 continuous day-and-night sittings, the repeal was passed on Oct. 30. Nebraska Populist William V. Allen, who held the floor without interruptions for 14 hours, set a new record. Allen's filibuster aroused widespread public concern over the conduct and viability of the Senate. "To vote without debating is perilous, but to debate and never vote is imbecile," wrote Sen. Henry Cabot Lodge (R-Mass.) shortly after the struggle ended. "As it is, there must be a change, for the delays which now take place are discrediting the Senate.... A body which cannot govern itself will not long hold the respect of the people who have chosen it to govern the country. . . ." [15]

Montana Republican Thomas H. Carter, who was about to retire from the Senate in a few hours, filibustered against a "pork-barrel" rivers and harbors bill from the night of March 3 until the Senate adjourned *sine die* at noon March 4, 1901 (legislative day of March 3). The bill was a raid on the Treasury, Carter claimed, and he was performing a "public service" in preventing it from becoming law. He readily yielded for other business but resumed his item-by-item denunciation of the bill whenever necessary. No determined attempt was made to stop him, and the bill died. [16]

Although the early filibusters had not been notably successful, senators gradually shifted to bolder techniques in the second half of the 19th century. By the beginning of the 20th century the filibuster had assumed scandalous proportions. This was, says historian Franklin Burdette, "the heyday of brazen and unblushing aggressors. The power of the Senate lay not in votes but in sturdy tongues and iron wills. The premium rested not upon ability and statesmanship but upon effrontery and audacity." [17]

Filibusters in Congress . . .

Filibustering is the practice by which a minority of a legislative body employs extended debate and dilatory tactics to delay or block action favored by the majority. The word filibuster is derived from the Dutch word *Vrijbuiter*, meaning freebooter. Passing into Spanish as *filibustero*, it was used to describe military adventurers from the United States who in the mid-1800s fomented insurrections against various Latin American governments.*

The first parliamentary use of the word is said to have occurred in the House in 1853, when a representative accused his opponents of "filibustering against the United States." ** By 1863 filibuster had come to mean delaying action on the floor, but the term was not widely used until the 1880s.

Although the word "filibuster" as applied to legislative obstruction is relatively new, the tactics it describes are as old as parliamentary government. What are now called filibusters occurred in the Colonial assemblies, and obstructive tactics were a feature of Congress from its earliest days. A bill to establish a "permanent residence" for the national government was subjected to a House filibuster early in the First Congress. When the same bill reached the Senate, Pennsylvania's Sen. William Maclay complained that "the design of the Virginians and the South Carolina gentlemen was to talk away the time so that we could not get the bill passed." ***

Obstruction in the House

Legislative obstruction was characteristic of the House long before it became common in the Senate. But the unwieldy size of the lower chamber's membership soon led to various curbs on debate. A motion adopted by the House in 1789, known as the previous question, has been used since 1811 to close debate and bring a matter under consideration to an immediate vote.

Under a 1798 rule, House members are permitted to speak only once during general debate, and for a specified period of time. Since 1847 debate

Senate Rules on Debate

The House must approve its rules at the beginning of each new Congress since its entire membership is elected anew every two years. But the Senate, which is considered a continuing body because only one-third

... An Age-Old Practice

on amendments has been limited to five minutes for each side, and since 1880 a rule of relevancy has been enforced by the Speaker. These limitations on debate curbed the practice of filibustering in the House, although delaying tactics continued to be used from time to time.

Obstruction in the Senate

The Senate, with its cherished tradition of unlimited debate, offered a more favorable climate for obstructionist tactics. By the end of the 19th century the upper chamber had become notorious as the home of the filibuster.

The first notable Senate filibuster occurred in 1841, when dissident senators held the floor for 10 days in opposition to a bill to shift the Senate's printing to new contractors. In the next 40 years filibusters were undertaken with increasing frequency, but usually they were not successful. In the last two decades of the 19th century, the practice assumed almost epidemic proportions, and as filibusterers used more daring techniques their rate of success increased.

The most important tool of the filibusterer, once he or she has gained control of the floor proceedings, is continued talk, for which a strong physical constitution is a prerequisite. Other techniques are dilatory motions, roll-call votes, quorum calls, points of order and appeals and the interjection of other business. Successful use of these devices calls for in-depth knowledge of parliamentary procedure. Senators with less than expert knowledge are likely to rely on talk, because a parliamentary blunder could spell defeat for their cause.

*Robert Luce, *Legislative Procedure: Parliamentary Practices and the Course of Business in the Framing of Statutes* (New York: Da Capo Press, 1972), p. 283.
**George B. Galloway, *The Legislative Process in Congress* (New York: Thomas Y. Crowell Co., 1953), pp. 559-560.
***Franklin L. Burdette, *Filibustering in the Senate* (New York: Russell & Russell, 1965), p. 14.

of its membership is newly elected at a time, faces no such task. Its rules remain in force from Congress to Congress unless the Senate decides to change them. Many revisions of the Senate's rules have occurred since the first rules were adopted in 1789, but these revisions have been chiefly codifications of changes that accumulated over a number of years.

Two such codifications occurred in the 1861-1901 period. The first, in 1868, increased the number of rules to an all-time high of 53, reflecting the wartime strains. Another codification, in 1884, reduced the number of rules to 40. Although many changes were made in the Senate's rules after 1884, another codification was not to take place for another 95 years.

"Rules are never observed in this body; they are only made to be broken. We are a law unto ourselves," said Republican John J. Ingalls of Kansas in 1876.[18] His comment may help to explain why rules reform has not played as significant a role in the history of the Senate as it has in the House, though efforts to limit the Senate filibuster provide a notable exception. In the last half of the 19th century many proposals were introduced to curtail debate, either through use of the previous question motion employed by the House or by some other means. Most of the proposals simply were ignored, but a few minor changes affecting debate were made.

"In consideration in secret session of subjects relating to the rebellion," the Senate resolved in 1862, "debate should be confined to the subject matter and limited to five minutes, except that five minutes be allowed any Member to explain or oppose a pertinent amendment."[19] Adoption of this resolution was attributable to the exigencies of wartime. In later years it also became customary for the Senate, at the end of a session when the need for haste was great, to apply a five-minute limit on debate on appropriations bills.

In 1870 the Senate adopted the Anthony Rule named after its originator, Sen. Henry B. Anthony (R-R.I.). The rule was the most important limitation on debate the Senate had yet agreed to as a means of expediting business. The rule was so successful in speeding action on non-controversial legislation that in 1880 it became part of the Standing Rules, where it now appears as Rule VIII:

> At the conclusion of the morning business for each day, unless upon motion the Senate shall at any time otherwise order, the Senate will proceed to the consideration of the Calendar of Bills and Resolutions, and continue such consideration until 2 o'clock; and bills and resolutions that are not objected to shall be taken up in their order, and each senator shall be entitled to speak once and for five minutes only upon any question; and the objection may be interposed at any stage of the proceedings, but upon motion the Senate may continue such consideration; and this order shall commence immediately after the call for "concurrent and other

resolutions," and shall take precedence of the unfinished business and other special orders. But if the Senate shall proceed with the consideration of any matter notwithstanding an objection, the foregoing provisions touching debate shall not apply.[20]

The Anthony Rule greatly speeded the handling of routine measures without prejudice to the right of senators to demand longer debate on controversial bills. Another change that helped to speed Senate business was an 1875 decision that action on an amendment to an appropriation bill could be postponed without jeopardizing or affecting the status of the bill itself. This rule was so successful that its application later was extended to amendments to any bill being considered by the Senate.

Notes

1. W. E. Binkley, *The Powers of the President* (New York: Russell & Russell, 1973), pp. 130-133.
2. Ibid., p. 207.
3. David J. Rothman, *Politics and Power: The United States Senate 1869-1901* (Cambridge, Mass.: Harvard University Press, 1966), p. 188.
4. Woodrow Wilson, *Congressional Government* (1885; reprint ed., Cleveland: Meridian, 1956), p. 147.
5. Rothman, *Politics and Power*, p. 44.
6. Ibid., pp. 56-57.
7. Ibid., p. 60.
8. Ibid., pp. 24-25.
9. Ibid., p. 97.
10. George H. Haynes, *The Senate of the United States: Its History and Practice*, 2 vols. (Boston: Houghton-Mifflin, 1938), I: 85.
11. Ibid., I: 95.
12. Rothman, *Politics and Power*, p. 146.
13. *Congressional Globe*, 37th Cong., 3rd sess., March 3, 1863, p. 1491.
14. *Congressional Globe*, 38th Cong., 2nd sess., Feb. 25, 1865, p. 1108.
15. Haynes, *The Senate of the United States*, I: 398-399.
16. Ibid., I: 400
17. Franklin L. Burdette, *Filibustering in the Senate* (New York: Russell & Russell, 1965), p. 80.
18. George B. Galloway, *The Legislative Process in Congress* (New York: Thomas Y. Crowell Co., 1953), p. 542.
19. Haynes, *The Senate of the United States*, I: 395.
20. Ibid., I: 395-396.

Chapter 22

ERA OF REFORM: 1901-1921

The "Progressive Era" in American history began with movements for economic reform in the 1880s and 1890s, gathered momentum and a radical democratic character after the turn of the century and gradually faded into the background during World War I. The platform of the Populist Party, which in 1892 polled more than a million votes for its presidential candidate, James B. Weaver, foreshadowed the progressive program. Although the party, centered in the agrarian Midwest and West, soon declined, many of its programs were adopted by the two major parties.

Some of the first "progressive" legislation passed by Congress included civil service reform (1883), the Interstate Commerce Act (1887), the Sherman Antitrust Act (1890), conservation legislation (1891) and an income tax law (1894). But the Supreme Court declared the income tax invalid in 1895 (*Pollock v. Farmers' Loan and Trust Co.*), and other measures were rendered ineffective by their vague language and loopholes, by court rulings and by unenthusiastic administration by the executive branch. Frustrated by these setbacks, which they blamed on the influence of vested interests, reformers concluded that more democratic control of the government was necessary to secure the laws they sought. Accordingly, the reform movement turned to institutional changes such as direct election of senators, direct primaries, women's suffrage and laws against corrupt election practices.

The power of the Senate declined during Theodore Roosevelt's presidency from 1901 to 1909. Roosevelt was an aggressive national leader who took an active role in championing progressive reforms. Although the House at this time was under the highly centralized rule of Speaker Joseph G. Cannon (R-Ill.), Roosevelt, through informal contacts with the leadership, was able to advance his legislative program. Under Cannon the House often tried to exert its authority over the Senate. By

1910, however, House reformers were strong enough to break the power of the Speaker.

Insurgent Movements in Congress

Congress went along, though somewhat reluctantly, with Roosevelt's progressive program, passing such measures as the Hepburn Act that strengthened the Interstate Commerce Commission, the pure food and drug laws and a workmen's compensation measure. But Republican William Howard Taft, who was elected president in 1908, failed to press for progressive reforms in the face of Old Guard opposition. The defeat of major legislation sought by progressives in both parties fueled an insurgent movement among western Republicans in Congress.

In the House, Republican insurgents led the revolt against Speaker Cannon, while in the Senate the "Band of Six" — Robert M. La Follette of Wisconsin, Albert J. Beveridge of Indiana, Jonathan P. Dolliver and Albert B. Cummins of Iowa, Francis Bristow of Kansas and Edwin Clapp of Minnesota — challenged the Nelson W. Aldrich machine on a tariff bill that Finance Chairman Aldrich had sponsored. Though they were unsuccessful in their efforts to defeat the bill, enactment of this distinctly protectionist measure led to resounding Republican defeats in the 1910 congressional elections and the formation of the Progressive (Bull Moose) Party, which nominated Roosevelt for president in 1912. The split between the Roosevelt and Taft wings of the Republican Party handed the Democrats an easy victory; under President Woodrow Wilson the government entered a period of progressive rule that lasted through most of Wilson's first term.

Wilson and Progressive Legislation

Wilson's relations with Congress at the beginning of his first term were harmonious. He returned to the pre-Jeffersonian practice of addressing Congress in person and frequently conferred with committees or individual members in the president's room in the Capitol. Under his leadership a caucus of Democratic senators was proposed in 1913 to marshal party support for a tariff-cutting bill sponsored by Oscar W. Underwood of Alabama. Other legislative victories included the income tax (made valid by a constitutional amendment submitted to the states in 1909 and belatedly ratified on the eve of Wilson's inauguration in 1913), direct election of senators, the Clayton Antitrust Act and the Federal Reserve and Federal Trade Commission acts.

This flow of progressive legislation ended when the United States entered World War I in 1917. During the war, Wilson assumed almost dictatorial powers over Congress, and criticism of his policies was muted. But with the president's ill-timed appeal for election of a Democratic Congress in the fall of 1918, the opposition surfaced. In the ensuing election, Republicans captured control of both houses of Congress, and the president went off to the Paris Peace Conference a rejected hero. Wilson's health broke in his futile efforts to enlist American support for the League of Nations, and the Republican Senate first emasculated and then rejected the Treaty of Versailles in which the League Covenant was embedded. With the election of a Republican Congress in 1918, a new period of congressional hegemony was at hand.

The 17th Amendment providing for direct election of senators undoubtedly was the most important development in the evolution of the Senate during the early 20th century, but there also were other significant changes. Political parties began to assume their modern place in the legislative structure, and as party leadership roles became institutionalized, formally identifiable majority and minority leaders emerged. With the admission of Arizona to statehood in 1912, the membership of the Senate increased to 96; no further changes in size would occur for nearly half a century. Finally, in 1917 the Senate was driven by the excesses of filibustering to adopt its first cloture (anti-debate) rule, permitting two-thirds of those senators present and voting to bring debate to a close.

Direct Election of Senators

'The Senate of the United States shall be composed of two Senators from each State, chosen by the Legislature thereof, for six years." Thus begins Article I, Section 3, of the Constitution. But in 1913, in response to popular pressure for more democratic control of government, the 17th Amendment providing for direct election of senators was ratified.

Being less immediately dependent on popular sentiment than the House, the Senate did not seek to reform itself. Only strong pressure from the public, expressed through the House, the state governments, pressure groups, petitions, referenda and other means, convinced the Senate that it must reform. It was common in this period to attribute legislative disappointments to behind-the-scenes dealings of vested interests. A Senate chosen by state legislatures, whose decisions often were made in closed-door party caucuses, could not easily escape suspicion. Moreover, the high-tariff views of the Senate served to link this body in the public mind with the great corporations that were widely accused of improper political influence.

History of Senate Election Reform. Andrew Johnson, who as president came within one vote of removal from office at the hands of the Senate, was an early advocate of Senate election reform. Twice as a representative, once as a senator and again as president in 1868, Johnson presented resolutions calling for direct election of senators. In the first 80 years of Congress, nine resolutions proposing a constitutional amendment to that effect were introduced in Congress. In the 1870s and 1880s the number increased significantly, but it was not until 1892 that a proposal for direct election of senators was approved in a House committee. In the next decade similar resolutions were passed five times by the House with only minor opposition. But the proposed amendment to the Constitution was not allowed to reach a vote in the Senate until 1911.

Petitions from farmers' associations and other organizations, particularly in the West, and party platforms in state elections pressured Congress until the national parties took it up. Direct election of senators was a plank in the Populist Party program in every election, beginning in 1892, and in the Democratic platform in each presidential election campaign from 1900 to 1912. Beginning with California and Iowa in 1894, state legislatures addressed Congress in favor of a constitutional amendment mandating direct election of the Senate. By 1905 the legislatures in 31 of the 45 states had taken this step, many of them on several occasions. Support was strongest in the West and North Central states, where every legislature petitioned Congress at least once, and weakest in the Northeast, where only Pennsylvania's legislature voted to address Congress in support of direct election. In 1900, when the House approved a constitutional amendment for direct election of senators by a vote of 240-15, it was favored by a majority of representatives from every state except Maine and Connecticut. [1]

Still the Senate did not act. Understandably, senators were wary of changing the way they were elected, and between 1902 and 1911 even the House did not vote on resolutions for direct election. But the states began to find ways to circumvent the need for a constitutional amendment. The spread of direct primaries in the 1890s led in many states to expressions of popular choice of senator on the primary ballot. Although not legally binding on the legislatures, the popular choice was likely to be accepted. In southern states the primary winners soon were being "elected" by the one-party legislatures almost as a matter of course. But in states that did not have a one-party system, and especially in those states lacking clearly defined party lines, primaries were less effective in guaranteeing that the popular choice would be ratified by the legislature.

Oregon led the way in devising a system to guarantee popular choice of senators in spite of the Constitution's assignment of this function exclusively to the legislatures. In 1901 an Oregon law was enacted enabling voters to express their choice for senator in the same manner as they voted for governor, except that the vote for senator had no legal force. But the law specified that when the legislature assembled to elect a senator, "it shall be the duty of each house to count the votes and announce the candidate having the highest number, and thereupon the houses shall proceed to the election of a senator." In the first test of this system, the man who led the field with 37 percent of the popular vote for senator secured scant support from the legislators, who scattered their votes among 14 candidates. After a five-week deadlock, the legislature chose a man who had not received a single vote in the popular election.

Far from being discouraged at this mockery of "the people's choice," the people of Oregon in 1904 used their new initiative and referendum powers to petition for and approve a new law. Henceforth, each candidate for senator was to be nominated by petition and allowed to include on the petition a 100-word statement of principles and on the ballot a 12-word statement to be printed after the candidate's name. The legislators, who could not be denied their constitutional power to name senators, were permitted to include in their nomination petitions their signatures on either "Statement No. 1" or "Statement No. 2." The former pledged the signer always to vote "for that candidate for United States Senator in Congress who has received the highest number of the people's votes ... without regard to my individual preference." The second statement was a pledge to regard the popular vote "as nothing more than a recommendation, which I shall be at liberty to wholly disregard...." Meanwhile, citizen groups circulated pledges, which were widely subscribed to, that the signer would not support or vote for any candidate to the legislature who did not endorse "Statement No. 1."

The first Oregon legislature elected after enactment of this law promptly ratified the "people's choice" for senator. And two years later, when 83 of the 90 members of the legislature were Republicans, the popular choice — a Democrat — was elected. He received 53 votes, including all 52 who had endorsed "Statement No. 1."

Other states adopted the "Oregon System" in modified form. By December 1910 it was estimated that 14 of the 30 senators about to be selected by state legislatures already had been designated by popular vote. [2]

Constitutional Amendment. Gradually the pressure for Senate election reform nationwide began to be felt in the Senate. Some of the senators themselves were products of the new form of popular election. The leader in the fight for the 17th Amendment, Sen. William E. Borah (R-Idaho), had entered the Senate through a popular mandate after an earlier defeat by the Idaho legislature.

By 1901 some state legislatures no longer were content to request Congress to submit a constitutional amendment to the states. They called for a convention to amend the Constitution, a method as yet untried in American history but obligatory once two-thirds of the states so petition Congress. Some senators opposed to popular election feared that such a convention, like the original Constitutional Convention in Philadelphia, might exceed its original mandate. Therefore, they agreed to vote for a specific amendment for direct election of senators that would be submitted to the states for ratification.

When a resolution embodying the constitutional amendment was referred to the Senate Judiciary Committee, rather than to the more hostile Committee on Privileges and Elections that had considered it on previous occasions, a favorable vote was at last obtained on Jan. 1, 1911. However, the resolution contained a committee amendment, supported by southern senators, modifying Congress' power under Article I, Section 4, to alter state regulations governing the "Times" and "Manner" of Senate and House elections.

The amendment provoked such a storm of controversy that at times it overshadowed the popular election issue itself. The amendment would have transferred to the states exclusive power to regulate the election of senators, while leaving unchanged Congress' power to regulate House elections. But northern opposition prevailed, and the committee amendment was dropped. On Feb. 28, 1911, the resolution itself failed to secure the necessary two-thirds majority support.[3]

In a special session later that year, the House passed the direct election resolution again, by a 296-16 vote. But the House version was the same as that reported by the Senate committee, giving the states exclusive power to regulate Senate elections. The Senate, on a 45-44 roll call decided by Vice President James S. Sherman's tie-breaking vote, again rejected the committee amendment and this time adopted the original resolution by the required two-thirds majority, 64-24. A deadlock between the two houses was broken in the next session, and on May 13, 1912, the House concurred in the Senate version, 238-39. By May 31, 1913, three-fourths of the states had ratified the amendment.[4]

The immediate effects of the 17th Amendment were difficult to assess. Even before its adoption, the direct primary movement had diminished the power of the legislatures. By 1913 three-fourths of the candidates for the Senate were being nominated in direct primaries. The terms of the senators in office at the time the amendment was ratified ended variously in 1915, 1917 and 1919, so the 66th Congress (1919-1921) was the first in which all members of the Senate were the products of direct election. As Senate historian George B. Galloway points out:

> By that time, 56 of the senators who owed their togas originally to state legislatures had been re-elected by the people, three had died, and 37 had disappeared from the scene either voluntarily or by popular verdict. In other words, more than half of those last chosen by legislative caucus were subsequently approved by the people. [5]

Restraining the Filibuster

Senate filibusters continued apace in the early 1900s, and with a high degree of success. But mounting opposition to the practice led, in 1908, to efforts to curb obstructionism through new interpretations of the rules and, in 1917, to the Senate's first cloture rule.

Meanwhile, 1903 proved to be a vintage year for the filibuster. Democratic Sen. Benjamin R. ("Pitchfork Ben") Tillman of South Carolina filibustered against an appropriation bill until an item for payment of war claims to his state was restored. The item was put back in the bill after Tillman threatened to read Byron's "Childe Harold" and other poems into the record until his colleagues surrendered from boredom.

While Tillman resorted to "legislative blackmail," in the words of House Speaker Cannon, Republican Sen. Beveridge chose a different method. Beveridge, chairman of the Territories Committee and an opponent of statehood for Arizona and New Mexico, initially led a filibuster against an omnibus statehood bill. Then, taking advantage of a custom that no votes were taken on a measure in the absence of the chairman of the committee that had handled it, Beveridge hid for days in Washington and finally slipped away to Atlantic City. The bill ultimately was dropped.

In 1908 a bitter two-day filibuster against an emergency currency measure sponsored by Sen. Aldrich and Rep. Edward B. Vreeland (R-N.Y.) brought the first significant steps to curb dilatory tactics. Wisconsin Republican Robert M. La Follette, Sr., had held the floor for 18 hours and 23 minutes (a record that stood until 1938), although he was interrupted by 29 quorum calls and three roll calls on questions of order. La Follette fortified himself periodically with eggnogs from the Senate restaurant. According to one account, he rejected one of the eggnogs as doped, and it later was found to contain a fatal dose of ptomaine. However, no charge of deliberate poisoning was ever made.

The filibusterers' cause finally was lost when Sen. Thomas P. Gore (D-Okla.), who was blind, yielded the floor believing that Sen. William J. Stone (D-Mo.), who was scheduled to relieve him, was in the chamber. But Stone had been called to the cloakroom, and Gore surrendered the floor. The bill then was approved on a hastily demanded roll call.

Three important rulings on obstruction resulted from the 1908 filibuster: 1) the chair could count a quorum if enough senators were present, even for a vote, whether or not they answered to a quorum call; 2) debate did not count as intervening business for the purpose of deciding if another quorum call was in order; and 3) senators could by enforcement of existing rules be prevented from speaking more than twice on the same subject in one day.

During a 1914 Republican filibuster against a rivers and harbors bill, the chair ruled that senators holding the floor could not yield for any purpose, even for a question, without unanimous consent. The Senate first tabled an appeal of this ruling on a 28-24 vote but reversed itself the next day. Thus the rule remained unchanged.

In 1915 a successful filibuster was organized against President Wilson's ship purchase bill. Republican Sen. Reed Smoot of Utah spoke for 11 hours and 35 minutes without relief and without deviating from the subject. After almost a month of delay, seven Democrats who thought the filibuster should give way to other important legislation joined the Republicans in moving that the bill be recommitted. But other Democrats supporting the bill then staged a five-day reverse filibuster until they regained control of the chamber. The Republican filibuster then was renewed. A Democratic motion to end debate was blocked, and the bill finally was dropped. As a result of the filibuster three important appropriation bills failed.

Eleven Willful Men

The public was disgusted by this episode, but it took one more great filibuster to force the Senate into action. The occasion came in 1917 when the Wilson administration's armed neutrality bill was talked to death by an 11-man bloc in the closing days of the 64th Congress. Seventy-five senators who signed a statement supporting the bill asked that it be entered in the record "to establish that the Senate favors the legislation and would pass it, if a vote could be had." [6]

Not all of the obstruction came from the Republican side of the aisle. On the last day of the session, when it was clear that the bill was doomed, the Democrats staged their own filibuster to keep an outraged La Follette from being able to speak against the measure before crowded Senate galleries.

No sooner had the session ended than Wilson issued this angry statement:

> The Senate of the United States is the only legislative body in the world which cannot act when its majority is ready for action. A little group of willful men, representing no opinion but their own, have rendered the great government of the United States helpless and contemptible. . . .

He immediately called the Senate into special session and demanded that it amend its rules so that it could act and "save the country from disaster." [7] The Senate yielded, and a conference of Republican and Democratic leaders hastily drew up the Senate's first cloture rule. After only six hours of debate, Rule 22 was adopted by the chamber March 8, 1917, by a vote of 76 to 3.

Rule 22 Limits Debate

The new rule restricted debate on any pending measure once a debate-limiting resolution was approved by two-thirds of senators present and voting. (The vote on the resolution was to be held two days after a cloture motion had been signed by 16 senators.) After such a resolution was agreed to, further debate was limited to one hour for each senator on the bill itself and on all amendments and motions affecting it. No new amendments could be offered except by unanimous consent.

Amendments that were not germane to the pending business, and amendments and motions clearly designed to delay action, were out of order.

During Senate debate on the proposed Rule 22, an amendment was offered to authorize cloture by majority vote instead of a two-thirds vote. But the amendment was attacked as a breach of faith by opponents and was withdrawn before a vote could be taken. In 1918 the Senate rejected, 34-41, a proposal to allow use of the so-called "previous question" motion to limit debate during the war period.

For a time it looked as if the Senate would never make use of its new tool against obstructionism, but the interminable debates on the Treaty of Versailles in 1919 finally provided an occasion. The Senate adopted its first cloture motion Nov. 15, 1919, on a 78-16 roll call, and four days later the treaty itself was brought to a vote after 55 days of debate.

Party Leadership

The system of party leadership that had evolved in the Senate at the end of the 19th century became institutionalized in the early years of the 20th with the creation of formally designated majority and minority leadership positions.

For many years both Republicans and Democrats had elected chairmen of their party caucuses, but each party's caucus chairman was not necessarily the actual leader of his party in the Senate. Sens. William B. Allison (R-Iowa) and Arthur P. Gorman (D-Md.) served as chairmen of their respective caucuses, but the position was not essential to their control. Aldrich, the most powerful member of the Senate until his retirement in 1911 after 30 years of service, never held any official position in the Senate other than the chairmanship of the Senate Finance Committee.

With the departure of these dynamic leaders from the chamber, power was fragmented within the parties. It became common for Republicans and Democrats to elect a different floor leader in each session, and the floor leadership did not necessarily correspond with the caucus chairmanship. Under these conditions party unity was hard to maintain.

In 1911 the Democrats — already in control of the House and looking forward to the election of a Democratic Senate in 1912 — instituted the practice of electing a single, readily identifiable leader to

245

hold the dual posts of floor leader and chairman of the party caucus. The Republicans, threatened by insurgents within their ranks, took a similar course in 1913. Subsequently, party whips (assistant floor leaders) were added to the leadership structure: in 1913 by the Democrats and in 1915 by the Republicans. From then on, the majority and minority leaders usually were the acknowledged spokesmen for their parties in the Senate.

The importance of the leadership role was underscored in 1913 when progressive Democrats deposed conservative leader Sen. Thomas S. Martin of Virginia and engineered the election of Indiana Sen. John W. Kern as majority leader, even though Kern had served in the Senate only two years. The Steering Committee, appointed by Kern and dominated by progressives, made committee assignments in such a way as to ensure that major committees would be sympathetic to the incoming Wilson administration's programs. Even seniority was ignored when necessary. The Steering Committee also recommended rules, later adopted by the caucus, that permitted a majority of committee members to call meetings, elect subcommittees and appoint conferees. Thus party authority was augmented, and the power of committee chairmen curbed in a movement that somewhat paralleled the revolt against Cannonism in the House.

Both parties at the turn of the century had replaced the title "caucus" with "conference," in formal recognition of the non-binding nature of these party meetings. The Democratic Caucus in 1903 had adopted a binding caucus rule, but when Kern in 1913 proposed holding a binding caucus on the tariff bill, opposition was so vigorous that the idea had to be dropped. The compromise finally achieved preserved the appearance of a non-binding "conference," though Democratic senators during this period were under such strong pressure to support caucus decisions that the effect of a binding caucus was maintained.

Notes

1. George H. Haynes, *The Senate of the United States: Its History and Practice*, 2 vols. (Boston: Houghton-Mifflin, 1938), I: 96-98.
2. Ibid., I: 100-104.
3. Ibid., I: 111-112.
4. Ibid., I: 112-115.
5. George B. Galloway, *Congress at the Crossroads* (New York: Thomas Y. Crowell Co., 1946), p. 38.
6. Haynes, *The Senate of the United States*, I: 402.
7. Ibid., I: 402-403.

Chapter 23

REPUBLICAN STALEMATE: 1921-1933

After its victory over Woodrow Wilson on the League of Nations, the Senate was in no mood to submit to presidential leadership. The Republican majority expected to assume control of the government in the Republican administrations that followed Wilson, but after the House revamped its appropriations procedures in 1920 the lower chamber increasingly challenged Senate primacy.

Wilson's three Republican successors, faithful to the GOP doctrine of congressional independence, made little effort to direct Congress in legislative matters. Wilson's immediate successor, Warren G. Harding, promised before his election in 1920 that he would take a hands-off approach with respect to lawmaking and that the Senate would "have something to say about the foreign relations, as the Constitution contemplates." He would "rather have the counsel of the Senate," Harding added, "than all the political bosses in any party." [1]

An ex-senator, Harding appeared before his former colleagues on several occasions. In an unprecedented move in 1921, he personally delivered his nominations for Cabinet positions to the Senate. But he came to regret his promise not to intervene in legislative matters. When he appeared before the Senate in 1921 to urge a balanced budget, the Senate berated him for interfering in its business, and the House was offended that the issue had not been raised in that chamber, where money bills had to originate. Harding's subsequent halfhearted efforts to exert leadership were rebuffed by Congress, and his administration was tarnished by scandals that were exposed by Senate investigators after his death in 1923.

Harding's successor, Calvin Coolidge, was even less inclined to direct congressional action than Harding had been. "I have never felt that it was my duty to attempt to coerce senators or representatives, or to make reprisals," Coolidge wrote. "The people sent them to Washington.

I felt I had discharged my duty when I had done the best I could with them."[2] The Senate rejected Coolidge's nomination of Charles Beecher Warren as attorney general, the first rejection of a Cabinet nomination since 1868, but in other respects it largely ignored the passive president.

More aggressive leadership was expected of President Herbert Hoover, but he lacked political experience and, as a recent convert to Republicanism, was distrusted by many members of his own party. Friction between the executive and legislative branches thwarted Hoover's efforts to end the economic depression that engulfed the nation early in his one term in office (1929-1933).

If the presidents of the 1920s were unable to lead the nation, Congress itself was not much more successful. Although Republicans controlled the White House from 1921 to 1933, the House from 1919 to 1931 and the Senate from 1919 to 1933, the party solidarity that had characterized the McKinley-Roosevelt presidencies no longer existed. Throughout the 1920s a "progressive" farm bloc dominated by western Republicans held the balance of power in Congress, and the decade was marked by persistent deadlocks on major issues.

Meanwhile, significant internal changes were taking place in the Senate. In 1921 the chamber consolidated its committee system and passed the Budget and Accounting Act, which returned to the Appropriations Committee exclusive authority over spending. In 1932 the Senate finally succeeded in winning House concurrence to the so-called "lame-duck" amendment altering the terms and sessions of Congress. Before the adoption of the 20th Amendment to the Constitution in 1933, Congress was required to meet annually in December. When Congress met in December of an even-numbered year, following the election of the succeeding Congress, it could remain in session until March 4 of the following year, when the term of the new Congress began. During this short or lame-duck session — in which members who had been defeated at the polls participated — filibusters were common. The amendment's sponsor, Sen. George W. Norris (R-Neb.), hoped that eliminating the lame-duck session would reduce the filibusters that had plagued the Senate in the 1920s. But of the nine cloture votes taken during that decade, only three succeeded.

Republican Insurgency

Farmers did not share in the prosperity of the 1920s, and congressional efforts to enact agricultural relief legislation split eastern and western Republicans in Congress and led to the establishment of a powerful bipartisan farm bloc. Although insurgent Republicans, mostly from the Great Plains and Rocky Mountain areas, maintained formal ties to the Republican Party, they cooperated with the Democrats on sectional economic legislation. In the House, Republican regulars for the most part kept the upper hand, but in the Senate Republican control often was only nominal. Insurgents frequently succeeded in blocking legislation sought by the administration, but they lacked the strength to initiate and carry out their own alternatives.

The 1922 congressional elections spelled disaster for the mainstream of the Republican Party. Although the Republicans managed to retain control of both houses in the 68th Congress, their 167-seat majority in the House declined to a slim 15-seat edge and their 22-seat majority in the Senate fell to an advantage of only 6 seats (51 Republicans to 43 Democrats and 2 Farmer-Labor members).

The insurgent Republicans and the two Farmer-Labor senators from Minnesota accepted committee assignments from the Republicans but did not caucus with them. When the committee lists for the 68th Congress came to the floor, Sen. Robert M. La Follette, Jr., of Wisconsin led an effort to remove party-regular Albert B. Cummins (R-Iowa) from the chairmanship of the Interstate Commerce Committee. A month-long deadlock ensued. La Follette was the second-ranking Republican on the committee, but the regular Republicans, unable to elect Cummins, had no intention of letting La Follette succeed to the chairmanship. Finally, on the 32nd ballot, the regulars threw their support to the committee's ranking Democrat, South Carolinian Ellison D. Smith, who was elected in spite of his minority party status. Cummins continued as a member of the committee and also retained his office as president pro tempore.

In 1924 La Follette ran for president under the Progressive banner, polling 16 percent of the popular vote but carrying only his home state of Wisconsin. The Republicans gained five seats in the Senate, and party leaders felt strong enough to retaliate against the farm-state insurgents who had supported the Progressive ticket. The Republican Conference adopted a resolution stating that the disloyal senators "be not invited to future Republican conferences and be not named to fill any Republican vacancies on Senate committees." [3] The irregulars were permitted to keep their committee assignments, but in many instances they lost their seniority. In the Senate reorganization two years later, however, they were welcomed back into the Republican fold.

The Progressives continued to be a thorn in the side of the Republican Party. In his last two years in office, President Herbert Hoover had to contend with a Democratic House in which the Republican Progressives regularly sided with the opposition. The situation in the Senate was not much better. The Senate in the 72nd Congress consisted of 48 Republicans, 47 Democrats and one Farmer-Labor member. Since some Progressive Republicans regularly voted with the Democrats, President Hoover advised Republican Sen. James E. Watson of Indiana to let the Democrats organize the Senate "to convert their sabotage into responsibility." Hoover said he "could deal more constructively with the Democratic leaders if they held full responsibility in both houses, than with an opposition in the Senate conspiring in the cloakrooms to use every proposal of his for demagoguery." [4] But Watson, who wanted to be majority leader, and his Republican colleagues, many of whom wanted to retain their committee chairmenships, rejected Hoover's proposal.

Cloture in Practice

Early experience with the Senate cloture rule (Rule 22) bore out the predictions of those who expected it to be used only sparingly. (Adopted in 1917, the rule required the vote of two-thirds of the senators present and voting to limit debate.) Between 1917 and the end of the Hoover administration in 1933, the Senate took only 11 cloture votes, of which five occurred in one two-week period in 1927.

Four of the 11 votes were successful. In addition to ending a filibuster on the Treaty of Versailles in 1919, the Senate in 1926 ended a 10-day talkathon against the World Court Protocol by invoking cloture on a 68-26 vote, and in 1927 it invoked cloture twice: on a branch banking bill, 65-18, and on a prohibition reorganization measure, 55-27. The seven measures on which cloture failed included two tariff bills, a bill for development of the Lower Colorado River Basin and a banking bill against which Huey P. Long (D-La.) staged his first filibuster early in 1933. On this occasion cloture failed by a single vote.

Some issues were too sensitive for a cloture vote even to be attempted. During the third session of the 67th Congress in 1922, a group of southern Democrats mounted a filibuster against an anti-lynching bill. On behalf of the obstructionists, Sen. Oscar Underwood of Alabama declared:

It is perfectly apparent that you are not going to get an agreement to vote on this bill. . . . I want to say right now to the Senate that if the majority party insist on this procedure, they are not going to pass the bill and they are not going to do any other business. . . . We are going to transact no other business until we have an understanding about this bill. . . . We are willing to take the responsibility, and we are going to do it." [5]

The obstructionists were as good as their word: the Senate was unable to transact any legislative business until the anti-lynching bill was formally put aside on the last day of the session, but cloture was not attempted.

Similarly, in 1927 no attempt was made to end a filibuster against extending the life of a special campaign-investigating committee headed by Sen. James A. Reed (D-Mo.). Although a majority of the Senate clearly favored its extension, a small group of senators succeeded in abolishing the committee, which had exposed corruption in the 1926 Senate election victories of Frank L. Smith (R-Ill., House, 1919-1921) and William S. Vare (R-Pa., House 1912-1927). Neither senator-elect was ever sworn-in.

As it became apparent that Rule 22 was not an effective weapon against the filibuster, new curbs on obstruction were proposed. During the 1922 filibuster on the anti-lynching bill, Republican Whip Charles Curtis of Kansas asked the Senate's presiding officer, Vice President Calvin Coolidge, to follow Speaker Thomas B. Reed's practice of ruling dilatory motions out of order — in the absence of a specific rule on the question — under general parliamentary law. Such a precedent would have established a significant tool against obstruction, but Coolidge declined to make a ruling.

The next vice president, however, showed more resolve. When Charles G. Dawes made his inaugural address to the Senate in 1925, he coupled a scathing denunciation of the existing Senate rules with a call for new curbs on debate. Not content with attacking the Senate on its own turf, Dawes took his campaign to the country, where he encountered the rather surprising opposition of the American Federation of Labor (AFL). The Dawes scheme, said the AFL ominously, "emanates from the secret chambers of the predatory interests." [6] Although Dawes aroused widespread public interest in rules reform, the Senate in this period took no action on the problem.

The Lame-Duck Amendment

One member of the Senate thought he saw a way to end the filibuster. Sen. Norris, the Progressive who had participated as a member of the House in the revolt against Speaker Cannon, proposed a constitutional amendment to eliminate the lame-duck sessions of Congress by starting the legislative and executive terms of office in January instead of March. By the time the House finally agreed to the Norris resolution in 1932, the Senate had approved it six times. The first Senate vote on the Norris amendment came early in 1923, during the short session of the 67th Congress. Approved by the Senate Agriculture Committee chaired by Norris, the amendment was passed by the Senate Feb. 13 by a 63-6 vote. In the House, the Election Committee reported the amendment and a majority of the Rules Committee approved it, but the Rules Chairman, himself a lame duck, managed to keep the legislation from reaching the floor for a vote.

In 1924 the Senate again approved the Norris amendment, 63-7; the House Election Committee again reported it; and the Rules Committee again blocked it. The same thing happened two years later when the Senate approved the amendment, 73-2.

The Norris amendment reached the House floor for the first time in 1928, after the Senate had approved it for a fourth time, 65-6. However, the House vote of 209 to 157 fell 35 short of the two-thirds required for approval under the Constitution. In the next Congress, the 71st, the Senate approved the amendment for a fifth time, 64-9. But the House adopted a different version, 290-93, and the measure died in a House-Senate conference committee.

Final action came during the 72nd Congress. Democrats now controlled the House. Early in 1932, the Senate adopted the Norris resolution for a sixth time, 63-7, and the House quickly approved it without amendment, 335-56. It became the 20th Amendment upon ratification by the 36th state in 1933.

The amendment established Jan. 3 of the year following a national election as the day on which members' terms would begin and end, and Jan. 20 as the day on which the president and vice president would take office. It provided also that Congress should meet annually on Jan. 3, instead of the first Monday in December, "unless they shall by law appoint a different day."

The second session of the 73rd Congress convened on Jan. 3, 1934, and President Franklin D. Roosevelt took office on Jan. 20, 1937, at the beginning of his second term. The changes in the legislative and executive terms of office worked smoothly enough, but it became apparent quickly that the amendment would not eliminate the filibuster, as Norris had hoped. The final sessions of the 73rd and 74th Congresses both ended in filibusters. *(See box, pp. 140-141.)*

Committee Reorganization

The Senate's standing committee system had expanded dramatically in the late 19th century, and by 1921 it was ripe for pruning. The 25 standing committees existing in 1853 had increased to 42 by 1889, and in the next quarter-century this number almost doubled. Five select committees graduated to standing committee status in 1884, three more did so in 1896 and all of the remaining select committees were made standing committees in 1909. At the same time, nine new standing committees were created, followed by three more in 1913, bringing the total number on the eve of World War I to an all-time high of 74.

The expansion of the committee system reflected the increasing complexity of Senate business. But committees also provided welcome clerical services and office space for their chairmen in the days before such assistance was available to all members. Thus "sinecure committees" had a way of surviving long after any need for them had disappeared. Benefits did not go only to the party in power. In 1907 the Republican Party took 61 chairmanships but assigned 10 others to the Democrats, who were in the minority, and several committees were established solely for the purpose of creating chairmanships.

When the 67th Congress convened in April 1921, the Senate effected a major consolidation of its committee system. The number of committees was cut drastically from 74 to 34, and several long-defunct bodies, such as the Committee on Revolutionary Claims, were abolished.

The committee system revision was initiated by the GOP Committee on Committees, which also proposed to increase the Republican margin on each of the major committees to reflect the 1920 gains in the Senate. To Democratic charges of "steamroller" tactics, committee chairman Frank B. Brandegee (R-Conn.) replied: "Criticisms are purely professional. The Republicans are responsible to the country for legislation and must have control of committees. That's not tyranny; that's representative government — the rule of the majority." [7] The Republican proposal was adopted, 45-25, without substantial change.

A further modification of the committee structure occurred in 1922 when the Senate, following the lead of the House, restored exclusive spending power to the Appropriations Committee. (This authority had been been taken away from the committee in 1899.) When each of the eight appropriation bills previously considered by a Senate legislative committee was taken up, three ad hoc members from the panel that previously considered the bill were allowed to serve on the Appropriations Committee. At the same time, Appropriations was deprived of its power to report amendments proposing new legislation.

The change in appropriations procedure was part of a larger effort to develop a more systematic approach to federal expenditures in both the executive and legislative branches. The 1921 budget act set up the Bureau of the Budget to assist the president in preparing an annual federal budget, including projections of surpluses or deficits. It also created the General Accounting Office (GAO) to strengthen congressional surveillance over federal government spending.

Notes

1. George H. Haynes, *The Senate of the United States: Its History and Practice*, 2 vols. (Boston: Houghton-Mifflin, 1938), II: 973.
2. W. E. Binkley, *The Powers of the President* (New York: Russell & Russell, 1973), p. 243.
3. Haynes, *The Senate of the United States*, I: 291.
4. Charles O. Jones, *The Minority Party in Congress* (Boston: Little, Brown & Co., 1970), p. 144.
5. Haynes, *The Senate of the United States*, I: 411.
6. Ibid., I: 416.
7. Ibid., I: 286.

Chapter 24

_____

DEMOCRATIC LEADERSHIP: 1933-1945

The United States was in the depths of its greatest economic depression when Franklin D. Roosevelt entered the White House in 1933 with an overwhelming popular mandate. Along with the presidency, Democrats commanded large majorities in both houses of Congress. Asked before his election what authority he would seek from Congress, Roosevelt had answered, "Plenty," which hardly conveyed the extent of the special powers Congress would give FDR to deal with the economic emergency.

Called into special session March 9, 1933, Congress in the next "hundred days" embarked on a whirlwind legislative course dictated by the president. On the first day of the special session, the House passed in 38 minutes an emergency banking bill, the provisions of which had not yet been printed. The Senate took a little longer, two hours and 15 minutes, but the measure was ready for the president's signature before the day ended.

In time, the pace slackened somewhat, but the pattern of action remained the same. The president would send a brief message to Congress, accompanied by a detailed draft of the legislation he proposed. Congress had been outraged when Lincoln dared to submit his own draft bills, but it readily accepted such action from Roosevelt. Given the president's popularity and the prevailing economic emergency, congressional opposition was often non-existent and his proposals were promptly enacted. Along with the extensive powers given the president, Congress at the beginning of Roosevelt's first term agreed to various legislative shortcuts to speed enactment of his economic recovery program. Congress did not long remain a rubber stamp, but throughout his first term (1933-1937) Roosevelt was able — through negotiation, compromise and the exercise of his patronage powers — to win enactment of a broad range of New Deal social and economic programs.

In his second term (1937-1941), a conservative coalition of Republicans and southern Democrats frequently opposed Roosevelt on domestic issues. The coalition thwarted his plan to enlarge the Supreme Court and blocked him on some some social legislation. During the president's unprecedented third term (1941-1945), wartime issues were paramount. As in previous wars, the executive branch assumed extraordinary powers, and Congress became restive under executive domination. As the war drew to a close, opposition to administration policies became more strident, and by the time Roosevelt died in April 1945 — just three months into his fourth term — Congress was in open revolt. His successor, Harry S Truman, won broad congressional support for his foreign policy measures, but his domestic programs were largely ignored.

In the mid-1940s, even before the war ended, Congress began to consider ways to modernize its internal machinery in response to complex international and domestic problems and the corresponding increase in its workload. The resulting Legislative Reorganization Act of 1946 was only partially successful in meeting those goals. For example, in the Senate no action was taken to strengthen the cloture rule, and filibusters were used repeatedly to defeat civil rights legislation. *(See box, p. 261.)* Another objective of the 1946 act was to regain some of the initiative the legislative branch had lost to the White House under Roosevelt. Here, too, the results were mixed at best.

Executive-Senate Relations

President Roosevelt, at times assisted by Vice President John Nance Garner (a former Speaker of the House), was his own legislative leader in the Senate during his first term. Most Senate Democratic leaders viewed themselves as the loyal lieutenants of the president. Although Senate rules and procedures precluded the close control exercised by party leaders in the House, Senate leaders were often more successful in advancing the administration's legislative programs than their House counterparts.

When Joseph T. Robinson of Arkansas became Senate majority leader in 1933, he revived the Democratic Caucus and won from Democratic senators an agreement, adopted by a vote of 50-3, to make caucus decisions on administration bills binding by majority vote. The caucus rule read:

> Resolved, That until further order the chairman [Robinson] is authorized to convene Democratic senators in caucus for the

purpose of considering any measure recommended by the president; and that all Democratic senators shall be bound by the vote of the majority of the conference; provided, that any senator may be excused from voting for any such measure upon his expressed statement to the caucus that said measure is contrary to his conscientious judgment or that said measure is in violation of pledges made to his constituents as a candidate. [1]

Although there is no evidence that Robinson ever made use of the binding caucus rule, non-binding caucuses frequently were held to mobilize party support. In the House the majority leadership worked through its Steering Committee and the whip organization, but in the Senate the Steering Committee served only as a committee on committees, while it is doubtful that the Senate Policy Committee ever met.

The Senate leadership had to contend with many southern Democrats who had risen to key committee chairmanships through the seniority system, but Roosevelt was remarkably successful at keeping them in line. Senate Agriculture Chairman Ellison D. Smith of South Carolina was not sympathetic to the proposed Agricultural Adjustment Act of 1933, but after a conference at the White House his committee reported the measure with this comment:

This bill . . . was drafted by the Department of Agriculture and is practically unchanged from the bill as presented to Congress. Considerable hearings were had by the Senate committee, but on account of the desire of the administration that no change be made the bill is presented to the Senate in practically an unchanged form. . . . [2]

As long as the Democrats maintained their tremendous margins in Congress and were able to curb the dissidents within their own party, the leadership could afford to ignore the minority, especially since many moderate and progressive Republicans supported early New Deal proposals. But by the beginning of Roosevelt's second term in 1937 these conditions no longer prevailed. A strong conservative coalition of Republicans and southern Democrats emerged to oppose much of the New Deal.

Court Packing Plan Fails

Stung by the Supreme Court's invalidation of major New Deal acts, Roosevelt sent to the Senate on Feb. 5, 1937, a proposal to enlarge the court by appointing additional justices, up to a total of six, to assist those who did not retire within six months of reaching the age of 70. For once, public opinion was against the president, and Senate Republicans sat on their hands while conservative and New Deal Democrats fought over the issue. A series of court decisions favorable to New Deal programs weakened support for the plan, as did the sudden death of Majority Leader Robinson on July 13. In the ensuing leadership contest, Alben W. Barkley of Kentucky, with the president's implied support, defeated Pat Harrison of Mississippi in a fight that brought to the surface the deep split in the Democrats' ranks. It also cost Roosevelt his plan to pack the court with justices of his choosing.

Struggling to reassert himself as leader of his party, Roosevelt decided to intervene in the 1938 Democratic primaries in an effort to block the renomination of conservative Democrats in Congress. The "purge" was notably unsuccessful. Many senators on the purge list triumphantly returned to office, and the president's only definite victory in the House was the unseating of Rep. John J. O'Connor (D-N.Y.), chairman of the House Rules Committee. As a further embarrassment, Republicans gained seven Senate seats in the November election.

With the onset of World War II, opposition to Roosevelt was muted. Wartime expenditures and programs were freely voted. And the Senate's Special Committee to Investigate the National Defense Program, set up in 1941 under the chairmanship of Sen. Harry S Truman (D-Mo.), earned the president's gratitude by serving as a "friendly watchdog" over defense spending without embarrassing the administration. As the war went on, however, growing opposition to Roosevelt on domestic issues became apparent.

Congress Challenges Roosevelt

The antagonism between Roosevelt and Congress came into the open in February 1944 when the president, against the advice of party leaders, vetoed a revenue bill, the first veto of a revenue measure by any president. On the floor of the Senate, Barkley denounced the action as "a calculated and deliberate assault upon the legislative integrity of every member of Congress." He said:

> Other members of Congress may do as they please, but as for me I do not propose to take this unjustifiable assault lying down. . . .
> I dare say that, during the last seven years of tenure as majority leader, I have carried the flag over rougher territory than ever traversed by any previous majority leader. Sometimes I have carried it with little help from the other end of Pennsylvania Avenue. [3]

The following day Barkley resigned as floor leader, but he was re-elected at once by unanimous vote of the Democratic Caucus.

Roosevelt's problems with Congress increased after his election to a fourth term in 1944. His proposals for postwar economic and social legislation were ignored, and his nomination of Henry A. Wallace as secretary of commerce was confirmed only after the Reconstruction Finance Corporation had been removed from Commerce Department control. By the time of his death in April 1945, his support in Congress had disintegrated.

When Vice President Harry S Truman succeeded Roosevelt as president, many observers predicted a renewal of the happy relationship between Congress and the executive branch that had prevailed in the McKinley administration. Like McKinley, Truman was a former member of Congress who enjoyed the goodwill of his colleagues, but his honeymoon with Congress did not last long. Although he was markedly successful in pushing his foreign policy programs, the conservative coalition stood ready to oppose him on domestic issues. With the election of a Republican House and Senate in 1946, the Democrats' 14-year reign in Congress came to an end.

Filibusters and Civil Rights

Parliamentary obstruction continued to plague the Senate in the latter stages of the New Deal era, but no concerted efforts were made to put new curbs on the filibuster. The Senate took no cloture votes in the 73rd and 74th Congresses, but between 1938 and 1946 eight votes were taken to shut off debate on various issues. None of the eight votes came close to the two-thirds majority needed to end debate.

The most notorious filibusterer of the early New Deal period was Sen. Huey Long (D-La.), who was at odds with the Roosevelt administration over patronage in his home state and other matters. Long staged his most famous filibuster in 1935, during debate on the proposed extension of the National Industrial Recovery Act. The "Kingfish," as he was called, spoke for 15 and a half hours, a record up to that time, filling 85 pages of the *Congressional Record* with remarks that ranged from commentaries on the Constitution to recipes for southern "potlikker," turnip greens and corn bread. He said his intent in delaying action on the bill was "to save to the sovereign states their rights and prerogatives" and "to preserve the right and prerogative of the Senate as to the qualifications of important officers." [4] Long conducted his last filibuster, against an emergency appropriation bill, less than two weeks before his assassination in the summer of 1935.

By the mid-1930s, the use of the filibuster increasingly came to be associated with attempts to frustrate civil rights legislation. Southern senators might lack the votes to defeat civil rights measures outright, but they found they could accomplish the same objective through obstruction. Proponents of civil rights legislation could not muster the requisite majority to invoke cloture on these filibusters, even though they often apparently had the support of a Senate majority. Accordingly, the southerners used the filibuster to keep civil rights bills from coming to a vote.

Most of the famous filibusters of the period involved civil rights. Anti-lynching bills were filibustered in 1935 and 1938 and anti-poll tax measures in 1942, 1944 and 1946. Fair employment practices legislation was filibustered in 1946.

It was hard to keep senators in the chamber during these exhibitions. At one point during the 1942 anti-poll tax debate a quorum could not be mustered and the business of the Senate had to be halted. The sergeant at arms was directed to "request the attendance" of absent senators, and after a long delay 44 senators, five short of a quorum, appeared. The sergeant at arms then was directed to "compel the attendance" of absent members. After more delay, he reported that 43 senators were out of town and eight others were in Washington but could not be located. The exasperated Senate leadership then ordered him to "execute warrants of arrest" upon absent senators. The sergeant at arms was saved from this embarrassing duty by the timely appearance of five senators to complete a quorum. (The sergeant at arms in the past had not always been so fortunate. During debate on the Lower Colorado River project in 1927, several infuriated senators actually were brought into the chamber under arrest warrants.)

Rule 22 proved totally ineffectual against these sustained and well-organized southern filibusters. Six of the eight unsuccessful cloture votes between 1938 and 1946 concerned civil rights issues. On four of those votes, cloture did not win even a simple majority. Therefore, Congress sought new ways of curbing dilatory tactics.

The first dealt with the quorum call, a favorite obstructionist tool. During a 1935 filibuster by Huey Long, the chair ruled that a quorum call constituted business and that senators who yielded for a quorum call would lose the floor. Under this ruling a senator who yields twice for a

Famous Filibusters

Efforts to curb filibusters in the 20th century had only limited effectiveness. The filibuster came to be identified with southern efforts to bloc civil rights legislation, although northern liberals occasionally found it a useful device as well. Until 1964 the Senate had never been able to end a filibuster on civil rights legislation.

The longest speech in the history of the Senate was made by Strom Thurmond (R-S.C.). During a filibuster against passage of a civil rights bill in 1957, Thurmond spoke for 24 hours and 18 minutes in a round-the-clock session on Aug. 28 and 29. Second place goes to Wayne Morse (Ind.-Ore.), who in April 1953 spoke for 22 hours and 26 minutes on the tidelands oil bill. The third longest individual filibuster was set by Robert M. La Follette, Sr. (R-Wis.), who in 1908 held the floor for 18 hours and 23 minutes in a fight over the Aldrich-Vreeland currency bill. William Proxmire (D-Wis.) takes fourth place for his 16-hour, 12-minute speech in 1981 against a bill to raise the public debt ceiling to more than a trillion dollars. Huey P. Long (D-La.) is next, for a June 1935 filibuster of 15 hours and 30 minutes in opposition to the extension of the National Industrial Recovery Act.

In this connection, special credit perhaps is due to Reed Smoot (R-Utah), who during a successful 1915 filibuster against President Woodrow Wilson's ship purchase bill spoke for 11 hours and 35 minutes without relief and without deviating from the subject.

Because the Senate has no germaneness rule, speakers do not always confine themselves to the subject under consideration. Sen. Long in 1935 entertained his colleagues with southern recipes, and Glen H. Taylor (D-Idaho), a former tent show performer, spent eight and one-half hours in 1947 expounding on fishing, baptism, Wall Street and his children in an effort to delay a vote to override President Harry S Truman's veto of the Taft-Hartley Act.

quorum call while the same question is before the Senate can be denied the right to speak again on that question during the same legislative day. The second curb, contained in reorganization measures passed in 1939 and 1945, limited debate on government reorganization recommendations submitted by the executive branch.

The Legislative Reorganization Act of 1946 contained no provisions on debate limitation since that subject was outside the purview of the Joint Committee on the Organization of Congress, but by 1946 many senators were convinced that further curbs on debate were needed if the Senate was to meet its postwar responsibilities.

Notes

1. Randall B. Ripley, *Majority Party Leadership in Congress* (Boston: Little, Brown & Co., 1969), p. 81.
2. Ibid., p. 77.
3. *Congressional Record,* 78th Cong., 2nd sess., Feb. 23, 1944, p. S 1966.
4. George H. Haynes, *The Senate of the United States: Its History and Practice*, 2 vols. (Boston: Houghton-Mifflin, 1938), I: 413.

Chapter 25

POSTWAR DEVELOPMENTS: 1945-1969

The election of a Republican Congress in 1946 marked the beginning of a period of divided government. For 16 of the 30 years between 1947 and 1976, the party in opposition to the president controlled Congress. Democratic President Harry S Truman (1945-1953) faced a Republican House and Senate in the 80th Congress (1947-1949). His successor, Republican Dwight D. Eisenhower (1953-1961), enjoyed Republican majorities in Congress only in his first two years in office. The Democrats controlled Congress throughout the terms of Democrats John F. Kennedy (1961-1963) and Lyndon B. Johnson (1963-1969), but when Republican Richard M. Nixon was elected in 1968, he became the first president since Zachary Taylor (1849-1850) to fail to win control of at least one house of the new Congress in a first-term election. The House and Senate remained in Democratic hands for the duration of the Nixon presidency (1969-1974).

In only two Congresses did Republicans organize the Senate. In the 80th Congress they enjoyed a 51-45 margin, but in the 83rd (1953-1955) their margin was so narrow that the death of Majority Leader Robert A. Taft of Ohio gave a numerical majority to the Democrats. In the 82nd, 84th and 85th Congresses, the Democratic margin of control was also razor-thin, but after the Democratic sweep in the 1958 congressional elections, the party maintained comfortable majorities in both houses.

Throughout the postwar period the parties themselves were often badly divided, and both Republican and Democratic presidents were forced to seek bipartisan support to win enactment of their programs. This proved to be easier on foreign than on domestic issues. Although Truman often was at loggerheads with the Republicans on domestic legislation, Sen. Arthur H. Vandenberg (R-Mich.) led his once-isolationist party colleagues into a new era of bipartisan foreign policy in cooperation with the Democratic administration. President Eisenhower often received more support from Democrats on foreign policy issues than from members of his own party, particularly in the early years of his administration. But partisanship increased as the 1960 elections approached, and many domestic bills were not enacted.

President Kennedy's relations with Congress were far from ideal, although the Senate generally was more responsive to his proposals than was the House. Much of Kennedy's program was enacted after his assassination in November 1963 during Lyndon B. Johnson's presidency. Johnson won spectacular legislative victories in 1965 and 1966, but with the escalation of the war in Vietnam and increasing civil and economic disorders at home, he lost favor in Congress and was forced into retirement in 1969. During the Nixon administration, Congress and the White House usually were at odds.

Congress Reorganizes

By the middle of the 20th century, the expanded powers of the executive branch had seriously weakened legislative authority. Pressures on Congress were intensified by the increased volume and complexity of its workload. At the same time, Congress as an institution suffered more and more public disfavor.

In an effort to reassert its eroded prerogatives and improve its legislative machinery, Congress enacted a major legislative reorganization measure in 1946. Then to improve their public image, both chambers in 1968 adopted ethics codes and financial disclosure requirements for members. But sensitive internal matters, such as the seniority system and limitations on Senate debate, remained vexing problems.

The tremendous expansion of the size and authority of the federal government under Roosevelt, especially through the plethora of New Deal programs and the wartime mobilization of the nation, spurred Congress to think about institutional reforms. Proposals ranged from granting the president constitutional power to dissolve Congress to minor administrative changes in the way the legislative branch was run. But two themes dominated the debate: the relationship between the organization of Congress and its increased workload, and relations between Congress and the executive branch.

Rep. Jerry Voorhis (D-Calif.) expressed the feelings of many members when he advocated the creation of a Joint Committee on the Organization of Congress. "[I]n the midst of this war," said Voorhis

Jan. 18, 1945, "we have to grant executive power ... of the most sweeping nature." But he wanted the groundwork laid

> in order that this Congress may perform its functions efficiently, effectively, and in accord with the needs of the people of this nation and so that it will become not merely an agency that says yes or no to executive proposals, but an agency capable of, and actually performing the function of, bringing forth its own constructive program [to benefit Americans]. Thus it will take its place and keep its place as an altogether coequal branch of our government. [1]

In February 1945 Congress set up the Joint Committee on the Organization of Congress with Sen. Robert M. La Follette, Jr. (Prog.-Wis.) as chairman and Rep. A. S. Mike Monroney (D-Okla.) as vice chairman. After extensive hearings the joint committee submitted a detailed report that formed the basis of the Legislative Reorganization Act of 1946. Passed with bipartisan support in both houses, the act made important changes in standing committees, committee staffs and congressional review of the federal budget. *(For more details on the Legislative Reorganization Act of 1946, see pp. 151-155.)*

Democratic Leadership

After World War II, Democratic leadership in the Senate was relatively stable. Alben W. Barkley of Kentucky remained majority leader from 1937 to 1947; he served as minority leader from 1947 until his resignation in 1949 to become Truman's vice president. The Democrats then had two majority leaders in as many Congresses: Scott W. Lucas of Illinois in the 81st and Ernest W. McFarland of Arizona in the 82nd.

When the 83rd Congress met in January 1953, with the Republicans back in control, the Democrats chose as their minority leader Lyndon B. Johnson of Texas, who had served only four years in the Senate. Johnson, a member of the House from 1937 to 1949, was a friend of House Speaker Sam Rayburn, a fellow Texan, and had the backing of powerful Senate conservatives, notably Robert S. Kerr (D-Okla.) and Richard B. Russell (D-Ga.). He promptly built bridges to the liberal Democrats in the Senate in an effort to heal the deep liberal-conservative split within the party. Johnson soon became one of the most powerful leaders in Senate history, serving as minority leader in 1953 and 1954 and as majority leader from 1955 until his resignation in 1961 to become Kennedy's vice president.

Johnson's powers of persuasion and manipulative skills are legendary. A system of rewards and punishments supplemented the famous Johnson "treatment." He revitalized the Senate Democratic Policy Committee, saw to it that liberals won seats on both that panel and on the Steering Committee (the party's committee on committees), and modified the seniority system to ensure freshman senators at least one major committee assignment, a practice later adopted by the Republicans as well. On the floor, efficiency was promoted through the use of such devices as unanimous consent agreements, simplified quorum calls and night sessions. Through an active intelligence operation headed by Robert G. "Bobby" Baker, secretary to the Senate majority, Johnson kept himself informed about the views and positions of the Senate membership. He also was adept at rounding up votes for compromises acceptable to both parties.

An apostle of "moderation" and "consensus government," Johnson supported the Eisenhower administration on many major policies and frequently solicited Republican support in the Senate. Such was his skill that in 1957 he was able to win passage of the first civil rights bill since Reconstruction without a filibuster and without splitting the Democratic Party.

Johnson's successor as majority leader in 1961 was party whip Mike Mansfield of Montana. Mansfield held the respect of his colleagues, but he shied away from the assertive leadership role Johnson had exercised. Under his more permissive rule, the Johnson style gave way to a collegial leadership pattern in which the Policy Committee and the legislative committees played commanding roles. Mansfield was called "the gentle persuader" because he felt that each senator should conduct his affairs with minimal pressure from the leadership. Despite his reticence on the national stage, Mansfield strongly defended Senate prerogatives during the Johnson and Nixon administrations, and differed openly with President Johnson on the Vietnam War.

Mansfield retired at the end of his term in January 1977. His 16-year tenure as majority leader was the longest in Senate history.

Republican Leadership

Party authority on the Republican side was less concentrated than in the Democratic Party at this time. Robert A. Taft of Ohio, the son of President William Howard Taft, had been the de facto Republican power in the Senate since the early 1940s. He had chaired the Policy Committee since its creation in 1947, but he did not feel it necessary to assume the leadership of his party until the Eisenhower administration took office in January 1953. After Taft's death only six months later, William F. Knowland of California became majority leader. Knowland was a conservative who frequently split with the Eisenhower administration on major issues, but H. Styles Bridges of New Hampshire often spoke for the Republicans as chairman of the Policy Committee.

When Democrats regained control of the Senate in the 84th Congress, Knowland became minority leader. In 1959 he was succeeded by one of the most colorful party leaders in recent history, Everett McKinley Dirksen of Illinois, a 16-year veteran of the House and a member of the Senate for eight years before his election as Senate majority leader. Dirksen's style, noted one observer, was "one of remaining vague on an issue, or taking an initial position from which he could negotiate: bargaining with the majority party, the president and his own colleagues, and eventually accepting a compromise." [2]

When Dirksen died in 1969, he was succeeded as minority leader by Hugh Scott of Pennsylvania, a liberal Republican who sometimes found it difficult to serve as spokesman for the Nixon, and later the Ford, administrations.

Changes in Rule 22

With increased demands in the 1950s and 1960s for enactment of civil rights legislation, liberals in the Senate made persistent, but largely unsuccessful, efforts to revise the cloture rule to make it easier to cut off filibusters. A change in Rule 22 in effect between 1949 and 1959 actually made it more difficult to invoke cloture.

As originally adopted in 1917, Rule 22 required a vote of two-thirds of the senators present and voting to invoke cloture. However, a series of rulings and precedents over the years rendered Rule 22 virtually inoperative by holding that it could not be applied to debate on procedural questions. Because of this, President Pro Tempore Vandenberg ruled in 1948, during a filibuster against an attempt to bring up an anti-poll-tax bill, that cloture could not be used against debate on a motion to proceed to consideration of a bill. In making this ruling, Vandenberg conceded: "In the final analysis, the Senate has no effective cloture rule at all." [3]

1949 Change. The Truman administration, desiring to clear the way for a broad civil rights program, backed a change in the cloture rule in

1949. After a long and bitter floor fight, the Senate adopted a proposal, supported by conservative Republicans and southern Democrats, that actually was more restrictive than the rule it replaced. The new rule required the votes of two-thirds of the entire Senate membership (instead of two-thirds of those present and voting) to invoke cloture, but the modification allowed cloture to operate on any pending business or motion with the exception of debate on motions to change the Senate rules themselves, on which Rule 22 previously had applied.

Since under the new interpretation cloture could not be used to cut off a filibuster against a change in the rules, and since any attempt to change Rule 22 while operating under this rule appeared hopeless, Senate liberals devised a new approach. They challenged the practice of continuing Senate rules from one Congress to the next, arguing that the Senate had a right to adopt new rules by a simple majority vote at the beginning of each Congress.

Accordingly, when the 83rd and 85th Congresses convened in 1953 and 1957, respectively, Sen. Clinton P. Anderson (D-N.M.) moved that the Senate consider the adoption of new rules. On both occasions his motion was tabled, but during the 1957 debate Vice President Richard M. Nixon offered a significant "advisory opinion" on how the Senate could proceed to change its rules.

Citing Article I, Section 5, of the Constitution which states that "each house may determine the rules of its proceedings," Nixon said he thought the Senate could adopt new rules "under whatever procedures the majority of the Senate approves." Although traditionally each incoming Senate had operated under the existing rules, Nixon said the Senate could not be bound by any previous rule "which denies the membership of the Senate the power to exercise its constitutional right to make its own rules." [4] Nixon said he regarded as unconstitutional the section in Rule 22 banning any limitation of debate on proposals to change the Senate's rules. The vice president explained that he was stating his personal opinion and that the question of the rule's constitutionality could be decided only by the Senate itself. But the Senate did not vote on the question.

1959 Change. A modest revision of Rule 22 was accomplished in 1959. Senate liberals hoped to make it possible to invoke cloture by a simple majority or by a three-fifths vote, but their efforts to bring about such a substantial change failed. Instead, a bipartisan leadership group under the direction of Majority Leader Johnson engineered a slight revision of the rule that the southern bloc opposed but did not really fight.

The change, adopted by a 72-22 roll call, permitted cloture to be invoked by two-thirds of those present and voting (rather than two-thirds of the full membership as the 1949 rule had required), and it also applied to debate on motions to change the Senate's rules. But at the same time the Senate added this new provision to Rule 32 (currently, section two of Rule 5), dealing with the continuation of Senate business from one session of Congress to another: "The rules of the Senate shall continue from one Congress to the next unless they are changed as provided in these rules." [5] The new language buttressed the position of those who maintained that the Senate was a continuing body, but liberal opponents of the filibuster never conceded the point.

During the 1960s 23 cloture votes were taken, four of which were successful. In 1962 the Senate voted 63-27 to shut off a liberal filibuster against the administration's communications satellite bill. This was the first successful cloture vote since 1927 and only the fifth since the adoption of Rule 22 in 1917. In 1964 the Senate for the first time in its history invoked cloture on a southern filibuster against a civil rights bill. This 71-29 vote was followed by successful cloture votes on two other civil rights measures: the Voting Rights Act of 1965 and, on the fourth try, the historic Housing and Urban Development Act of 1968.

Humphrey Ruling Reversed. The discovery that it was possible to vote cloture on civil rights bills under the existing rule took some of the steam out of the liberals' efforts to reform Rule 22. In 1969 their strategy focused on obtaining from Vice President Hubert H. Humphrey a ruling that at the start of a new Congress a simple majority could invoke cloture against filibusters on proposed changes in the Senate rules.

After a cloture motion was filed on the liberals' proposal to reduce the cloture requirement from two-thirds to three-fifths of those present and voting, Humphrey announced that if a majority, but less than two-thirds, of those present and voting voted for cloture he would rule that the majority prevailed. Because such a ruling could be appealed by the Senate, Humphrey said, it would enable the Senate to decide the constitutional issue by a simple majority vote without debate. Humphrey added that if he held that the cloture motion had failed because of the lack of a two-thirds vote, he would be inhibiting the Senate from deciding the constitutional question. In explaining the ruling he proposed to make, Humphrey declared: "On a par with the right of the Senate to determine its rules, though perhaps not set forth so specifically in the Constitution, is the right of the Senate, a simple majority of the Senate, to decide constitutional questions." [6]

When the cloture motion came to a vote Jan. 16, 1969, a slim majority (51-47) voted for cloture, and Humphrey ruled that debate would proceed under the limitations in Rule 22. Opponents of the rules change immediately appealed his decision, and Humphrey's ruling was not upheld, 45-53. The vote on the appeal meant that cloture was not invoked, thus leaving those opposed to changing Rule 22 free to continue their filibuster. Proponents of the change did not have enough support to limit debate through a two-thirds vote, so they ended their efforts in that Congress. (The real breakthrough for senators seeking a change in Rule 22 would not come until 1975.)

Other Rules Changes

Two minor changes in Senate rules were adopted in 1964. The first amended Rule 8 (currently, clause 1B of Rule 19) to provide for a three-hour period after the "morning hour" — a period of up to two hours at the beginning of each legislative day when routine business is conducted — when debate on a pending measure, or amendments to that measure, must be germane. The period could be waived by unanimous consent. The intent of the proposal was to speed passage of pending bills by preventing speeches on irrelevant matters until late in each day's session. It was adopted in place of proposals for more stringent germaneness rules. But senators immediately found a loophole: a non-germane amendment could be offered to a bill, and later withdrawn, and debate on that amendment would be in order. Thus the rule was seldom applied in practice.

In the second change, the Senate amended Rule 25 (currently, clause 5A of Rule 26) to permit Senate standing committees to meet until completion of the morning hour. Previously, unanimous consent had been required in order for committees to meet at any time when the Senate was in session.

The Senate in the Public Image

In the postwar period, the Senate's public image became tarnished. By virtue of its antiquated procedures, the Senate often seemed unable to accomplish the work the public expected it, and the integrity of its members and employees frequently came under attack. The Senate is not a body to be stampeded by public pressures, and it approached its image problem in its own way and in its own time.

McCarthy Controversy. From 1950 until 1954 Joseph R. McCarthy (R-Wis.) was by all odds the most controversial member of the Senate. Sen. McCarthy's career as a communist-hunter began in February 1950 with a speech in Wheeling, West Virginia, in which he charged that 205 communists were working in the State Department with the knowledge of the secretary of state. From that time until his formal censure by the Senate in 1954 by a 67-22 vote, McCarthy and his freewheeling accusations of communist sympathies among high- and low-placed government officials, former officials and private citizens captivated public attention.

The phenomenon of "McCarthyism" had a major impact on the psychological climate of the early 1950s. As chairman of the Senate Government Operations Committee, McCarthy investigated the State Department, the Voice of America, the Department of the Army and other agencies. An opinion-stifling climate of fear throughout the country was said to be one of the results of his probes.

For several years McCarthy's colleagues showed no disposition to tangle with him, but the Army-McCarthy hearings, televised in the spring of 1954, led finally to his censure by the Senate in a special session held after the midterm elections of 1954. The first Republican to attack McCarthy's tactics was Sen. Margaret Chase Smith of Maine. In June 1950 she startled her colleagues with these words:

> I do not like the way the Senate has been made a rendezvous for vilification, for selfish political gain at the sacrifice of individual reputations and national unity. I am not proud of the way we smear outsiders from the floor of the Senate. . . . I do not want to see the Party ride to political victory on the Four Horsemen of Calumny — fear, ignorance, bigotry and smear.

In the end McCarthy was censured, not for what Sen. Ralph E. Flanders (R-Vt.) called his "habitual contempt of people," but for his contemptuous treatment of the Senate itself — for his failure to cooperate with the Subcommittee on Privileges and Elections in 1952 and for his abuse of the select committee that had considered the censure charges against him. The censure resolution asserted that McCarthy had "acted contrary to senatorial ethics and tended to bring the Senate into dishonor and disrepute, to obstruct the constitutional processes of the Senate, and to impair its dignity. And such conduct is hereby condemned." [7]

McCarthy remained in the Senate until his death in 1957, but he lost his committee and subcommittee chairmanships when the Democrats took control of Congress in 1955, and his activities no longer attracted much attention in the Senate, the press or elsewhere.

Meanwhile, alleged excesses in treatment of witnesses by congressional committees led in 1954 to an extensive search for a "fair-play" rule to govern congressional investigations. Most of the criticism was directed at McCarthy's Permanent Investigations Subcommittee and at the House Un-American Activities Committee. In 1955 the House amended its rules to provide a minimum standard of conduct for House committees. The Senate adopted no general rules on the subject, but the Permanent Investigations Subcommittee under its new chairman, John L. McClellan (D-Ark.), adopted safeguards for the protection of witnesses. *(See pp. 164-165.)*

Bobby Baker Scandal. In 1963 the Senate was shaken by charges that Robert G. "Bobby" Baker had used his position as secretary to the Senate majority to promote outside business interests. Baker, who served as secretary from 1955 until his resignation under fire in August 1963, was no ordinary Senate functionary. Exposure of his numerous "improprieties" led to criticism of the Senate as a whole and prompted a review of congressional ethics.

A protégé of Lyndon B. Johnson, to whom the case was particularly embarrassing, Baker had access to leadership councils and was known as the Senate's "most powerful employee." He headed Johnson's intelligence network in the Senate and was celebrated for his ability to forecast the outcome of close votes. Johnson once hailed "his tremendous fund of knowledge about the Senate, which is almost appalling in one so young." [8]

In the wake of disclosures about Baker's wide-ranging business ventures, the Senate instructed its Rules and Administration Committee to investigate his activities from the standpoint of congressional ethics. The committee's Democratic majority, in reports issued in 1964 and 1965, accused Baker of "many gross improprieties" but cited no actual violations of law. Committee Republicans charged that the investigation was incomplete and a "whitewash." Both Republicans and Democrats called for rules requiring financial disclosure statements by members of Congress and their employees.

Baker ultimately was convicted in court and imprisoned for income tax evasion, theft and conspiracy to defraud the government. Meanwhile, largely because of embarrassments caused by the Baker scandal, the Senate in 1964 created a Select Committee on Standards and Conduct to investigate allegations of improper activities by Senate members and staff, to recommend disciplinary action where relevant and to draw up a code of ethical conduct. The House established a similar committee in 1967.

Dodd Investigation. Charges by syndicated columnists Drew Pearson and Jack Anderson that Sen. Thomas J. Dodd (D-Conn.) had misused political campaign contributions prompted the select committee's first investigation. The committee in April 1967 recommended that the Senate censure Dodd for misuse of political funds and for double-billing for official and private travel. The Senate on June 23 censured Dodd on the first charge by a 92-5 roll-call vote but refused, on a 45-51 vote, to censure him on the second charge. The action marked the seventh time in its history that the Senate had censured one of its members. After the vote, the issue was closed, and Dodd continued to serve in the Senate until he was defeated for re-election in 1970.

Ethics Code Adopted

Concern over conflicts of interest at all levels of government had been growing since World War II, but Congress showed no inclination to adopt self-policing measures. Pressure generated by the Baker and Dodd cases in the Senate and by investigations of the activities of Rep. Adam Clayton Powell, Jr. (D-N.Y.) in the House were largely responsible for the adoption of limited financial disclosure requirements in both chambers in 1968.

In the Senate, a code of conduct proposed by the Select Committee on Standards and Conduct was adopted without substantial change on March 22, 1968, by a 67-1 vote. Included were provisions to regulate the outside employment of Senate employees, to require a full accounting of campaign contributions and restrict the uses to which they could be put, and to require senators and top employees to file detailed financial reports each year. However, these reports were to be made available only to the select committee. The only public accounting required was of campaign contributions of $50 or more and honoraria of $300 or more.

Censured Members of the Senate

Year	Member	Grounds
1811	Timothy Pickering (Fed-Mass.)	Breach of confidence
1844	Benjamin Tappan (D-Ohio)	Breach of confidence
1902	John L. McLaurin (D-S.C.)	Assault
1902	Benjamin R. Tillman (D-S.C.)	Assault
1929	Hiram Bingham (R-Conn.)	Bringing Senate into disrepute
1954	Joseph R. McCarthy (R-Wis.)	Obstruction of legislative process, insult to senators, etc.
1967	Thomas J. Dodd (D-Conn.)	Financial misconduct

Source: U.S. Senate, Committee on Rules and Administration, Subcommittee on Privileges and Elections, *Senate Election, Expulsion and Censure Cases from 1793 to 1972*, compiled by Richard D. Hupman, S. Doc. 92-7, 92nd Cong., 1st sess., 1972.

The Senate rejected, 40-44, a proposal for full public disclosure of members' finances. The proposal had been pressed by Sen. Joseph S. Clark (D-Pa.), a persistent advocate of congressional reform.

The code of conduct was embodied in four additions to the Senate rules concerning outside employment, campaign contributions, political fund raising and financial disclosure.

Officers and employees of the Senate were prohibited from engaging in any employment or paid activity that was inconsistent with their official Senate duties. Employees were required to report any outside employment to their supervisors, who were required to monitor their employees' outside activities to prevent conflicts of interest.

Senators and declared candidates for the Senate were required to maintain a full accounting of the sources and amounts of all campaign contributions and to give their express approval to all fund-raising efforts conducted on their behalf. Campaign funds were to be limited to a candidate's nomination and election expenses and to be used only for "the reasonable expenses," past or future, of the candidate's Senate office.

Senate staff members generally were prohibited from receiving, soliciting or distributing funds collected in connection with any election campaign for the Senate or any other federal office. Aides specifically designated by senators to help raise campaign funds were exempted from the rule, which required senators to file the names of such aides with the secretary of the Senate, and such information was to be available to the public.

Senators, declared candidates for the Senate and Senate employees earning more than $15,000 a year were required to file by May 15 each year two financial disclosure reports, one to remain sealed and the other to be available for public inspection. The sealed report was to contain a copy of the filer's U.S. income tax returns and a detailed disclosure of his financial interests, including major businesss interests, holdings, liabilities, legal fees of $1,000 or more and gifts exceeding $50 in value. This report was to remain sealed in the custody of the U.S. comptroller general for a period of seven years, after which it was to be returned. The Select Committee on Standards and Conduct could examine the sealed report's contents only if a majority of the committee's members voted to do so as part of an investigation. The public report, to be filed with the secretary of the Senate, was to list all campaign contributions received in the previous year and the amount, value and source of any honorarium of $300 or more.

For a while the 1968 code of conduct quieted the public's uneasiness over ethical standards in the Senate. But in the following decade, the Watergate scandal was to cause the 1968 rules to be superceded by a more restrictive ethics code, more detailed public financial disclosure requirements and more rigorous reporting of campaign finances.

Senate-Executive Rivalry

One of the principal purposes of the Legislative Reorganization Act of 1946 was to help Congress hold its own against the rapidly expanding power of the executive branch. In this it was only partly successful. By the end of World War II it seemed clear that legislative initiative had shifted, apparently irretrievably, from Congress to the president, and during the postwar era Congress struggled to preserve its powers to approve, revise or reject presidential programs.

In 1954 the Senate came within one vote of approving a proposed constitutional amendment — known as the Bricker Amendment after its sponsor, John W. Bricker (R-Ohio) — to restrict the president's power to negotiate treaties and other international agreements. Other conflicts arose over the spending power, the war power and to a lesser extent the appointment power. Frequently the Senate was in contention with the House as well as with the executive branch in its attempts to guard its constitutional prerogatives.

Disputes Over the Spending Power

In the 1946 reorganization act Congress tried to tighten its control over the budget process through the creation of a congressionally drafted budget for the federal government that would be separate from the funding recommendations submitted by the executive branch. After three unsuccessful attempts to use this device, it was abandoned as an unqualified failure.

In 1947 the Joint Committee on the Legislative Budget, composed of members of the House Ways and Means and Appropriations committees and the Senate Finance and Appropriations committees, approved a resolution setting ceilings on federal appropriations and expenditures that were substantially lower than the amounts projected in President Truman's budget. The House approved the ceilings, but the Senate raised them and insisted that an expected budget surplus be applied to debt retirement rather than to a reduction in taxes as House leaders proposed. A stalemate resulted, and that year's congressional budget initiative died in conference.

In 1948 both houses reached agreement on a budget resolution, but Congress then went on to appropriate $6 billion more than the agreed-upon ceiling in the resolution. In 1949 the process broke down entirely when the deadline for a budget resolution was moved from Feb. 15 to May 1. By that date 11 of the annual appropriation bills for government departments had been passed by the House and nine by the Senate, and the budget resolution never was approved.

The failure of the budget process under the Legislative Reorganization Act of 1946 prompted a serious effort in 1950 to combine the numerous separate appropriation bills into one omnibus measure. That year an omnibus measure was approved by Congress about two months earlier than the last of the separate funding measures had been passed in 1949. In addition, the appropriations total was about $2.3 billion below President Truman's combined budget requests. House Appropriations Committee Chairman Clarence A. Cannon (D-Mo.) hailed the omnibus approach as "the most practical and efficient method of handling the annual budget." [9]

Despite Cannon's support for the new approach, the House Appropriations Committee in 1951 voted 31-18 to return to the traditional method of considering the appropriation for each government department in separate bills. One reason was that the omnibus approach had undercut the authority of the full committee's subcommittees and their chairmen. (Under the traditional procedure, each subcommittee considered a different appropriations bill and was responsible for most of the funding decisions for an entire department or departments.) After the vote, Cannon charged that "every predatory lobbyist, every pressure group seeking to get its hands into the U.S. Treasury, every bureaucrat seeking to extend his empire downtown is opposed to the consolidated bill." [10]

The Senate in 1953 decided to try the omnibus appropriation bill approach again, but the House, which must initiate funding measures, did not act on the Senate proposal. A Senate proposal to create a Joint Budget Committee was approved by the Senate eight times between 1952 and 1967 but never accepted by the House.

By the 1950s Congress belatedly discovered that the world war and the expansion of government under the New Deal had diluted one of its most cherished prerogatives — the "power of the purse." Congress generally managed to authorize less spending than was proposed by the postwar presidents, but it proved unable to consider the budget as a whole or to enforce funding priorities as a means of controlling expenditures. "Backdoor spending" by Congress and executive branch impoundment of appropriated funds intensified legislative-executive tensions over the appropriations process. Congressional frustration frequently found expression in mandatory spending ceilings imposed on executive branch agencies and written into program authorizations.

Meanwhile, longstanding disagreements between the Senate and House over their respective roles in the appropriations process caused new rifts between the two chambers. In 1962 this feud delayed final action on appropriation bills. The squabble began as a disagreement over the physical location of conference committee meetings, but it soon engulfed the larger issues of whether the Senate could initiate its own appropriation bills and whether it could add to the House-passed money bills funds for items not previously considered, or considered and rejected, by the House.

When the Senate drafted and passed a resolution to provide emergency financing for federal agencies pending final congressional action on their regular appropriations, the House called the action an infringement on its "immemorial" right to initiate appropriation bills. In retaliation, the Senate adopted a resolution that "the acquiescence of the Senate in permitting the House to first consider appropriation bills cannot change the clear language of the Constitution nor affect the Senate's coequal power to originate any bill not expressly 'raising revenue.' " [11] Although the two chambers eventually reached a truce, the basic issues were not resolved. It was not until a decade later that the House and Senate agreed on new procedures for handling the federal budget.

Exercise of the War Power

Events of the postwar era reminded Congress that its constitutional power to declare war (Article I, Section 8) counted for little in the modern world. But in the late 1960s the Senate began to mount a substantial challenge to presidential authority over military involvement.

Truman. At issue in the early 1950s was the president's authority to dispatch troops to South Korea and Western Europe. Republican Sen. Robert A. Taft opened a three-month-long debate on Jan. 5, 1951, by asserting that Truman had "no authority whatever to commit American troops to Korea without consulting Congress and without congressional approval." Moreover, he said, the president had "no power to agree to send American troops to fight in Europe in a war between members of the Atlantic Pact and Soviet Russia." [12]

The troops-to-Europe debate ended on April 4 when the Senate adopted two resolutions approving the dispatch of four divisions to Europe. One of the resolutions stated that it was the sense of the Senate that "no ground troops in addition to such four divisions should be sent to Western Europe . . . without further congressional approval." [13] But neither resolution had the force of law because the House took no action.

Truman never asked Congress for a declaration of war in Korea, and he waited until Dec. 16, 1950 — six months after the outbreak of hostilities — to proclaim a national emergency. In defense of this course, it was argued that the Russians or the Chinese or both had violated post-World-War-II agreements on Korea and that emergency powers authorized during World War II still could be applied.

The Korean conflict provided two further tests of presidential power. In 1951 Truman dismissed Gen. Douglas A. MacArthur from his post as commander of United Nations' and U.S. forces in the Far East because of a dispute over policy. The Senate Foreign Relations and Armed Services committees reviewed the ouster of the popular general, and their joint hearings were credited with cooling the atmosphere throughout the country. So bitter was the controversy that the committees refrained from making any formal report, but the president's right to remove MacArthur was conceded, and the principle of civilian control over the military upheld.

In 1952 Congress ignored Truman's request for approval of his seizure of the nation's steel mills. The Supreme Court later ruled that the seizure was without statutory authority and constituted a usurpation of the powers of Congress by the chief executive.

Eisenhower. Presidents who followed Truman made frequent use of their constitutional power as commander in chief (Article II, Section 2). Sometimes they exercised their war powers unilaterally, at other times in cooperation with Congress. President Eisenhower, for example, asked Congress in 1955 for advance approval to use American armed forces in the event of a Chinese communist attack on Formosa or the Pescadores Islands. A resolution to that effect was adopted within a week. But without consulting Congress, Eisenhower landed troops in Lebanon in July 1958. In this instance he acted strictly on his own authority. In a special message to Congress on July 15, Eisenhower said his action was designed to protect American lives and "to assist the Government of Lebanon in the preservation of Lebanon's territorial integrity and independence, which have been deemed vital to U.S. national interests and world peace." [14]

Kennedy. President Kennedy, responding to Soviet threats to the rights of American allies in West Berlin, asked Congress on July 16, 1961, for authority to call up ready reservists and to extend the enlistments of men already on active duty. Such authority was granted in a joint resolution signed by the president Aug. 1. But Kennedy did not wait for congressional approval of his actions in the Cuban missile crisis of October 1962. Confronted with a buildup of Soviet missile bases in Cuba, he ordered an immediate "naval quarantine" of Cuba to prevent delivery of additional Russian missiles. More than any other crisis of the postwar period, the Cuba episode illustrated the vast sweep of presidential power in times of great emergency. [15]

Johnson. Congress virtually abdicated its power to declare war in Vietnam when it adopted the Gulf of Tonkin resolution authorizing the president to "take all necessary measures" to stop aggression in Southeast Asia.[16] The resolution was requested by President Johnson and adopted in August 1964 by a vote of 88-2 in the Senate and 414-0 in the House. The president considered the resolution adequate authority for expanding U.S. involvement in the Vietnam War, but in following years, as public support for the war deteriorated, Congress was to have second thoughts about its 1964 action. The Tonkin Gulf resolution was repealed in January 1971.

Notes

1. *Congressional Record*, 79th Cong., 1st sess., Jan. 18, 1945, p. H349.
2. Charles O. Jones, *The Minority Party in Congress* (Boston: Little, Brown & Co, 1970), p. 168.
3. *Congress and the Nation*, 5 vols., *Congress and the Nation, 1945-1964*, vol. 1 (Washington, D.C.: Congressional Quarterly, 1965), I: 1426.
4. Ibid., I: 1427.
5. Ibid.
6. *Congress and the Nation, 1969-1972*, vol. 3 (Washington, D.C.: Congressional Quarterly, 1973), III: 357.
7. *Congress and the Nation, 1945-1964*, I: 1726.
8. Ibid., I: 1774.
9. George B. Galloway, *The Legislative Process in Congress* (New York: Thomas Y. Crowell, 1946), p. 659.
10. Ibid.
11. *Congressional Record*, 87th Cong., 2nd sess., Oct. 13, 1962, p. S23470.
12. *Congress and the Nation, 1945-1964*, I: 264.
13. Ibid., I: 265.
14. Ibid., I: 122.
15. Ibid., I: 132-133.
16. Ibid., I: 138-139.

Chapter 26

CHANGING OF THE GUARD: 1969-1981

Conservative southern Democrats dominated the Senate power structure during the 1960s; through the seniority system, they slowly gained and tenaciously held onto many of the chamber's most prestigious leadership positions and committee chairmanships. But big election victories by the Democrats in the late 1950s and early 1960s began to push into the seniority pipeline a predominance of northern liberals. By the 1970s many of these senators had worked their way to the top leadership posts and had begun displacing their more conservative colleagues. The liberals' ascendancy led to important changes in Senate procedures as well as in its legislative product.

Legislation enacted in the 1970s stressed the role of government in answering society's diverse needs and curing its ills. Lyndon Johnson's Great Society programs of the mid-1960s, created to bring the poor into the mainstream of American life, were expanded during this decade to offer aid to individuals and communities of greater means. State and local governments, themselves strapped for cash, eagerly accepted federal funding.

In the Senate, institutional reforms were adopted that paralleled this democratic surge, making the chamber more open and egalitarian. Organizational and procedural changes enabled less senior members to gain power at the expense of older and more experienced legislators. With more staff, more money and more power, individual senators were able to maintain a new degree of independence from party leaders and could pursue more easily their own interests and legislative goals.

Senate reforms were not as broad as those in the House; the 100-member Senate already was a more accessible and less structured institution than the 435-member upper chamber. Unlike the House, the Senate, did not use a closed rule to govern the handling of a particular measure on the floor. Any senator was free to propose floor amendments, even if they were opposed by the Senate leadership or committee chairmen. Similarly, the Senate did not rely on non-recorded votes in acting upon major bills and controversial amendments, as did the House until its age-old floor procedures were modernized in 1970. Thus individual senators could be held more closely accountable for their positions on legislation. And the Senate had admitted television and radio coverage of Senate committees, sanctioned in the Legislative Reorganization Act of 1946, long before the House ended its general broadcast ban on committee hearings through enactment of the Legislative Reorganization Act of 1970.

Several of the most important Senate reforms centered on the filibuster. Many reformers felt the principal obstacle to a more democratic and responsible Senate was unlimited debate, which enabled a minority to use the filibuster to obstruct the majority. After years of trying, the reformers in 1975 reduced the number of votes needed to invoke cloture. This modification to Rule 22 did not prevent a minority from talking legislation to death, but it diminished the possibility by reducing the number of senators needed to end debate from two-thirds of those present and voting to three-fifths of the 100-member Senate.

A second major filibuster reform occurred in 1979 when the Senate agreed to curb the so-called "post-cloture" filibuster, a delaying tactic that had been used by a handful of senators to get around the 1975 cloture rule.

Reforms in other areas had a major impact on the way the Senate operated. In 1977 the Senate overhauled its committee system and adopted a new ethics code for members. The relationship between the Senate and the executive branch also changed. As public respect for the presidency waned in the aftermath of Watergate, the Senate took the lead in Congress in reasserting many of the powers of the legislative branch that slowly had been ceded to the president since World War II.

During the 1970s members of Congress were more willing to challenge the content and form of legislation drafted by the president. Particularly during the final years of the Nixon administration, fine tuning legislation became a contest of wills between a strong-minded executive and partisan legislators. The Budget Act of 1974 established congressional budget committees and involved Congress more deeply in the federal budget process. Congress also improved its oversight of executive agencies and assumed a higher profile in defense and foreign policy issues.

Congressional restrictions on the president's ability to carry out his basic foreign policy and military plans became commonplace. In 1973, the Democratic-controlled Congress won passage — over President Nixon's veto — of the War Powers Act, which attempted to delineate the extent of presidential war powers. Further incursions into the executive branch's domain occurred in 1975, when Congress defeated President Ford's proposals for emergency military aid for South Vietnam and Cambodia. Congress also temporarily placed an embargo on the transfer of U.S. military aid to Turkey and legislated against presidential proposals to provide military aid to anti-communist factions in a civil war in Angola.[1]

The Senate played an important role in reforming federal campaign laws and in exposing the crimes of Watergate. It was the Senate Watergate Committee that discovered the existence of the secret tape recordings that led eventually to President Nixon's resignation.

Changes in Party Leadership

The decade saw new Senate leadership on both sides of the aisle. Both Majority Leader Mike Mansfield (D-Mont.) and Minority Leader Hugh Scott (R-Pa.) announced their retirement from Congress effective at the conclusion of the 94th Congress in January 1977. Their departure coincided with the change in administrations in the White House from Gerald R. Ford (1974-1977) to Jimmy Carter (1977-1981).

The Democratic leader in the Senate since 1961, Mansfield capitalized during his final years as majority leader on his early opposition to the Vietnam War and his party's differences with the Nixon administration. Despite his low-key approach to the job, he ended his career as a respected party leader. But Scott completed his 18-year Senate career under a cloud of disfavor. He defended U.S. actions in Indochina long after many of his constituents had turned against the war. And his promise that the White House tapes would exonerate President Nixon caused him considerable embarrassment.[2]

Succeeding Mansfield as majority leader was Robert C. Byrd (D-W.Va.), who had assumed much of the responsibility for the day-to-day operations of the Senate while Mansfield still was leader. Other Senate Democrats — particularly Hubert H. Humphrey of Minnesota and Edward M. Kennedy of Massachusetts — built their reputations on national issues and oratorical flair. But Byrd built his by working quietly behind the scenes; his power base was constructed on a foundation of fa-

Senate Committee Changes

The Legislative Reorganization Act of 1946 reduced the number of standing committees in the Senate from 33 to 15 by dropping inactive committees and merging others with related functions. During the next 30 years only minor changes were made. But in 1977 the Senate agreed to another major overhaul of its committee structure. Fifteen standing committees with revised jurisdictions remained after the 1977 reorganization. The number increased to 16 at the beginning of the 97th Congress in 1981 when the Select Small Business Committee was made a standing committee.

Committee roster under 1946 act: Agriculture and Forestry; Appropriations; Armed Services; Banking and Currency; District of Columbia; Expenditures in the Executive Departments; Finance; Foreign Relations; Interstate and Foreign Commerce; Judiciary; Labor and Public Welfare; Post Office and Civil Service; Public Works; and Rules and Administration.

Four new standing committees were created between 1946 and 1981: Aeronautical and Space Sciences (1958, abolished in 1977); Veterans' Affairs (1970); Budget (1974) and Small Business (1981).

Six existing committees changed their names during this period: Public Lands became Interior and Insular Affairs in 1948 and Energy and Natural Resources in 1977; Expenditures in the Executive Departments became Government Operations in 1952 and Governmental Affairs in 1977; Interstate and Foreign Commerce became Commerce in 1961 and Commerce, Science and Transportation in 1977; Banking and Currency became Banking, Housing and Urban Affairs in 1970; Agriculture and Forestry became Agriculture, Nutrition and Forestry in 1977; Labor and Public Welfare became Human Resources in 1977 and Labor and Human Resources in 1979; and Public Works became Environment and Public Works in 1977.

Two of the committees created in 1946 were abolished in 1977; the jurisdiction of the District of Columbia and the Post Office and Civil Service committees were given to Governmental Affairs.

vors and parliamentary skills. A conservative by ideology, Byrd rarely let his own views shape his leadership functions. Instead, he viewed his task as one of sounding out his colleagues and then carrying out their wishes. Strengthening his hand in the Senate was his superb knowledge of Senate rules and procedures.

An aloof individual, Byrd confined his relationships with fellow Democrats purely to Senate business. His pompous manner also made him a somewhat stilted spokesman for the Democratic Party. But this did not prevent him from keeping a tight personal rein on the party apparatus in the chamber. The Senate Democratic Conference met rarely during his tenure as majority leader, and party staffers reported solely to him.

Howard H. Baker, Jr. (R-Tenn.) succeeded Scott as minority leader in January 1977. Although Baker mounted a last-minute campaign for the post, he defeated Minority Whip Robert P. Griffin (R-Mich.) by one vote. The job was to pay him rich dividends. It first served as a launching pad for his 1980 presidential campaign. Even when that effort failed, the 1980 congressional elections produced a Republican takeover of the Senate that in January 1981 catapulted Baker into the post of majority leader.

Baker's principal leadership tools were his relaxed manner and personal friendships with his Republican colleagues. Like Byrd, he downplayed his own political views in favor of reaching compromises through gentle persuasion. Though some conservatives held against him a handful of votes he took on such key conservative issues as Senate approval of the Panama Canal treaties, he enjoyed great popularity with most Republicans as well as with Democrats. As a result, a bipartisan spirit prevailed during his tenure as minority leader, and the majority of Republicans were able to cooperate with Democrats in fashioning legislation.

Baker became majority leader after the November 1980 elections propelled Ronald Reagan into the White House and gave the Republicans 12 new Senate seats for a total of 53 — the first Republican sweep of the Senate in 28 years. But some conservatives still harbored doubts about Baker's commitment to their particular brand of politics. The House remained in the Democrats' hands with 243 seats compared with the Republicans' 192, which constituted a second stumbling block to enactment of the new president's programs.

Baker overcame the conservatives' doubts in the first session of the 97th Congress (1981-1982) by stressing GOP unity over ideology. As a result, he enjoyed extraordinary success in guiding through the Senate a far-reaching package of tax and budget cuts that Reagan claimed would revitalize the American economy. At the same time, working closely with House Republican Leader Robert H. Michel of Illinois, Baker used his leverage as Senate leader to help prevent House Democrats from obstructing the Reagan program in the House.

Legislative Reorganization

The Legislative Reorganization Act of 1970 marked the first significant changes in Senate procedures since the major overhaul of the legislative branch in 1946. It authorized additional congressional staff, beefed up Congress' research and information resources and required the administration to provide Congress with more information about the federal budget. A separate section, consisting of rules changes applying only to the Senate, focused on improving the accountability, openness and efficiency of Senate committees.

The new legislation directed the U.S. comptroller general and Library of Congress to devote more of their resources to legislative research and permitted committees to hire consultants as well as to expand their permanent professional staffs. A Joint Committee on Congressional Operations was created to study the operations and organization of Congress and make recommendations on how to improve them. (The Senate abolished the joint committee at the end of the 94th Congress in 1977; a successor House Select Committee on Congressional Operations survived until 1979, when it too was abolished.)

Among the Senate rules changes were provisions 1) allowing a committee majority to call a meeting when the chairman refused to do so, 2) guaranteeing a committee's minority members the right to call witnesses and 3) requiring committees to adopt and publish their rules of procedure. Other rules changes made the committee assignment process more egalitarian by limiting the ability of senior senators to snap up all the choice seats. Under the new regulations, senators could be members of only two major committees and one minor, select or joint committee; no senator could serve on more than one of the most prestigious committees, and no senator could hold the chairmanship of more than one full committee and one subcommittee of a major committee.

To provide senators with more information on which to base their votes, the new rules prohibited Senate consideration of a bill — exceptions included declarations of war and other emergencies — unless the committee report on the measure was available three days before it was brought to the floor. In addition, conference committees were required to explain the actions taken on bills during House-Senate conferences.[3]

Seniority System Challenged

In 1971 Sens. Fred R. Harris (D-Okla.) and Charles McC. Mathias, Jr. (R-Md.) led an unsuccessful move to scrap the seniority system for selecting committee chairmen, a custom practiced since the mid-19th century, in favor of what they called "a standard of merit" in making the top choices. Their plan called for amending Rule 24, which stated that the Senate "shall proceed by ballot to appoint severally the chairmen of each committee, and then, by one ballot, the other members necessary to complete the same." Harris and Mathias favored changing the rule to require that committee chairmen and ranking minority members be nominated individually by a majority vote of the party caucuses and elected individually by majority vote of the full Senate at the beginning of each new Congress. But the proposal was reported adversely by the Senate Rules and Administration Committee.

Democratic reformers were more successful in January 1975 when they revised party rules to establish a method by which committee chairmen would have to face an election every two years, but a vote was not mandatory, as it was in the House. The Democratic Caucus voted to require selection of chairmen by secret ballot whenever one-fifth of the caucus requested it. The modification did not affect chairmen in the 94th Congress.

The rules change was intended to make it easier for senators to depose a chairman without fear of retribution. Under the procedure, a list of proposed committee chairmen nominated by the Democratic Steering Committee would be distributed to all Democrats. Party members then would check off the names of the nominees they wished to subject to a secret ballot and would submit the list without signing it. If at least 20 percent of the caucus members wanted a secret vote on any nominee it would be held automatically two days later.

Senate in the 'Sunshine'

The Senate lagged behind the House in opening to the public many of its committee meetings. Almost three years after the House voted in March 1973 to open up its committee bill-drafting sessions to the public

Postwar Secret Sessions

Although treaties and nominations are no longer considered in closed sessions, as they were until the late 19th century, the Senate occasionally holds secret sessions, usually to discuss classified information. In such sessions, the public, the press and most Senate aides are required to leave the chamber and galleries. Frequently a censored transcript of the proceedings is released later.

From the end of World War II to the adjournment of the first session of the 97th Congress on Dec. 16, 1981, the Senate held 23 secret sessions: April 11, 1963, to discuss classified information concerning missile defenses; July 14, 1966, to consider establishment of a special committee to oversee the activities of the Central Intelligence Agency; Oct. 2, 1968, and July 17, 1969, to consider classified material connected with the anti-ballistic missile program; Dec. 15, 1969, to discuss U.S. military actions in Laos and Thailand; Sept. 10 and Dec. 18, 1970, to discuss legislative impasses; June 7, 1971, to discuss a report on American military and related activities in Laos; twice on May 2, 1972,* and once on May 4, 1972, to consider a request to print classified National Security Council documents in the *Congressional Record*; Sept. 25, 1973, to debate the need for an accelerated Trident submarine program; June 10, 1974, to consider development of a new strategic missile system; June 4, 1975, again to discuss strategic missiles; Nov. 20, 1975, to consider releasing a study on the Central Intelligence Agency and political assassinations; Dec. 17 and 18, 1975, to consider U.S. activities in Angola; July 1, 1977, to consider sensitive information about the neutron bomb; Feb. 21 and 22, 1978, during debate on the then-pending Panama Canal treaties; May 15, 1978, to discuss the Carter administration's request to sell $4.8 billion worth of jet fighters to Israel, Egypt and Saudi Arabia; Sept. 21, 1979, to discuss classified data on a U.S. military exercise called "Nifty Nugget" that tested the military's readiness to mobilize for war; and Feb. 1, 1980, during debate on a military pay and benefits bill, to discuss personnel retention and recruitment problems in the military.**

* Technically, two separate secret meetings of the Senate were held on May 2, 1972, although the period of time between them was less than a minute.
**United States Senate, Office of the Secretary, Historical Office.

and the press, the Senate in November 1975 adopted a similar rule, requiring most of its committees to work in public. At the same time, the Senate approved open conference committee sessions, as the House had done in January, thereby ending one of the last bastions of congressional committee secrecy.

The new rules required all meetings to be public unless a majority of a committee voted in open session to close a meeting or series of meetings on the same subject. Meetings could not be closed for more than 14 days and only if they concerned: 1) national security; 2) committee personnel or internal staff management matters; 3) charges against a person that might harm a person professionally or otherwise represent an invasion of privacy; 4) disclosure of the identity of an informer or undercover agent or of the existence of a criminal investigation that should be kept secret; 5) disclosure of trade secrets or other confidential business information; or 6) disclosure of "matters required to be kept confidential under other provisions of law or government regulation."

The new Senate rules also required committees to prepare transcripts or electronic recordings of each of their sessions, including conference committee meetings, unless a majority of the committee voted not to comply with this rule.

In another 1975 reform, junior senators obtained committee staff assistance to aid them on legislative issues. In the past, committee staff members were controlled by chairmen and other senior members. Few junior members had regular and dependable access to staff personnel.[4]

Overhaul of Committee System

A top priority of the Senate when the 95th Congress convened in 1977 was reorganizing its committee structure. The reorganization, the first major overhaul of standing committees since 1946, was the product of the temporary Select Committee to Study the Senate Committee System, chaired by Sen. Adlai E. Stevenson III (D-Ill.).

The committee reforms approved by the Senate were more modest in scope than those originally proposed by the Stevenson committee. For example, the Veterans' Affairs and Select Small Business committees were saved, as well as the Joint Economic and Joint Taxation committees, although all would have been abolished under the Stevenson plan. But the reorganization did reduce the number of standing, select and partisan Senate committees from 31 to 25 and revised the jurisdictions of the remaining panels. The overhaul also limited the number of committees and subcommittees a senator could belong to and provided committees' minority members with additional staff support.[5]

Filibuster Reforms

After years of effort, Senate reformers in March 1975 modified Rule 22 to make it easier for the Senate to terminate filibusters mounted by a minority of its members. The existing rule had required two-thirds of senators present and voting — 67 senators if all 100 senators voted — to invoke cloture and thus bring a controversial bill or amendment to a vote. The 1975 change set the number of votes required to invoke cloture at three-fifths of the full Senate — 60 if there were no vacancies.

Before 1975, Senate liberals had attempted to modify the cloture rule every two years since 1959, with the exception of 1973. In 1971, the last time a concerted effort was made before the successful attempt in 1975, reformers failed on a series of four votes to amend Rule 22. The last few months of the 91st Congress had seen the Senate become embroiled in a confusion of filibusters on a variety of major questions. Although this spectacle led to soul-searching within the Senate and to calls from President Nixon for procedural reforms, the Senate refused to make any change at the beginning of the 92nd Congress.

The change in the cloture rule finally was adopted in March 1975 after a bitter three-week struggle on the Senate floor. One reason for the reformers' success was that many of the younger senators felt less vehemently about preserving the old rule than had their predecessors in previous Congresses. Historically, the filibuster had been most important to southern senators interested in blocking civil rights legislation. But by 1975 the big battles over civil rights already had taken place. *(See box, Famous Filibusters, p. 261.)*

Initially, the reformers had sought to permit a simple majority or a three-fifths majority of senators present and voting to end a filibuster, but they subsequently settled for a compromise that set the number at three-fifths of the Senate membership, called "a constitutional majority." The new rule applied to any matter except a proposed change in the Standing Rules of the Senate — including Rule 22, of course — for which the old two-thirds majority rule for ending debate still held.

As it turned out, the change in the filibuster rule made it only marginally easier for a Senate faction to invoke cloture. The record of voting patterns shows that the three-fifths "constitutional" majority rule would have made little difference in the actual outcome of legislation on which filibusters and cloture votes had occurred since Rule 22 was adopted in 1917. During the 20 years immediately preceding the 1975 change, for example, on only five of 79 cloture attempts were 60 votes or more (but not a two-thirds majority) obtained. And in four of these cases where bills were being filibustered, cloture was obtained on a subsequent vote. At the time, however, reformers expected the new rule to speed up the Senate's work as well as cut down on the number of filibusters on controversial legislation.

A second, less publicized change in the filibuster rule was approved by a coalition of Senate liberals and conservatives in April 1976. The change allowed the introduction of amendments to a bill being filibustered up until the announcement of the outcome of a cloture vote. Under the previous version of the rule, no amendment was to be considered after cloture was invoked that had not been formally read or considered prior to the cloture vote. In practice, the Senate routinely agreed by unanimous consent to consider all amendments at the Senate desk at the time of a cloture vote, so supporters said the change merely formalized the existing informal practice. But opponents argued that the change made it possible to delay bringing an amendment or bill to a final vote after cloture had been invoked.[6]

Over the next couple of years, the Senate paid increasing attention to the period following a cloture vote on a bill or amendment. The so-called "post-cloture filibuster" was to become a new form of delay and the new focus of reform efforts in the Senate.

Rule 22 already allowed each senator just one hour to talk on a bill after cloture was invoked. Technically, the hour-per-senator limit did not include such parliamentary maneuvers as quorum calls and votes on amendments submitted before the cloture vote. In 1976 Sen. James B. Allen (D-Ala.) stretched the rule to the limit by making frequent quorum calls and bringing up amendment after amendment for a vote, even after cloture had been invoked on bills he opposed. These shrewd parliamentary tactics soon made Allen a hero to conservatives but earned him the scorn of colleagues forced to accept compromises they otherwise would have opposed once a filibuster had been broken.

Majority Leader Byrd attempted to end such tactics in early 1977, but his effort never gained momentum, and in the ensuing 95th Congress use of the post-cloture filibuster mushroomed. Most of the time, use of

Senate Filibusters and the . . .

Several techniques can be employed against the filibuster: the most spectacular, and probably least effective, is the use of prolonged sessions to break the strength of the obstructionists. A second technique is strict observance of existing Senate rules. A widely ignored rule requires a speaker to stand, rather than sit or walk about. The rules also permit the presiding officer to take a senator "off his feet" for using unparliamentary language; require that business intervene between quorum calls; and prohibit the reading of speeches or other material by a clerk without Senate consent. Finally, a senator may be refused an opportunity to speak more than twice on a subject in any one day. (A legislative day may spread over several calendar days if the Senate recesses rather than adjourns.)

Senate Cloture Rule

The Senate's ultimate check on the filibuster is the provision for cloture, or limitation on debate, contained in Rule 22 of its Standing Rules. The original Rule 22 was adopted in 1917 following a furor over the "talking to death" of a proposal by President Wilson to arm American merchant ships before the United States entered World War I. The new cloture rule required the votes of two-thirds of all of the senators present and voting to invoke cloture. In 1949, during a parliamentary skirmish preceding scheduled consideration of a Fair Employment Practices Commission bill, the requirement was raised to two-thirds of the entire Senate membership.

A revision of the rule in 1959 provided for limitation of debate by a vote of two-thirds of the senators present and voting, two days after a cloture petition was submitted by 16 senators. If cloture was adopted by the Senate, further debate was limited to one hour for each senator on the bill itself and on all amendments affecting it. No new amendments could be

that technique was confined to conservatives. However, during a highly charged debate on legislation proposing to deregulate natural gas prices, two liberal Democrats — Howard Metzenbaum of Ohio and James Abourezk of South Dakota — mounted a post-cloture filibuster that tied up the Senate for nine days.[7]

The natural gas debate provided Byrd with one more reason to try

. . . Cloture Rule: A Recapitulation

offered except by unanimous consent. Amendments that were not germane to the pending business and dilatory motions were out of order. The rule applied both to regular legislation and to motions to change the Standing Rules.

Rule 22 was revised significantly in 1975 by lowering the vote needed for cloture to three-fifths of the Senate membership. That revision applied to any matter except proposed rules changes, for which the old requirement of a two-thirds majority of senators present and voting still applied.

Post-Cloture Curbs

The 1975 revision succeeded in making it easier for a Senate majority to invoke cloture and thus cut off an extended debate mounted by a minority. But much of the revision's success relied on the willingness of the senators to abide by the spirit as well as the letter of the chamber's rules. When cloture was invoked on a particular measure, senators generally conceded defeat and proceeded to a vote without further delay.

But in 1976 Sen. James B. Allen (D-Ala.) began violating this unwritten rule of conduct by using his mastery of parliamentary technique and the Senate's rules to eat up far more time than the one hour allotted him under the 1959 rules revision. He did so by capitalizing on a loophole that permitted unlimited post-cloture quorum calls, parliamentary motions and roll-call votes on amendments introduced before cloture was invoked.

The Senate closed this loophole in 1979 when it agreed to an absolute limit on post-cloture delaying tactics. The rule provided that once cloture was invoked, a final vote had to be taken after no more than 100 hours of debate. All time spent on quorum calls, roll-call votes and other parliamentary procedures was to be included in the 100-hour limit.

again to curb the practice, and his second effort, begun in January 1979, met with greater success. Byrd initially proposed a package of seven changes in the filibuster rule, including an absolute time limit on post-cloture filibusters, a limit on debate on motions to bring up a bill, a procedure to limit non-germane amendments to bills being filibustered, and a method to speed up consideration of cloture petitions. He pressed for adoption of the package for six weeks before a group of senators working behind the scenes agreed to a compromise.

As adopted by the full Senate in February, the change included only the absolute time limit on post-cloture filibusters. It required that after the Senate voted to invoke cloture on a bill, a final vote had to occur after no more than 100 hours of post-cloture debate. The new limitation appeared to put an end to the practice of post-cloture filibusters, but Senate leaders warned that the rules still could be abused by a senator who was skillful enough and willing to incur the wrath of his colleagues.

Budget Control

Under the Congressional Budget Act of 1974, Congress strengthened its control over government spending. The new budget process, which took effect in fiscal year 1977, forced Congress into more measured and timely action on appropriations legislation, combining Congress' separate spending decisions with fiscal policy objectives in a congressionally determined budget package. The Senate worked closely with the House on the drafting of the legislation.

Among other changes, the budget act moved back the beginning of the government's fiscal year from July 1 to Oct. 1 and mandated a series of deadlines imposing changes in Congress' consideration of its annual appropriations bills. This was to allow Congress time to complete the entire budget process before the fiscal year began. It had been decades since Congress had enacted its appropriations legislation by July 1. The act also curbed presidential impoundment of funds as a means of cutting government spending. President Nixon's use of impoundment to override Congress' fiscal and legislative decisions was one of the principal reasons for the budget act's support in Congress.[8] *(See History of the House, pp. 173-174.)*

Campaign Practices

Long criticized for doing little to control the use of money in federal election campaigns, Congress approved two comprehensive federal election campaign finance reform bills: the Federal Election Campaign Act of 1971 and the Federal Election Campaign Act Amendments of 1974. Another major overhaul of election laws occurred in 1976 after a Supreme Court decision declared key portions of the 1971 and 1974 laws unconstitutional.

Before enactment of the 1971 and 1974 measures, the entire history of campaign finance legislation had been one of non-enforcement. No candidate for Congress had ever been prosecuted under the Corrupt Practices Act of 1925, which was repealed by the 1971 law. But the abuses of Watergate and widespread allegations of illegal congressional fund-raising activities prompted the reforms.

The new laws strengthened the requirements for reporting, and making available for public inspection, the sources and amounts of a candidate's campaign contributions and how the money was spent. All candidates and political committees were required to report the names and addresses of all persons making contributions and loans in excess of $100 and of all persons to whom expenditures of $100 were made. The disclosure requirements were viewed by many as the most useful feature of the laws because they enabled scholars, journalists and investigators to obtain a better picture of spending patterns and to uncover formerly concealed contributions and expenditures.[9]

The 1974 act established the Federal Election Commission to collect the finance reports and oversee federal campaigns to ensure compliance. It also provided for public financing of presidential campaigns, though it did not include public financing of congressional races, a feature approved by the Senate but dropped in conference at the insistence of House conferees.

The new laws limited campaign contributions and campaign spending and, with the help of a key Federal Election Commission decision, opened the door to union and corporate financial participation in political campaigns. By limiting the role individuals could play in campaigns while enabling unions and corporations to establish political action committees, the laws changed the face of campaign financing in America. In the future, candidates turned away from the political parties and other traditional kingmakers in favor of small donors, corporations and unions. The rapid increase in the number of political action committees and the cost of political campaigns led to widespread criticism that corporations and unions could in effect buy members' friendship with offers of campaign contributions. But Congress appeared to have little interest in curbing the committees' activities beyond requiring the public disclosure of their financial activities.

The Supreme Court held unanimously on January 30, 1976, that the Federal Election Commission was unconstitutional because it violated the Constitution's separation-of-powers and appointment clauses by being congressionally appointed but exercising executive branch power. The court also threw out the 1974 law's limitations on independent political expenditures as a clear violation of the First Amendment.

The Federal Election Campaign Act Amendments of 1976 reorganized the commission as a six-member panel appointed by the president and confirmed by the Senate; established new contribution limits for individuals and political committees and cut off matching funds for presidential candidates who receive less than a specific percentage of the votes cast during the primaries. No limit was imposed on spending for congressional races and individual candidates were exempted from any limits on contributions they make to themselves. The 1976 revisions did not alter the public financing provisions for presidential campaigns and the spending limits on the presidential pre-nomination and general election campaigns.

On Jan. 8, 1980, President Carter signed the Federal Campaign Act Amendments of 1979, which simplified reporting and registration requirements that apply to political committees and candidates and lifted some restrictions on volunteer activities and on party assistance to federal candidates.[10]

CIA, FBI Probe

Senate investigations into the activities of the Central Intelligence Agency (CIA) and the Federal Bureau of Investigation (FBI) earned the Senate a reputation as a tough overseer of executive agencies in the mid-1970s.

In the post-World War II era, the CIA and the FBI routinely were excluded from congressional oversight, even during Congress' annual consideration of the budgets of those agencies. But in a series of hearings in 1975, the Senate Select Committee to Study Government Operations with Respect to Intelligence Activities revealed that the CIA had illegally kept deadly poisons, snooped into Americans' mail and conducted extensive domestic spying operations, in violation of the agency's charter.

The select committee in the spring of 1976 issued reports stating that since World War II Republican and Democratic administrations alike had used the FBI for secret surveillance of citizens. The report prompted FBI Director Clarence M. Kelley, in a May 1976 speech, to place the blame for FBI wrongdoing on his predecessor, J. Edgar Hoover.[11]

Watergate

The Senate launched its inquiry into the Watergate scandal on Feb. 7, 1973, when it approved by a 77-0 vote a resolution creating a Select Committee on Presidential Campaign Activities (known as the Senate Watergate Committee), to investigate and study "the extent . . . to which illegal, improper, or unethical activities" occurred in the 1972 presidential campaign and election. The nationally televised committee hearings were the major focus of Watergate developments during the summer of 1973.

Numerous former employees of the Committee for the Re-election of the President, which directed Nixon's 1972 campaign, as well as former White House aides appeared — some to admit perjury during earlier investigations. They drew a picture of political sabotage that went far beyond the break-in and attempted burglary of the headquarters of the Democratic National Committee in the Watergate Hotel.

The hearings brought forth details of a special White House investigative unit, known as the "plumbers," that had been responsible for "plugging leaks" in the administration through such tactics as harassment of Daniel Ellsberg, who had released the classified "Pentagon Papers" on the Vietnam War to the press. During a four-day appearance before the panel, former White House counsel John Dean turned over about 50 documents to the Senate committee, including a memorandum written by Dean on "dealing with our political enemies." White House lists subsequently made public named about 200 important "enemies." Dean was the only witness to implicate the president directly in the Watergate cover-up.

Another important revelation to come out of the committee hearings resulted from questioning of Federal Aviation Administration chief Alexander P. Butterfield, a former White House aide. Butterfield testified publicly in July that the president's offices were equipped with a special voice-activated system that secretly recorded all conversations. The subsequent emergence of the taped evidence completely changed the course of the Watergate investigation and ultimately led to President Nixon's dramatic resignation on Aug. 9, 1974.[12]

New Ethics Code

In the wake of revelations of political wrongdoing during the Watergate years, the Senate in 1977 adopted a new code of conduct drafted by a special committee headed by Sen. Gaylord Nelson (D-Wis.).

The ethics code required expanded disclosure requirements of the financial activities of both senators and highly paid Senate employees, imposed tight restrictions on senators' outside employment activities, ended unofficial office accounts and strengthened rules governing the use of the frank. The code also restructured the Senate's Ethics Committee. To sweeten the reform package, legislators got a 29 percent pay raise.[13]

The code recommended by Nelson's committee was weakened slightly before the Senate approved it. Spirited debate was prompted by a controversial provision, to take effect in 1979, limiting senators' outside earnings each year to 15 percent of their official salary. Senators relying to a significant extent on their official salaries alone argued bitterly that the rule favored their wealthier colleagues, who could continue to live on unearned income — in the form of rent, dividends and interest payments — which were not affected by the code's restrictions. Despite the opposition, the 15 percent limit was upheld on the Senate floor. But in January 1979 senators reversed themselves and voted to delay the limit's effective date until 1983.

The adoption of the ethics code and other rules changes increased the total number of Senate rules to 50. So the Senate in November 1979 and again in March 1980 revised, consolidated and renumbered certain rules without changing either their substance or interpretation. These two recodifications brought the total number of Senate rules down to 42.[14]

Two major misconduct cases shook the Senate during the decade. In October 1979 Sen. Herman E. Talmadge (D-Ga.) was "denounced" for financial misconduct. And on March 11, 1982, Sen. Harrison A. Williams, Jr. (D-N.J.) resigned on the eve of a Senate vote to expel him for his involvement in an FBI undercover political corruption investigation dubbed "Abscam."

The action against Talmadge was taken after press reports surfaced that the senior Georgia Democrat had collected reimbursements from the Senate for expenses that he never incurred or were not reimbursable under Senate rules, that he had accepted reimbursements from his campaign funds that were not reported to the Federal Election Commission, and that he lived for years off unreported gifts of cash, food, lodging and even clothes from friends and constituents. After a lengthy investigation, a divided Senate Ethics Committee recommended that Talmadge be "denounced" by his colleagues rather than "censured" — the more traditional punishment — apparently to enable Talmadge's

Senate supporters to claim the punishment was less severe than censure. The denunciation was voted amidst lengthy testimonials to Talmadge's character. Talmadge was defeated for re-election in November 1980.

Sen. Williams' expulsion was debated by the Senate after a federal jury in Brooklyn, N.Y., found him guilty of bribery and conspiracy in May 1981. Williams resigned only hours before the Senate was expected to vote on his expulsion — a vote that seemed certain to go against the 23-year Senate veteran. By resigning, Williams avoided becoming the first senator to be expelled since the Civil War and the first in history on grounds other than treason or disloyalty. The New Jersey Democrat had been accused of accepting a hidden interest in a Virginia titanium mine in return for a promise to use his influence to obtain government contracts to buy the mine's output. As part of the deal, government agents posing as wealthy Arabs and their associates promised to loan $100 million to the mining venture, owned by friends of Williams. Williams also was accused of promising to use his influence to help an undercover agent posing as a wealthy Arab gain permanent U.S. residency.

Both in his federal trial and in hearings before the Senate Ethics Committee, Williams maintained his innocence. He explained that he had been "entrapped" and "fooled" by the undercover agents into making seemingly incriminating statements.[15]

Vietnam and War Powers Act

Concerted Senate efforts to reassert its voice in the conduct of foreign affairs dated back to the late 1960s and the opposition to the Vietnam War. The result was passage in 1973 of the War Powers Act, the first law ever passed by Congress defining and limiting presidential war powers. The legislation was approved after Congress overrode President Nixon's veto of the bill.

Although the final version of the act was closer to the House-passed bill, much of the credit for its enactment belonged to its Senate supporters, for the legislation culminated several years of Senate attempts to limit executive war powers. Under the law, the president could commit U.S. armed forces to hostilities only pursuant to a declaration of war, specific statutory authorization or a national emergency created by an attack upon the United States or its armed forces, territories or possessions. And the president "in every possible instance" was expected to consult with Congress before committing U.S. forces to hostilities, and to consult Congress regularly after such a commitment.

The law also required the president to report to Congress in writing within 48 hours on any commitment or substantial enlargement of U.S. combat forces abroad, except for deployments related solely to supply, replacement, repair or training. Finally, the law required U.S. troops to be withdrawn within 60 days after the president submitted his initial report to Congress, unless Congress declared war, specifically authorized the commitment of troops or was physically unable to convene because of an armed attack on the United States.

Congress again asserted its determination to take a forceful role in the conduct of foreign policy in 1975. As communist forces were overrunning South Vietnam and Cambodia, the Senate Armed Services Committee refused to approve President Ford's request for $722 million in additional military aid to South Vietnam. Then on May 12 Cambodian communist forces captured the American merchant ship *Mayaguez* and its crew of 39. President Ford ordered combined Navy, Air Force and Marine units to retake the ship and crew. Ford's action was questioned in Congress, but there was general agreement that he had authority to commit U.S. troops under the War Powers Act. Ford complied with the letter of the law by later issuing a report to Congress on his actions.[16]

SALT Talks, Panama Canal

After another tangle between the Senate and the executive branch over the conduct of foreign policy, the Senate in 1978 ratified two treaties with Panama relinquishing American control over the Panama Canal. The Carter administration argued that the treaties were in the best long-term interests of the nation, but conservatives mounted a fierce campaign to convince Americans and their legislators that the treaties would compromise U.S. national security. The treaties ultimately were approved, but only after 38 days of Senate debate. No other single foreign policy issue since the Vietnam War had attracted as much attention, aroused as many emotions and consumed as much of an administration's time and effort. Senators' votes on the treaties remained a key issue in their re-election campaigns for years afterward.

In 1979 a similarly intense executive-legislative struggle developed over approval of a new U.S.-Soviet arms limitation treaty (SALT II). But on the eve of what observers expected to be a protracted Senate debate on the matter, the Soviet Union invaded Afghanistan. President Carter then withdrew the treaty from Senate consideration, explaining that the Soviet action had convinced him the treaty no longer served the nation's best interests. Both SALT II supporters and opponents, however, agreed that Carter's decision simply reflected the political reality that the pact would not have come even close to winning the necessary two-thirds Senate majority had it come up for a vote.[17]

Republican Advances

The contentious debates over the Panama Canal and SALT II treaties hinted that the liberals' domination of the Senate was drawing to a close. The November 1980 general election confirmed this supposition, and 1980 proved to be a watershed year for Congress.

In a stunning Republican victory, the GOP gained control of the White House as well as the Senate. Adding to the election's impact was the defeat of many of the Senate's most senior Democrats, many of them liberals. And though the House remained in Democratic hands, Republicans discovered they could in effect control both chambers by luring to their side in the House the votes of many conservative southern Democrats.

This change in the congressional power balance signaled a reversal of two and a half decades of uninterrupted Democratic rule on Capitol Hill, and it put a halt to a decade of liberal domination in Congress. As the 97th Congress began, the Senate's committees were taken over by Republican chairmen who were in many instances dramatically more conservative, younger and less experienced than the Democrats they replaced. In the ensuing months, even liberals began to act more like conservatives, out of fear that the 1980 election reflected a fundamental realignment of the political spectrum rather than a single instance of conservative success at the polls.

The Republicans elected to the 97th Congress were proud to follow the conservative president who had led their national ticket, Ronald Reagan. This was in marked contrast to the Democrats' independence from Jimmy Carter during his administration. Rather than set out on their own in an attempt to assert their independence, most congressional Republicans quickly fell in line behind Reagan and his free market economic policies, even though it meant clipping their own wings.

During its first year, at least, the Reagan presidency appeared to prove that the era of the strong executive and the submissive legislature had not ended decades before.

Notes

1. Arthur M. Schlesinger Jr., *The Imperial Presidency* (Boston: Houghton-Mifflin Company, 1973), p. 201; *Congressional Record*, 90th Cong., 1st sess., July 31, 1967, pp. S20706, S20718; *Congressional Quarterly Almanac, 1972* (Washington, D.C.: Congressional Quarterly, 1973), pp. 905-917; *Congressional Quarterly Almanac, 1975* (Washington, D.C.: Congressional Quarterly, 1976), p. 5.

2. *Congressional Quarterly Weekly Report*, Dec. 6, 1975, p. 2657; *Congressional Quarterly Weekly Report*, March 6, 1976, p. 507.

3. *Congress and the Nation*, 5 vols., *Congress and the Nation, 1969-1972*, vol. 3 (Washington, D.C.: Congressional Quarterly, 1973), III: 382-396.

4. *Inside Congress*, p. 15.

5. *Congressional Quarterly Almanac, 1977* (Washington, D.C.: Congressional Quarterly, 1978), p. 781.

6. *Inside Congress* (Washington, D.C.: Congressional Quarterly, 1976), pp. 11-14; *Congressional Quarterly Weekly Report*, April 10, 1976, pp. 838-839.

7. *Almanac, 1977*, p. 735.

8. Ibid., pp. 127-133; *Congressional Quarterly Almanac, 1974* (Washington, D.C.: Congressional Quarterly, 1975), pp. 145-153.

9. *Congressional Quarterly Almanac, 1971* (Washington, D.C.: Congressional Quarterly, 1972), pp. 875-896; *Almanac, 1974*, pp. 611-633.

10. *Congressional Quarterly Almanac, 1976* (Washington, D.C.: Congressional Quarterly, 1977), pp. 459-462; *Federal Regulatory Directory, 1981-1982* (Washington, D.C.: Congressional Quarterly, 1981), p. 468.

11. *The Washington Post*, May 10, 1976.

12. *Congressional Quarterly Almanac, 1973* (Washington, D.C.: Congressional Quarterly, 1974), p. 1008; *Watergate: Chronology of a Crisis* (Washington, D.C.: Congressional Quarterly, 1975), pp. 192, 620.

13. *Almanac, 1977*, pp. 763-781.

14. For a history of Senate rules from 1789 to 1981 by Sen. Robert C. Byrd, see *Congressional Record*, 97th Cong., 1st sess, Feb. 16, 1981, S1284-S1295.

15. *Congressional Quarterly Weekly Report*, March 13, 1982, p. 555.

16. *Almanac, 1973*, pp. 905-917; *Almanac, 1975*, pp. 291, 306-311, 344-349, 885-887.

17. *Congressional Quarterly Almanac, 1979* (Washington, D.C.: Congressional Quarterly, 1980), p. 411.

CONSTITUTION
OF THE UNITED STATES

We the People of the United States, in Order to form a more perfect Union, establish Justice, insure domestic Tranquility, provide for the common defence, promote the general Welfare, and secure the Blessings of Liberty to ourselves and our Posterity, do ordain and establish this Constitution for the United States of America.

Article I

Section 1. All legislative Powers herein granted shall be vested in a Congress of the United States, which shall consist of a Senate and House of Representatives.

Section 2. The House of Representatives shall be composed of Members chosen every second Year by the People of the several States, and the Electors in each State shall have the Qualifications requisite for Electors of the most numerous Branch of the State Legislature.

No Person shall be a Representative who shall not have attained to the age of twenty five Years, and been seven Years a Citizen of the United States, and who shall not, when elected, be an Inhabitant of that State in which he shall be chosen.

Representatives and direct Taxes shall be apportioned among the several States which may be included within this Union, according to their respective Numbers, which shall be determined by adding to the whole Number of free Persons, including those bound to Service for a Term of Years, and excluding Indians not taxed, three fifths of all other Persons. The actual Enumeration shall be made within three Years after the first Meeting of the Congress of the United States, and within every subsequent Term of ten Years, in such Manner as they shall by Law direct. The Number of Representatives shall not exceed one for every thirty Thousand, but each State shall have at Least one Representative; and until such enumeration shall be made, the State of New Hampshire shall be entitled to chuse three, Massachusetts eight, Rhode-Island and Providence Plantations one, Connecticut five, New-York six, New Jersey four, Pennsylvania eight, Delaware one, Maryland six, Virginia ten, North Carolina five, South Carolina five, and Georgia three.

When vacancies happen in the Representation from any State, the Executive Authority thereof shall issue Writs of Election to fill such Vacancies.

The House of Representatives shall chuse their Speaker and other Officers; and shall have the sole Power of Impeachment.

Section 3. The Senate of the United States shall be composed of two Senators from each State, chosen by the Legislature thereof, for six Years; and each Senator shall have one Vote.

Immediately after they shall be assembled in Consequence of the first Election, they shall be divided as equally as may be into three Classes. The Seats of the Senators of the first Class shall be vacated at the Expiration of the second Year, of the second Class at the Expiration of the fourth Year, and of the third Class at the Expiration of the sixth Year, so that one third may be chosen every second Year; and if Vacancies happen by Resignation, or otherwise, during the Recess of the Legislature of any State, the Executive thereof may make temporary Appointments until the next Meeting of the Legislature, which shall then fill such Vacancies.

No Person shall be a Senator who shall not have attained to the Age of thirty Years, and been nine Years a Citizen of the United States, and who shall not, when elected, be an Inhabitant of that State for which he shall be chosen.

The Vice President of the United States shall be President of the Senate, but shall have no Vote, unless they be equally divided.

The Senate shall chuse their other Officers, and also a President pro tempore, in the Absence of the Vice President, or when he shall exercise the Office of President of the United States.

The Senate shall have the sole Power to try all Impeachments. When sitting for that Purpose, they shall be on Oath or Affirmation. When the President of the United States is tried the Chief Justice shall preside: And no Person shall be convicted without the Concurrence of two thirds of the Members present.

Judgment in Cases of Impeachment shall not extend further than to removal from Office, and disqualification to hold and enjoy any Office of honor, Trust or Profit under the United States: but the Party convicted shall nevertheless be liable and subject to Indictment, Trial, Judgment and Punishment, according to Law.

Section 4. The Times, Places and Manner of holding Elections for Senators and Representatives, shall be prescribed in each State by the Legislature thereof; but the Congress may at any time by Law make or alter such Regulations, except as to the Places of chusing Senators.

The Congress shall assemble at least once in every Year, and such Meeting shall be on the first Monday in December, unless they shall by Law appoint a different Day.

Section 5. Each House shall be the Judge of the Elections, Returns and Qualifications of its own Members, and a Majority of each shall constitute a Quorum to do Business; but a smaller Number may adjourn from day to day, and may be authorized to compel the Attendance of absent Members, in such Manner, and under such Penalties as each House may provide.

Each House may determine the Rules of its Proceedings, punish its Members for disorderly Behaviour, and, with the Concurrence of two thirds, expel a Member.

Each House shall keep a Journal of its Proceedings, and from time to time publish the same, excepting such Parts as may in their Judgment require Secrecy; and the Yeas and Nays of the Members of either House on any question shall, at the Desire of one fifth of those Present, be entered on the Journal.

Neither House, during the Session of Congress, shall, without the Consent of the other, adjourn for more than three days, nor to any other Place than that in which the two Houses shall be sitting.

Section 6. The Senators and Representatives shall receive a Compensation for their Services, to be ascertained by Law, and paid out of the Treasury of the United States. They shall in all Cases, except Treason, Felony and Breach of the Peace, be privileged from Arrest during their Attendance at the Session of their respective Houses, and in going to and returning from the same; and for any Speech or Debate in either House, they shall not be questioned in any other Place.

No Senator or Representative shall, during the Time for which he was elected, be appointed to any civil Office under the Authority of the United States, which shall have been created, or the Emoluments whereof shall have been encreased during such time; and no Person holding any Office under the United States, shall be a Member of either House during his Continuance in Office.

Section 7. All Bills for raising Revenue shall originate in the House of Representatives; but the Senate may propose or concur with amendments as on other Bills.

Every Bill which shall have passed the House of Representatives and the Senate, shall, before it become a Law, be presented to the President of the United States; If he approve he shall sign it, but if not he shall return it, with his Objections to that House in which it shall have originated, who shall enter the Objections at large on their Journal, and proceed to reconsider it. If after such Reconsideration two thirds of that House shall agree to pass the Bill, it shall be sent, together with the Objections, to the other House, by which it shall likewise be reconsidered, and if approved by two thirds of that House, it shall become a Law. But in all such Cases the Votes of both Houses shall be determined by yeas and Nays, and the Names of the Persons voting for and against the Bill shall be entered on the Journal of each House respectively. If any Bill shall not be returned by the President within ten Days (Sunday excepted) after it shall have been presented to him, the Same shall be a Law, in like Manner as if he had signed it, unless the Congress by their Adjournment prevent its Return, in which Case it shall not be a Law.

Every Order, Resolution, or Vote to which the Concurrence of the Senate and House of Representatives may be necessary (except on a question of Adjournment) shall be presented to the President of the United States; and before the Same shall take Effect, shall be approved by him, or being disapproved by him, shall be repassed by two thirds of the Senate and House of Representatives, according to the Rules and Limitations prescribed in the Case of a Bill.

Section 8. The Congress shall have Power To lay and collect Taxes, Duties, Imposts and Excises, to pay the Debts and provide for the common Defence and general Welfare of the United States; but all Duties, Imposts and Excises shall be uniform throughout the United States;

To borrow Money on the credit of the United States;

To regulate Commerce with foreign Nations, and among the several States, and with the Indian Tribes;

To establish an uniform Rule of Naturalization, and uniform Laws on the subject of Bankruptcies throughout the United States;

To coin Money, regulate the Value thereof, and of foreign Coin, and fix the Standard of Weights and Measures;

To provide for the Punishment of counterfeiting the Securities and current Coin of the United States;

To establish Post Offices and post Roads;

To promote the Progress of Science and useful Arts, by securing for limited Times to Authors and Inventors the exclusive Right to their respective Writings and Discoveries;

To constitute Tribunals inferior to the supreme Court;

To define and punish Piracies and Felonies commited on the high Seas, and Offences against the Law of Nations;

To declare War, grant Letters of Marque and Reprisal, and make Rules concerning Captures on Land and Water;

To raise and support Armies, but no Appropriation of Money to that Use shall be for a longer Term than two Years;

To provide and maintain a Navy;

To make Rules for the Government and Regulation of the land and naval Forces;

To provide for calling forth the Militia to execute the Laws of the Union, suppress Insurrections and repel Invasions;

To provide for organizing, arming, and disciplining, the Militia, and for governing such Part of them as may be employed in the Service of the United States, reserving to the States respectively, the Appointment of the Officers, and the Authority of training the Militia according to the discipline prescribed by Congress;

To exercise exclusive Legislation in all Cases whatsoever, over such District (not exceeding ten Miles square) as may, by Cession of Particular States, and the Acceptance of Congress, become the Seat of the Government of the United States, and to exercise like Authority over all Places purchased by the Consent of the Legislature of the State in which the Same shall be, for the Erection of Forts, Magazines, Arsenals, dock-Yards, and other needful Buildings; — And

To make all Laws which shall be necessary and proper for carrying into Execution the foregoing Powers, and all other Powers vested by this Constitution in the Government of the United States, or in any Department or Officer thereof.

Section 9. The Migration or Importation of such Persons as any of the States now existing shall think proper to admit, shall not be prohibited by the Congress prior to the Year one thousand eight hundred and eight, but a Tax or duty may be imposed on such Importation, not exceeding ten dollars for each Person.

The Privilege of the Writ of Habeas Corpus shall not be suspended, unless when in Cases of Rebellion or Invasion the public Safety may require it.

No Bill of Attainder or ex post facto Law shall be passed.

No capitation, or other direct, Tax shall be laid, unless in Proportion to the Census of Enumeration herein before directed to be taken.

No Tax or Duty shall be laid on Articles exported from any State.

No Preference shall be given by any Regulation of Commerce or Revenue to the Ports of one State over those of another; nor shall Vessels bound to, or from, one State, be obliged to enter, clear or pay Duties in another.

No Money shall be drawn from the Treasury, but in Consequence of Appropriations made by Law; and a regular Statement and Account of the Receipts and Expenditures of all public Money shall be published from time to time.

No Title of Nobility shall be granted by the United States: And no Person holding any Office of Profit or Trust under them, shall, without the Consent of the Congress, accept of any present, Emolument, Office, or Title, of any kind whatever, from any King, Prince or foreign State.

Section 10. No State shall enter into any Treaty, Alliance, or Confederation; grant Letters of Marque and Reprisal; coin Money; emit Bills of Credit; make any Thing but gold and silver Coin a Tender in Payment of Debts; pass any Bill of Attainder, ex post facto Law, or Law impairing the Obligation of Contracts, or grant any Title of Nobility.

No State shall, without the Consent of the Congress, lay any Imposts or Duties on Imports or Exports, except what may be absolutely necessary for executing it's inspection Laws: and the net Produce of all Duties and Imposts, laid by any State on Imports or Exports, shall be for the Use of the Treasury of the United States; and all such Laws shall be subject to the Revision and Controul of the Congress.

No State shall, without the Consent of Congress, lay any Duty of Tonnage, keep Troops, or Ships of War in time of Peace, enter into any Agreement or Compact with another State, or with a foreign Power, or engage in War, unless actually invaded, or in such imminent Danger as will not admit of delay.

Article II

Section 1. The executive Power shall be vested in a President of the United States of America. He shall hold his Office during the Term of four Years, and, together with the Vice President, chosen for the same Term, be elected, as follows.

Each State shall appoint, in such Manner as the Legislature thereof may direct, a Number of Electors, equal to the whole Number of Senators and Representatives to which the State may be entitled in the Congress: but no Senator or Representative, or Person holding an Office of Trust or Profit under the United States, shall be appointed an Elector.

The Electors shall meet in their respective States, and vote by Ballot for two Persons, of whom one at least shall not be an Inhabitant of the same State with themselves. And they shall make a List of all the Persons voted for, and of the Number of Votes for each; which List they shall sign and certify, and transmit sealed to the Seat of the Government of the United States, directed to the President of the Senate. The President of the Senate shall, in the Presence of the Senate and House of Representatives, open all the Certificates, and the Votes shall then be counted. The Person having the greatest Number of Votes shall be the President, if such Number be a Majority of the whole Number of Electors appointed; and if there be more than one who have such Majority, and have an equal Number of Votes, then the House of Representatives shall immediately chuse by Ballot one of them for President; and if no Person have a Majority, then from the five highest on the list the said House shall in like Manner chuse the President. But in chusing the President, the Votes shall be taken by States, the Representation from each State having one Vote; a quorum for this Purpose shall consist of a Member or Members from two thirds of the States, and a Majority of all the States shall be necessary to a Choice. In every Case, after the Choice of the President, the Person having the greatest Number of Votes of the Electors shall be the Vice President. But if there should remain two or more who have equal Votes, the Senate shall chuse from them by Ballot the Vice President.

The Congress may determine the Time of chusing the Electors, and the Day on which they shall give their Votes; which Day shall be the same throughout the United States.

No Person except a natural born Citizen, or a Citizen of the United States, at the time of the Adoption of this Constitution, shall be eligible to the Office of President; neither shall any Person be eligible to that Office who shall not have attained to the Age of thirty five Years, and been fourteen Years a Resident within the United States.

In Case of the Removal of the President from Office, or of his Death, Resignation, or Inability to discharge the Powers and Duties of the said Office, the Same shall devolve on the Vice President, and the Congress may by Law provide for the Case of Removal, Death, Resignation or Inability, both of the President and Vice President, declaring what Officer shall then act as President, and such Officer shall act accordingly, until the Disability be removed, or a President shall be elected.

The President shall, at stated Times, receive for his Services, a Compensation, which shall neither be encreased nor diminished during the Period for which he shall have been elected, and he shall not receive within that Period any other Emolument from the United States, or any of them.

Before he enter on the Execution of his Office, he shall take the following Oath or Affirmation: — "I do solemnly swear (or affirm) that I will faithfully execute the Office of President of the United States, and will to the best of my Ability, preserve, protect and defend the Constitution of the United States."

Section 2. The President shall be Commander in Chief of the Army and Navy of the United States, and of the Militia of the several States, when called into the actual Service of the United States; he may require the Opinion, in writing, of the principal Officer in each of the executive Departments, upon any Subject relating to the Duties of their respective Offices, and he shall have Power to grant Reprieves and Pardons for Offenses against the United States, except in Cases of Impeachment.

He shall have Power, by and with the Advice and Consent of the Senate, to make Treaties, provided two thirds of the Senators present concur; and he shall nominate, and by and with the Advice and Consent of the Senate, shall appoint Ambassadors, other public Ministers and Consuls, Judges of the supreme Court, and all other Officers of the United States, whose Appointments are not herein otherwise provided for, and which shall be established by Law: but the Congress may by Law vest the Appointment of such inferior Officers, as they think proper, in the President alone, in the Courts of Law, or in the Heads of Departments.

The President shall have Power to fill up all Vacancies that may happen during the Recess of the Senate, by granting Commissions which shall expire at the End of their next Session.

Section 3. He shall from time to time give to the Congress Information of the State of the Union, and recommend to their Consideration such Measures as he shall judge necessary and expedient; he may, on extraordinary Occasions, convene both Houses, or either of them, and in Case of Disagreement between them, with Respect to the Time of Adjournment, he may adjourn them to such Time as he shall think proper; he shall receive Ambassadors and other public Ministers; he shall take Care that the Laws be faithfully executed, and shall Commission all the Officers of the United States.

Section 4. The President, Vice President and all Civil Officers of the United States, shall be removed from office on Impeachment for, and Conviction of, Treason, Bribery, or other high Crimes and Misdemeanors.

Article III

Section 1. The judicial Power of the United States, shall be vested in one supreme Court, and in such inferior Courts as the Congress may from time to time ordain and establish. The Judges, both of the supreme and inferior Courts, shall hold their Offices during good Behaviour, and shall, at stated Times, receive for their Services, a Compensation, which shall not be diminished during their Continuance in Office.

Section 2. The judicial Power shall extend to all Cases, in Law and Equity, arising under this Constitution, the Laws of the United States, and Treaties made, or which shall be made, under their Authority; — to all Cases affecting Ambassadors, other public Ministers and Consuls; — to all Cases of admiralty and maritime Jurisdiction; — to Controversies to which the United States shall be a Party; — to Controversies between two or more States; — between a State and Citizens of another State; — between Citizens of different States; — between Citizens of the same State claiming Lands under Grants of different States, and between a State, or the Citizens thereof, and foreign States, Citizens or Subjects.

In all Cases affecting Ambassadors, other public Ministers and Consuls, and those in which a State shall be Party, the supreme Court shall have original Jurisdiction. In all the other Cases before mentioned, the supreme Court shall have appellate Jurisdiction, both as to Law and

Fact, with such Exceptions, and under such Regulations as the Congress shall make.

The Trial of all Crimes, except in cases of Impeachment, shall be by Jury; and such Trial shall be held in the State where the said Crimes shall have been committed; but when not committed within any State, the Trial shall be at such Place or Places as the Congress may by Law have directed.

Section 3. Treason against the United States, shall consist only in levying War against them, or in adhering to their Enemies, giving them Aid and Comfort. No Person shall be convicted of Treason unless on the Testimony of two Witnesses to the same overt Act, or on Confession in open Court.

The Congress shall have Power to declare the Punishment of Treason, but no Attainder of Treason shall work Corruption of Blood, or Forfeiture except during the Life of the Person attainted.

Article IV

Section 1. Full Faith and Credit shall be given in each State to the public Acts, Records, and judicial Proceedings of every other State. And the Congress may by general Laws prescribe the Manner in which such Acts, Records and Proceedings shall be proved, and the Effect thereof.

Section 2. The Citizens of each State shall be entitled to all Privileges and Immunities of Citizens in the several States.

A Person charged in any State with Treason, Felony, or other Crime, who shall flee from Justice, and be found in another State, shall on Demand of the executive Authority of the State from which he fled, be delivered up, to be removed to the State having Jurisdiction of the Crime.

No Person held to Service or Labour in one State, under the Laws thereof, escaping into another, shall, in Consequence of any Law or Regulation therein, be discharged from such Service or Labour, but shall be delivered up on Claim of the Party to whom such Service or Labour may be due.

Section 3. New States may be admitted by the Congress into this Union; but no new State shall be formed or erected within the Jurisdiction of any other State; nor any State be formed by the Junction of two or more States, or Parts of States, without the Consent of the Legislatures of the States concerned as well as of the Congress.

The Congress shall have Power to dispose of and make all needful Rules and Regulations respecting the Territory or other Property belonging to the United States; and nothing in this Constitution shall be so construed as to Prejudice any Claims of the United States, or of any particular State.

Section 4. The United States shall guarantee to every State in this Union a Republican Form of Government, and shall protect each of them against Invasion; and on Application of the Legislature, or of the Executive (when the Legislature cannot be convened) against domestic Violence.

Article V

The Congress, whenever two thirds of both Houses shall deem it necessary, shall propose Amendments to this Constitution, or, on the Application of the Legislatures of two thirds of the several States, shall call a Convention for proposing Amendments, which, in either Case, shall be valid to all Intents and Purposes, as Part of this Constitution, when ratified by the Legislatures of three fourths of the several States, or by Conventions in three fourths thereof, as the one or the other Mode of Ratification may be proposed by the Congress; Provided that no Amendment which may be made prior to the Year One thousand eight hundred and eight shall in any Manner affect the first and fourth Clauses in the Ninth Section of the first Article; and that no State, without its Consent, shall be deprived of its equal Suffrage in the Senate.

Article VI

All Debts contracted and Engagements entered into, before the Adoption of this Constitution, shall be as valid against the United States under this Constitution, as under the Confederation.

This Constitution, and the Laws of the United States which shall be made in Pursuance thereof; and all Treaties made, or which shall be made, under the Authority of the United States, shall be the supreme Law of the Land; and the Judges in every State shall be bound thereby, any Thing in the Constitution or Laws of any State to the Contrary notwithstanding.

The Senators and Representatives before mentioned, and the Members of the several State Legislatures, and all executive and judicial Officers, both of the United States and of the several States, shall be bound by Oath or Affirmation, to support this Constitution; but no religious Test shall ever be required as a Qualification to any Office or public Trust under the United States.

Article VII

The Ratification of the Conventions of nine States, shall be sufficient for the Establishment of this Constitution between the States so ratifying the Same. Done in Convention by the Unanimous Consent of the States present the Seventeenth Day of September in the Year of our Lord one thousand seven hundred and Eighty seven and of the Independence of the United States of America the Twelfth In witness whereof We have hereunto subscribed our Names, George Washington, President and deputy from Virginia.

New Hampshire:	John Langdon, Nicholas Gilman.
Massachusetts:	Nathaniel Gorham, Rufus King.
Connecticut:	William Samuel Johnson, Roger Sherman.
New York:	Alexander Hamilton
New Jersey:	William Livingston, David Brearley, William Paterson, Jonathan Dayton.
Pennsylvania:	Benjamin Franklin, Thomas Mifflin, Robert Morris, George Clymer, Thomas FitzSimons, Jared Ingersoll, James Wilson, Gouverneur Morris.
Delaware:	George Read, Gunning Bedford Jr., John Dickinson, Richard Bassett, Jacob Broom.

Maryland:	James McHenry,
	Daniel of St. Thomas Jenifer,
	Daniel Carroll.
Virginia:	John Blair,
	James Madison Jr.
North Carolina:	William Blount,
	Richard Dobbs Spaight,
	Hugh Williamson.
South Carolina:	John Rutledge,
	Charles Cotesworth Pinckney,
	Charles Pinckney,
	Pierce Butler.
Georgia:	William Few,
	Abraham Baldwin.

Amendments

Amendment I

(First ten amendments ratified Dec. 15, 1791.)

Congress shall make no law respecting an establishment of religion, or prohibiting the free exercise thereof; or abridging the freedom of speech, or of the press; or the right of the people peaceably to assemble, and to petition the Government for a redress of grievances.

Amendment II

A well regulated Militia, being necessary to the security of a free State, the right of the people to keep and bear Arms, shall not be infringed.

Amendment III

No Soldier shall, in time of peace be quartered in any house, without the consent of the Owner, nor in time of war, but in a manner to be prescribed by law.

Amendment IV

The right of the people to be secure in their persons, houses, papers, and effects, against unreasonable searches and seizures, shall not be violated, and no Warrants shall issue, but upon probable cause,

Constitution

supported by Oath or affirmation, and particularly describing the place to be searched, and the persons or things to be seized.

Amendment V

No person shall be held to answer for a capital, or otherwise infamous crime, unless on a presentment or indictment of a Grand Jury, except in cases arising in the land or naval forces, or in the Militia, when in actual service in time of War or public danger; nor shall any person be subject for the same offence to be twice put in jeopardy of life or limb; nor shall be compelled in any criminal case to be a witness against himself, nor be deprived of life, liberty, or property, without due process of law; nor shall private property be taken for public use, without just compensation.

Amendment VI

In all criminal prosecutions, the accused shall enjoy the right to a speedy and public trial, by an impartial jury of the State and district wherein the crime shall have been committed, which district shall have been previously ascertained by law, and to be informed of the nature and cause of the accusation; to be confronted with the witnesses against him; to have compulsory process for obtaining witnesses in his favor, and to have the Assistance of Counsel for his defence.

Amendment VII

In Suits at common law, where the value in controversy shall exceed twenty dollars, the right of trial by jury shall be preserved, and no fact tried by a jury, shall be otherwise re-examined in any Court of the United States, than according to the rules of the common law.

Amendment VIII

Excessive bail shall not be required, nor excessive fines imposed, nor cruel and unusual punishments inflicted.

Amendment IX

The enumeration in the Constitution, of certain rights, shall not be construed to deny or disparage others retained by the people.

Amendment X

The powers not delegated to the United States by the Constitution, nor prohibited by it to the States, are reserved to the States respectively, or to the people.

Amendment XI *(Ratified Feb. 7, 1795)*

The Judicial power of the United States shall not be construed to extend to any suit in law or equity, commenced or prosecuted against one of the United States by Citizens of another State, or by Citizens or Subjects of any Foreign State.

Amendment XII *(Ratified June 15, 1804)*

The Electors shall meet in their respective states and vote by ballot for President and Vice-President, one of whom, at least, shall not be an inhabitant of the same state with themselves; they shall name in their ballots the person voted for as President, and in distinct ballots the person voted for as Vice-President, and they shall make distinct lists of all persons voted for as President, and of all persons voted for as Vice-President, and of the number of votes for each, which lists they shall sign and certify, and transmit sealed to the seat of the government of the United States, directed to the President of the Senate; — The President of the Senate shall, in the presence of the Senate and House of Representatives, open all the certificates and the votes shall then be counted; — The person having the greatest number of votes for President, shall be the President, if such number be a majority of the whole number of Electors appointed; and if no person have such majority, then from the persons having the highest numbers not exceeding three on the list of those voted for as President, the House of Representatives shall choose immediately, by ballot, the President. But in choosing the President, the votes shall be taken by states, the representation from each state having one vote; a quorum for this purpose shall consist of a member or members from two-thirds of the states, and a majority of all the states shall be necessary to a choice. And if the House of Representatives shall not choose a President whenever the right of choice shall devolve upon them, before the fourth day of March next following, then the Vice-President shall act as President, as in the case of the death or other constitutional disability of the President — The person having the greatest number of votes as Vice-President, shall be the Vice-President, if such number be a majority of the whole number of Electors appointed, and if no person have a majority, then from the two highest numbers on the list, the Senate shall choose the Vice-President; a quorum for the purpose shall consist of two-thirds of the whole number of Senators, and a majority of the whole number shall be necessary to a choice. But no person constitutionally ineligible to the office of President shall be eligible to that of Vice-President of the United States.

Amendment XIII *(Ratified Dec. 6, 1865)*

Section 1. Neither slavery nor involuntary servitude, except as a punishment for crime whereof the party shall have been duly convicted, shall exist within the United States, or any place subject to their jurisdiction.

Section 2. Congress shall have power to enforce this article by appropriate legislation.

Amendment XIV *(Ratified July 9, 1868)*

Section 1. All persons born or naturalized in the United States and subject to the jurisdiction thereof, are citizens of the United States and of the State wherein they reside. No State shall make or enforce any law which shall abridge the privileges or immunities of citizens of the United States; nor shall any State deprive any person of life, liberty, or property, without due process of law; nor deny to any person within its jurisdiction the equal protection of the laws.

Section 2. Representatives shall be apportioned among the several States according to their respective numbers, counting the whole number of persons in each State, excluding Indians not taxed. But when the right to vote at any election for the choice of electors for President and Vice President of the United States, Representatives in Congress, the Executive and Judicial officers of a State, or the members of the Legislature thereof, is denied to any of the male inhabitants of such State, being twenty-one years of age, and citizens of the United States, or in any way abridged, except for participation in rebellion, or other crime, the basis of representation therein shall be reduced in the proportion which the number of such male citizens shall bear to the whole number of male citizens twenty-one years of age in such State.

Section 3. No person shall be a Senator or Representative in Congress, or elector of President and Vice President, or hold any office, civil or military, under the United States, or under any State, who, having previously taken an oath, as a member of Congress, or as an officer of the United States, or as a member of any State legislature, or as an executive or judicial officer of any State, to support the Constitution of the United States, shall have engaged in insurrection or rebellion against the same, or given aid or comfort to the enemies thereof. But Congress may by a vote of two-thirds of each House, remove such disability.

Section 4. The validity of the public debt of the United States, authorized by law, including debts incurred for payment of pensions and bounties for services in suppressing insurrection or rebellion, shall not be questioned. But neither the United States nor any State shall assume or pay any debt or obligation incurred in aid of insurrection or rebellion against the United States, or any claim for the loss or emancipation of any slave; but all such debts, obligations and claims shall be held illegal and void.

Section 5. The Congress shall have power to enforce, by appropriate legislation, the provisions of this article.

Amendment XV *(Ratified Feb. 3, 1870)*

Section 1. The right of citizens of the United States to vote shall not be denied or abridged by the United States or by any State on account of race, color, or previous condition of servitude.

Section 2. The Congress shall have power to enforce this article by appropriate legislation.

Amendment XVI *(Ratified Feb. 3, 1913)*

The Congress shall have power to lay and collect taxes on incomes, from whatever source derived, without apportionment among the several States, and without regard to any census or enumeration.

Amendment XVII *(Ratified Apr. 8, 1913)*

The Senate of the United States shall be composed of two Senators from each State, elected by the people thereof, for six years; and each Senator shall have one vote. The electors in each State shall have the qualifications requisite for electors of the most numerous branch of the State legislatures.

When vacancies happen in the representation of any State in the Senate, the executive authority of such State shall issue writs of election to fill such vacancies: *Provided,* That the legislature of any State may empower the executive thereof to make temporary appointments until the people fill the vacancies by election as the legislature may direct.

This amendment shall not be so construed as to affect the election or term of any Senator chosen before it becomes valid as part of the Constitution.

Amendment XVIII *(Ratified Jan. 16, 1919)*

Section. 1. After one year from the ratification of this article the manufacture, sale, or transportation of intoxicating liquors within, the importation thereof into, or the exportation thereof from the United States and all territory subject to the jurisdiction thereof for beverage purposes is hereby prohibited.

Section 2. The Congress and the several States shall have concurrent power to enforce this article by appropriate legislation.

Section 3. This article shall be inoperative unless it shall have been ratified as an amendment to the Constitution by the legislatures of the several States, as provided in the Constitution, within seven years from the date of the submission hereof to the States by the Congress.

Amendment XIX *(Ratified Aug. 18, 1920)*

The right of citizens of the United States to vote shall not be denied or abridged by the United States or by any State on account of sex.

Congress shall have power to enforce this article by appropriate legislation.

Amendment XX *(Ratified Jan. 23, 1933)*

Section 1. The terms of the President and Vice President shall end at noon on the 20th day of January, and the terms of Senators and Representatives at noon on the 3d day of January, of the years in which such terms would have ended if this article had not been ratified; and the terms of their successors shall then begin.

Section 2. The Congress shall assemble at least once in every year, and such meeting shall begin at noon on the 3d day of January, unless they shall by law appoint a different day.

Section 3. If, at the time fixed for the beginning of the term of the President, the President elect shall have died, the Vice President elect shall become President. If a President shall not have been chosen before the time fixed for the beginning of his term, or if the President elect shall have failed to qualify, then the Vice President elect shall act as President until a President shall have qualified; and the Congress may by law provide for the case wherein neither a President elect nor a Vice President elect shall have qualified, declaring who shall then act as President, or the manner in which one who is to act shall be selected, and such person shall act accordingly until a President or Vice President shall have qualified.

Section 4. The Congress may by law provide for the case of the death of any of the persons from whom the House of Representatives may choose a President whenever the right of choice shall have devolved upon them, and for the case of the death of any of the persons from whom the Senate may choose a Vice President whenever the right of choice shall have devolved upon them.

Section 5. Sections 1 and 2 shall take effect on the 15th day of October following the ratification of this article.

Section 6. This article shall be inoperative unless it shall have been ratified as an amendment to the Constitution by the legislatures of three-fourths of the several States within seven years from the date of its submission.

Amendment XXI *(Ratified Dec. 5, 1933)*

Section 1. The eighteenth article of amendment to the Constitution of the United States is hereby repealed.

Section 2. The transportation or importation into any State, Territory or possession of the United States for delivery or use therein of intoxicating liquors, in violation of the laws thereof, is hereby prohibited.

Section 3. This article shall be inoperative unless it shall have been ratified as an amendment to the Constitution by conventions in the several States, as provided in the Constitution, within seven years from the date of the submission hereof to the States by the Congress.

Amendment XXII *(Ratified Feb. 27, 1951)*

Section 1. No person shall be elected to the office of the President more than twice, and no person who has held the office of President, or acted as President, for more than two years of a term to which some other person was elected President shall be elected to the office of the President more than once. But this Article shall not apply to any person holding the office of President when this Article was proposed by the Congress, and shall not prevent any person who may be holding the office of President, or acting as President, during the term within which this Article becomes operative from holding the office of President or acting as President during the remainder of such term.

Section 2. This Article shall be inoperative unless it shall have been ratified as an amendment to the Constitution by the legislatures of three-fourths of the several States within seven years from the date of its submission to the States by the Congress.

Amendment XXIII *(Ratified March 29, 1961)*

Section 1. The District constituting the seat of Government of the United States shall appoint in such manner as the Congress may direct:

A number of electors of President and Vice President equal to the whole number of Senators and Representatives in Congress to which the District would be entitled if it were a State, but in no event more than the least populous State; they shall be in addition to those appointed by the States, but they shall be considered, for the purposes of the election of President and Vice President, to be electors appointed by a State; and they shall meet in the District and perform such duties as provided by the twelfth article of amendment.

Section 2. The Congress shall have power to enforce this article by appropriate legislation.

Amendment XXIV *(Ratified Jan. 23, 1964)*

Section 1. The right of citizens of the United States to vote in any primary or other election for President or Vice President, for electors for President or Vice President, or for Senator or Representative in Congress, shall not be denied or abridged by the United States or any State by reason of failure to pay any poll tax or other tax.

Section 2. The Congress shall have power to enforce this article by appropriate legislation.

Amendment XXV *(Ratified Feb. 10, 1967)*

Section 1. In case of the removal of the President from office or of his death or resignation, the Vice President shall become President.

Section 2. Whenever there is a vacancy in the office of the Vice President, the President shall nominate a Vice President who shall take office upon confirmation by a majority vote of both Houses of Congress.

Section 3. Whenever the President transmits to the President pro tempore of the Senate and the Speaker of the House of Representatives his written declaration that he is unable to discharge the powers and duties of his office, and until he transmits to them a written declaration to the contrary, such powers and duties shall be discharged by the Vice President as Acting President.

Section 4. Whenever the Vice President and a majority of either the principal officers of the executive departments or of such other body as Congress may by law provide, transmit to the President pro tempore of the Senate and the Speaker of the House of Representatives their written declaration that the President is unable to discharge the powers and duties of his office, the Vice President shall immediately assume the powers and duties of the office as Acting President.

Thereafter, when the President transmits to the President pro tempore of the Senate and the Speaker of the House of Representatives his written declaration that no inability exists, he shall resume the powers and duties of his office unless the Vice President and a majority of either the principal officers of the executive department or of such other body as Congress may by law provide, transmit within four days to the President pro tempore of the Senate and the Speaker of the House of Representatives their written declaration that the President is unable to discharge the powers and duties of his office. Thereupon Congress shall decide the issue, assembling within forty-eight hours for that purpose if not in session. If the Congress, within twenty-one days after receipt of the latter written declaration, or, if Congress is not in session, within twenty-one days after Congress is required to assemble, determines by two-thirds vote of both houses that the President is unable to discharge the powers and duties of his office, the Vice President shall continue to discharge the same as Acting President; otherwise, the President shall resume the powers and duties of his office.

Amendment XXVI *(Ratified July 1, 1971)*

Section 1. The right of citizens of the United States, who are eighteen years of age or older, to vote shall not be denied or abridged by the United States or by any State on account of age.

Section 2. The Congress shall have power to enforce this article by appropriate legislation.

SELECTED BIBLIOGRAPHY

Part I Constitutional Beginnings

Andrews, Charles M. *The Colonial Period of American History.* 4 vols. New Haven: Yale University Press, 1934.

Beard, Charles A. *An Economic Interpretation of the Constitution of the United States.* New York: Macmillan, 1935.

____, ed. *The Enduring Federalist.* Garden City, N.Y.: Doubleday, 1948.

Brant, Irving. *James Madison: Father of the Constitution, 1787-1800.* Indianapolis: Bobbs-Merrill, 1950.

Burnett, Edmund C. *The Continental Congress.* New York: Macmillan, 1941.

Butterfield, L. H., ed. *Adams Family Correspondence.* 4 vols. *December 1761-May 1776.* vol. 1. Cambridge, Mass.: The Belknap Press of Harvard University Press, 1963.

Commager, Henry Steele, ed. *Documents of American History.* 2 vols. *Documents of American History to 1898.* vol. 1. Englewood Cliffs, N. J.: Prentice-Hall, 1973.

Elliot, Jonathan, ed. *The Debates in the Several State Conventions on the Adoption of the Federal Constitution.* 5 vols. Philadelphia: J. B. Lippincott, 1937.

Farrand, Max. *The Framing of the Constitution of the United States.* New Haven: Yale University Press, 1913.

____, ed. *The Records of the Federal Convention of 1787.* 4 vols. New Haven: Yale University Press, 1973.

Fisher, Louis. *The Politics of Shared Power: Congress and the Executive.* Washington, D.C.: CQ Press, 1981.

Greene, Jack P., ed. *Great Britain and the American Colonies, 1606-1763.* New York: Harper Paperbacks, 1970.

Hamilton, Alexander; Madison, James; and Jay, John. *The Federalist Papers.* Introduction by Clinton Rossiter. New York: Mentor, 1961.

Jensen, Merrill. *The Articles of Confederation.* Madison, Wis.: University of Wisconsin Press, 1940.

Kelly, Alfred H., and Harbison, Winfred A. *The American Constitution: Its Origins and Development.* New York: Norton, 1955.

Lingley, Charles Ramsdell. *The Transition in Virginia from Colony to Commonwealth.* New York: Columbia University, 1910.

McLaughlin, Andrew C. *The Confederation and the Constitution, 1783-1789.* Foreword by Henry Steele Commager. New York: Collier Books, 1962.

Morgan, Edmund S. *The Birth of the Republic.* Chicago: University of Chicago Press, 1956.

Nevins, Allan. *The American States During and After the Revolution, 1775-1789.* New York: Macmillan, 1966.

Smith, David G. *The Convention and the Constitution.* New York: St. Martin's Press, 1965.

Van Doren, Carl. *Benjamin Franklin.* Westport, Conn.: Greenwood Press, 1973.

——. *The Great Rehearsal: The Story of the Making and Ratifying of the Constitution.* Boston: Little, Brown, 1928.

Warren, Charles. *The Making of the Constitution.* Boston: Little, Brown, 1928.

Wilson, Woodrow. *Congressional Government.* 1885. Reprint ed. Baltimore: The Johns Hopkins University Press, 1981.

Wright, Benjamin F. *Consensus and Continuity, 1776-1787.* Boston: Boston University Press, 1958.

Part II History of the House

Bolling, Richard H. *House Out of Order.* New York: E. P. Dutton, 1965.

——. *Power in the House.* New York: E. P. Dutton, 1968.

Brown, George Rothwell. *The Leadership of Congress.* New York: Arno Press, 1974.

Burns, James MacGregor. *Congress on Trial.* New York: Harper & Brothers, 1949.

Carroll, Holbert N. *The House of Representatives and Foreign Affairs.* Pittsburgh: University of Pittsburgh Press, 1958.

Chiu, Chang-Wei. *The Speaker of the House of Representatives Since 1896.* New York: Columbia University Press, 1928.

Clapp, Charles L. *The Congressman: His Work As He Sees It.* Washington, D.C.: Brookings Institution, 1963.

Congress and the Nation, 1945-1964. vol. 1. Washington, D.C.: Congressional Quarterly Inc., 1965.

Congress and the Nation, 1965-1968. vol. 2. Washington, D.C.: Congressional Quarterly Inc., 1969.

Congress and the Nation, 1969-1972. vol. 3. Washington, D.C.: Congressional Quarterly Inc., 1973.

Congress and the Nation, 1973-1976. vol. 4. Washington, D.C.: Congressional Quarterly Inc., 1977.

Congress and the Nation, 1977-1980. vol. 5. Washington, D.C.: Congressional Quarterly Inc., 1981.

Congressional Quarterly Almanac: 97th Congress, 1st Session, 1981. Washington, D.C.: Congressional Quarterly Inc., 1982.

Davidson, Roger H., and Oleszek, Walter J. *Congress and Its Members.* Washington, D.C.: CQ Press, 1981.

Dodd, Lawrence C., and Oppenheimer, Bruce I., eds. *Congress Reconsidered.* 2nd ed. Washington, D.C.: CQ Press, 1981.

Fenno, Richard F., Jr. *Congressmen in Committees.* Boston: Little, Brown, 1973.

_____. *Home Style: House Members in Their Districts.* Boston: Little, Brown, 1978.

_____. *The Power of the Purse: Appropriations Politics in Congress.* Boston: Little, Brown, 1966.

Follett, Mary P. *The Speaker of the House of Representatives.* New York: Burt Franklin Reprints, 1974.

Ford, Paul Leicester, ed. *The Writings of Thomas Jefferson.* 10 vols. New York: G. P. Putnam's, 1895.

Froman, Lewis A., Jr. *Congressmen and their Constituencies.* Chicago: Rand-McNally Co., 1963.

Galloway, George B. *Congress at the Crossroads.* New York: Thomas Y. Crowell Co., 1946.

_____. *History of the House of Representatives.* rev. ed. by Sidney Wise. New York: Thomas Y. Crowell Co., 1976.

_____. *The Legislative Process in Congress.* New York: Thomas Y. Crowell Co., 1953.

Griffith, Ernest S. *Congress: Its Contemporary Role.* New York: New York University Press, 1951.

Hasbrouck, Paul DeWitt. *Party Government in the House of Representatives.* New York: Macmillan, 1927.

Hecht, Marie B. *John Quincy Adams: A Personal History of an Independent Man*. New York: Macmillan, 1972.

Hinds, Asher C. *Precedents of the House of Representatives of the United States*. 5 vols. Washington, D.C.: U.S. Government Printing Office, 1907.

Huitt, Ralph K., and Peabody, Robert L. *Congress: Two Decades of Analysis*. New York: Harper & Row, 1972.

MacNeil, Neil. *Forge of Democracy: The House of Representatives*. New York: David McKay Co., 1963.

Mann, Thomas E., and Ornstein, Norman J., eds. *The New Congress*. Washington, D.C.: American Enterprise Institute for Public Policy Research, 1981.

Mayo, Bernard. *Henry Clay: Spokesman of the New West*. Boston: Houghton-Mifflin, 1937.

McConachie, Lauros G. *Congressional Committees: A Study of the Origins and Development of Our National and Local Legislative Methods*. New York: Burt Franklin Reprints, 1973.

Riddick, Floyd M. *The United States Congress: Organization and Procedure*. Manassas, Va.: National Capitol Publishers, 1949.

Ripley, Randall B. *Party Leaders in the House of Representatives*. Washington, D.C.: Brookings Institution, 1967.

Robinson, James A. *The House Rules Committee*. Indianapolis: Bobbs-Merrill Co., 1963.

Sundquist, James L. *The Decline and Resurgence of Congress*. Washington, D.C.: Brookings Institution, 1981.

Williams, T. Harry. *Hayes: The Diary of a President, 1875-1881*. New York: David McKay Co., 1964.

Wilson, Woodrow. *Congressional Government*. 1885. Reprint ed. Baltimore: The Johns Hopkins University Press, 1981.

Young, Roland. *The American Congress*. New York: Harper & Brothers, 1958.

Part III History of the Senate

Asbell, Bernard. *The Senate Nobody Knows*. Garden City, N.Y.: Doubleday & Co., 1978.

Baker, Bobby, and King, Larry L. *Wheeling and Dealing: Confessions of a Capitol Hill Operator*. New York: Norton, 1978.

Bates, Ernest Sutherland. *The Story of Congress, 1789-1935.* New York: Harper & Brothers, 1936.

Benton, Thomas Hart. *Thirty Years' View.* 2 vols. New York: Greenwood Press, 1968.

Bibby, John F., and Davidson, Roger H. *On Capitol Hill.* 2nd ed. Hinsdale, Ill.: Dryden Press, 1972.

Binkley, Wilfred E. *President and Congress.* New York: Alfred A. Knopf, 1947.

———. *The Powers of the President.* New York: Russell & Russell, 1973.

Burdette, Franklin L. *Filibustering in the Senate.* New York: Russell & Russell, 1965.

Clark, Joseph S. *Congress: The Sapless Branch.* New York: Harper & Row, 1964.

———. *The Senate Establishment.* New York: Hill & Wang, 1963.

Congress and the Nation, 1945-1964. vol. 1. Washington, D.C.: Congressional Quarterly Inc., 1965.

Congress and the Nation, 1965-1968. vol. 2. Washington, D.C.: Congressional Quarterly Inc., 1969.

Congress and the Nation, 1969-1972. vol. 3. Washington, D.C.: Congressional Quarterly Inc., 1973.

Congress and the Nation, 1973-1976. vol. 4. Washington, D.C.: Congressional Quarterly Inc., 1977.

Congress and the Nation, 1977-1980. vol. 5. Washington, D.C.: Congressional Quarterly Inc., 1981.

Congressional Quarterly Almanac: 97th Congress, 1st Session, 1981. Washington, D.C.: Congressional Quarterly Inc., 1982.

Cotton, Norris. *In the Senate: Amidst the Conflict and the Turmoil.* New York: Dodd, Mead, 1978.

Davidson, Roger H., and Oleszek, Walter J. *Congress and Its Members.* Washington, D.C.: CQ Press, 1981.

de Tocqueville, Alexis. *Democracy in America.* 2 vols. New York: Schocken Books, 1967.

Dodd, Lawrence C., and Oppenheimer, Bruce I., eds. *Congress Reconsidered.* 2nd ed. Washington, D.C.: CQ Press, 1981.

Drew, Elizabeth. *Senator.* New York: Simon & Schuster, 1979.

Evans, Rowland, and Novak, Robert. *Lyndon B. Johnson: The Exercise of Power.* New York: New American Library, 1966.

Fiorina, Morris P. *Congress: Keystone of the Washington Establishment.* New Haven: Yale University Press, 1977.

Galloway, George B. *Congress at the Crossroads.* New York: Thomas Y. Crowell Co., 1946.

——. *The Legislative Process in Congress.* New York: Thomas Y. Crowell Co., 1953.

Hamilton, Alexander; Madison, James; and Jay, John. *The Federalist Papers.* Introduction by Clinton Rossiter. New York: Mentor, 1961.

Harris, Joseph P. *The Advice and Consent of the Senate.* New York: Greenwood Press, 1968.

Haynes, George H. *The Senate of the United States: Its History and Practice.* 2 vols. Boston: Houghton-Mifflin, 1938.

Huitt, Ralph K., and Peabody, Robert L. *Congress: Two Decades of Analysis.* New York: Harper & Row, 1972.

Jones, Charles O. *The Minority Party in Congress.* Boston: Little, Brown, 1970.

Josephy, Alvin M., Jr. *On the Hill: A History of the American Congress.* New York: Simon & Schuster, 1980.

Luce, Robert. *Legislative Procedure: Parliamentary Practices and the Course of Business in the Framing of Statutes.* New York: Da Capo Press, 1972.

Mackaman, Frank H., ed. *Understanding Congressional Leadership.* Washington, D.C.: CQ Press, 1981.

MacNeil, Neil. *Dirksen: Portrait of a Public Man.* New York: World, 1970.

Madison, James. *Notes of Debates in the Federal Convention of 1787.* Introduction by Adrienne Koch. Athens, Ohio: Ohio University Press, 1966.

Mann, Thomas E., and Ornstein, Norman J., eds. *The New Congress.* Washington, D.C.: American Enterprise Institute for Public Policy Research, 1981.

Matthews, Donald R. *U.S. Senators and Their World.* New York: Norton, 1973.

Mayhew, David. *Congress: The Electoral Connection.* New Haven, Conn.: Yale University Press, 1974.

McConachie, Lauros G. *Congressional Committees: A Study of the Origins and Development of Our National and Local Legislative Methods.* New York: Burt Franklin Reprints, 1973.

Oleszek, Walter J. *Congressional Procedures and the Policy Process.* Washington, D.C.: CQ Press, 1978.

Price, David E. *Who Makes the Laws: Creativity and Power in Senate Committees.* Cambridge, Mass.: Schenkman Publishing Co., 1972.

Reid, T. R. *Congressional Odyssey: The Saga of a Senate Bill.* San Francisco: W. H. Freeman & Co., 1980.

Ripley, Randall B. *Majority Party Leadership in Congress.* Boston: Little, Brown, 1969.

____. *Power in the Senate.* New York: St. Martin's Press, 1969.

Rogers, Lindsay. *The American Senate.* New York: Alfred A. Knopf, 1926.

Rothman, David J. *Politics and Power: The United States Senate, 1869-1901.* Cambridge, Mass.: Harvard University Press, 1966.

Schwarz, John E., and Shaw, L. Earl. *The United States Congress in Comparative Perspective.* Hinsdale, Ill.: Dryden Press, 1976.

Sundquist, James L. *The Decline and Resurgence of Congress.* Washington, D.C.: Brookings Institution, 1981.

Swanstrom, Roy. *The United States Senate, 1787-1801.* Senate Document No. 64, 87th Cong., 1st sess.. Washington, D.C.: U.S. Government Printing Office, 1962.

Warren, Charles. *The Making of the Constitution.* Boston: Little, Brown, 1928.

White, William S. *The Citadel: The Story of the United States Senate.* New York: Harper & Row, 1956.

Wilson, Woodrow. *Congressional Government.* 1885. Reprint ed. Baltimore: The Johns Hopkins University Press, 1981.

Young, James S. *The Washington Community, 1800-1828.* New York: Columbia University Press, 1966.

INDEX

A

Abourezk, James - 292
Abscam investigation - 187-188
Adams, John - 24, 28, 92, 196, 200, 206, 207
Adams, John Quincy - 108, 110, 112, 209-211
Adams, Samuel - 23, 24
Adams, Sherman - 152
Agricultural Adjustment Act of 1933 - 148, 257
Aiken, William - 112
Albany Plan of the Union of 1754 - 19, 25 (box)
Albert, Carl B. - 157, 175
Aldrich, Nelson W. - 225, 237, 243
Allen, James B. - 291, 293
Allen, William V. - 231
Allison, William B. - 225-227, 245
American Federation of Labor (AFL) - 251
Ames, Fisher - 99, 102
Anderson, Clinton P. - 268
Annapolis convention - 39
Anthony, Henry B. - 234-235
Anthony rule (1870) - 234-235
Anti-Federalists
    First elections - 91-93
    Ratification of Constitution - 88-91
Appropriations. *See Spending powers.*
Appropriations Committee
    House - 117, 118, 132, 134, 277
    Senate - 134, 235, 248, 254
Articles of Confederation - 33-37
    Powers and provisions - 1, 34-35

Proposed revision - 11, 38-39
Ratification - 35
Weaknesses and defects - 35-36

B

Baker, Howard H. - 285-286
Baker, Robert G. "Bobby" - 165, 266, 272
Bankhead, William B. - 147, 148
Banking and Currency Committee (House) - 117
Banks, Nathaniel P. - 111
Barbour, Henry E. - 143
Barbour, James - 213
Barbour, Philip P. - 110
Barkley, Alben W. - 258, 259, 265
Beecher, Charles - 248
Bell, John - 110
Benton, Thomas Hart - 212, 215, 217
Beveridge, Albert J. - 226, 237, 242, 243
Bill of Rights - 32, 68, 89
Blaine, James G. - 119
Blair, Henry W. - 230
Boggs, Hale - 157, 175
Bolling, Richard - 183
Borah, William E. - 241
Boston Tea Party - 23
Boutwell, George - 119
Boyd, Linn - 111
Brandegee, Frank B. - 253
Bricker, John W. - 275
Bridges, H. Styles - 158, 267
Bristow, Francis - 237
Brooks, Preston - 190 (photo), 219

Index

Structure of Congress - 48, 49
Wilson, Woodrow
Budget system proposal - 133
Legislative-executive relations - 129-130, 247
Parlimentary obstruction - 244
Power in the House - 118

Progressive era, reforms - 237-238
Senate role - 3-4, 225
Winthrop, James - 88
Winthrop, Robert C. - 111
Woolens Act of 1699 - 17
World War I - 132, 238
Wright, Jim - 176